DAYS OF THE BLACKTHORN

FACTION FIGHTERS OF KERRY

SEÁN MORAGHAN

MERCIER PRESS

MERCIER PRESS
Cork
www.mercierpress.ie

ISBN: 978 1 78117 750 1

A CIP record for this title is available from the British Library.

Printed and bound in the EU.

CONTENTS

AUTHOR'S NOTE

This book contains quotes from primary sources, many of which date from the nineteenth century. Original spellings have been maintained throughout, despite certain inconsistencies and misspellings. Punctuation has been altered, on occasion, in order to make the source material clearer for the modern reader.

PREFACE

In a study of homicide in nineteenth-century Ireland, it was observed that faction fighting has received surprisingly little attention from historians.[1] This for a phenomenon that lasted for over 200 years, involving gangs of men attacking each other heartily with various cudgels, sticks, reaping hooks and sometimes guns. Similarly, only a single analysis of the activity was undertaken while it was actually occurring.[2] Regarded as an embarrassment by nationalist Ireland both before and after independence, this practice was rarely discussed afterwards.

The present volume is the first county-level survey of faction fighting. Kerry had a strong reputation for the practice, perhaps second in Munster only to Tipperary. The county featured several long-lived factions, as well as one of the most infamous fights ever – the clash at Ballyeagh strand in 1834.

Information about faction activity in the county is not bountiful, but enough exists to give us a sense of who fought where and, occasionally, why. Reports on fights and factions have been drawn mostly from local newspapers, chiefly *The Kerry Evening Post*, the *Tralee Mercury* and *The Tralee Chronicle*. It is important to stress, however, that the fights reported by newspapers are not likely to constitute a comprehensive record of the incidents. Many of the fights occurred in what was still, in the nineteenth century, the obscurity of the wilds of Iveragh or the Dingle peninsula, far from the press rooms of Tralee. Faction fights in which no participants were injured or killed, or which were otherwise unremarkable, are also likely to have been considered unworthy of print. Moreover, a dearth of surviving copies of Kerry newspapers from the earliest decades of the 1800s, as well as from the late eighteenth century, leaves the records incomplete. In addition, accounts of court proceedings that mentioned men charged or convicted for assaults at fairs or for riotous assembly often left out any details that would confirm that their cases had to do with faction fighting.

The fights featured here might best be considered as representative of a much wider spread of such events. Molahiffe fair, for example, already had a reputation for hosting faction fights by 1840, one which was commented on again in 1873, yet that reputation is unlikely to have arisen on the basis of just fifteen reports that appeared in the press over the decades. Similarly, the mere six newspaper accounts of fights in Castleisland hardly tally with the claim made in 1846 that the town hosted gangs that had been established since the 1740s or 1760s, or with the testimony of folklore that states that two particular parties fought each other at every fair held in the town.

Press sources have been supplemented with eyewitness tales presented by contemporary writers, particularly foreign travellers, which regularly provide a more visceral sense of the activity than the bare facts in news items, or in press accounts of court cases. Songs, ballads, poems and a little fiction have also been quoted, wherever possible, to give an impression of how factions and fighters were viewed by contemporaries. More importantly, much use has been made of the material housed in the National Folklore Collection; it is mostly due to that trove that we know anything about factions such as the Casúraigh of

Mastergeehy, or anything remotely personal about some of the most famous Kerry fighters.

'Partly because of their alleged primitivism, factions have been largely ignored by sober, cultured academics,' it has been said. Here, however, is a glimpse into their once infamous and semi-heroic milieu, into what has been characterised as their 'vengeful, brutal, drunken, petty world'.[3]

INTRODUCTION

THE CURIOUS PHENOMENON OF FACTION FIGHTING

> 'Nearly every village forms a kind of faction, which has a soubriquet. Factions that began nobody knows when and continue nobody knows why.'
>
> Alexis de Tocqueville, 1835[1]

On town streets or in green fields, at fairs and race meetings, on Sundays and saints' patron days, rival gangs of Irishmen used to meet to battle and beat each other with cudgels and sticks. Tens, hundreds, and on rare occasions, thousands of people might take part. Skill and brutality, bravery and blackguardism were displayed. Magistrates, policemen and clergymen waded into the crowds of fighters in often vain attempts to thwart these encounters, sometimes at a cost to themselves. Fighters risked terrible injuries and sometimes death, while arrested participants faced jail sentences, fines or transportation to Australia. The practice, which appears to have taken place from the 1600s, flourished most visibly during the early 1800s, and lingered on in isolated episodes until the turn of the century. Here was a phenomenon which spanned at least 200 years of Irish life, which puzzled visitors, appalled or entertained Irish commentators, and confounded the civil and clerical authorities.

With a somewhat different emphasis, Sir Jonah Barrington, a former member of the Irish parliament, in 1809 commented of the Irish peasantry:

> Battle is their pastime: whole parishes and districts form themselves into parties, which they denominate factions; they meet, by appointment, at their country fairs; there they quarrel without a cause, and fight without an object; and having indulged their propensity, and bound up their wounds, they return satisfied to their own homes generally without anger, and frequently in perfect friendship with each other.[2]

The factions often sported unusual names. In Tipperary there were the Caravats and the Shanavests, afterwards rebranded as the Three Year Olds and the Four Year Olds. The original name of the first group appears to have been derived from the fact that the men wore cravats, while that of their rivals arose from their wearing of old waistcoats (*sean bheisteanna*). In that county, too, were the Black Hens and the Magpies. Abbeyfeale, Co. Limerick, was the home of the Boccaghs ('the Beggarmen').[3] In Kerry, factions generally bore the surname of the most prominent, or founding, family of the faction, the only variations being the Cooleens and the Ballymacks of North Kerry, and the 'Poul-na-mucks' of Killarney, who instead carried the names of the districts associated with them.

Rural factions were run by farmers. 'Of what class in life are the leaders of those clans?', a parliamentary committee asked in 1824. 'They are generally farmers, or the sons of farmers,' replied a witness from Co. Cork.[4] In particular, they were the better off, what were later called 'strong', farmers. Those involved were 'well-dressed, apparently wealthy', noted a judge in Limerick in 1878.[5] The factions of the Sullivans and the Riordans of Castlemaine were 'headed by the richest farmers on the banks of the Main', it was stated in 1845.[6] Another fighting family, the Foleys of Killorglin, were wealthy enough to buy out the ownership of their lands during the eighteenth century and lived in a fine Georgian farmhouse.[7] It was stated by a local historian in 1868, in relation to the factions of the Cooleens and the Lawlors:

> Compared with the majority of the fighting men, the leaders were respectable; they were, for the most part, farmers, while the rank and file were tradesmen, farm-servants, and that great number who had a house of their own, however wretched the hut might be … There were many others who were distinguished for personal bravery, but whose social standing did not warrant higher ranks than lieutenants and aide[s]-de-camp.[8]

The factions were usually comprised of a prominent local family and its extended kinship network, intermixed with a collection of neighbours, allies and associates who felt an attachment or loyalty to them, all fighting under a common moniker. 'Some farmers, according to their means and connections, could bring into the field from 200 to 1000 men, whenever their honor or that of their adherents was called into question,' noted a newspaper in 1845.[9]

Women also played their part. Typical interventions consisted of hectoring the opposition, cheering on their own party and supplying men with sticks and stones. Some women also fought. Thomas Reid, a Royal Navy surgeon from Co. Tyrone, visited Cahersiveen in 1822:

> This happening to be the fair-day in the little town … I went to see the country people assembled; and never did I see a village fair so crowded. … In the course of the afternoon a battle took place, in which about a dozen persons of both sexes were engaged, and mauled one another without the least mercy. One man appeared to be an object of general hostility, and he defended himself with wonderful address; but the prowess of a woman vanquished him at last. This Amazon took off her apron, and enclosed in it a large angular stone, and winding this terrific catapult two or three times round her head, she then let fly at the head of her towering antagonist, still holding the ends of the apron in both her hands. The blow brought him to the ground streaming with blood; it was not necessary to repeat it; he lay along as senseless as a log.[10]

Natives and visitors alike have left us portraits of the gangs' fighting scenes. Barrington recalled regularly attending a fair in Queen's County (later Co. Laois) 'solely in order to see the fight which was sure to conclude it'.[11]

> To this fair resorted sundry factions, as they were termed – a *faction* consisting of one or two parishes, baronies or town-lands, that were very good friends in small parties or individually, but had a prescriptive deadly hatred to each other at all great meetings, fairs, returns from alehouses …
>
> Their weapon was almost exclusively an oaken cudgel … The friends and neighbours of the pugnacious factions, always in bodies, joined more or less warmly in the fray. In truth, it would be totally impossible to keep an Irish peasant, man or woman (if *the drop* was in), from joining in any battle going merrily on … Two hours, or thereabouts, was considered as a decent period for a beating-match …

> Sometimes one faction had clearly the best of it; then they ran away in their turn, for there was no determined stand made by any party – so that their alternate advancing, retreating, running away, and rallying, were productive of huge diversion.[12]

In North Kerry, an army officer, seemingly an Englishman, had a close encounter with a fight between two unnamed factions in 1827:

> I suddenly found myself surrounded by a host of combatants, who, at that instant, commenced operations. One fellow seized my horse, that I might not disturb them, and the rest leathered away most famously. Cudgels twinkled and Paddies fell in every direction … and a man who seemed a sort of leader of his faction broke his shillelah on his neighbour's pate. As I happened to be provided with one myself, and was unwilling to spoil sport, or see sport spoiled, I handed it out, and bade him play out the play. He received the gift with a grim smile of welcome, and in an instant I saw men tumbling like nine-pins 'beneath his sturdy stroke'. In something more than half an hour, a loud hurrah of 'The Boys of Ballinageary [Ballingarry] for ever!' announced that the fray was ended – my friend with the stick had won. He came up to where I stood, took off his hat, and with great propriety of speech and gesture, apologized for the delay I had met with, assuring me that once the signal was given, it was impossible to stop for any gentleman; and as he handed back my stick with eloquent thanks, he hoped I 'took no offence at the taste of a scrimmage that had detained my honour'.[13]

In 1828 a German prince who toured parts of Ireland, including Kerry, attempted to describe the character of the Irish people and noted:

> their utter inability to resist ardent spirits, so long as they have a penny in their pockets; the sudden and continual wild quarrels and national pitched battles with the shillelagh (a murderous sort of stick which every man keeps hidden under his rags) in which a hundred take part in a minute, and desist not till several are left dead or wounded on the field; the frightful war-whoop which they set up on these occasions; the revenge for an affront or injury, cherished and inherited by whole villages.[14]

THE SHILLELAGH AND OTHER STICKS

A letter writer to the *Dublin Penny Journal* observed in 1832 that 'an Irishman cannot walk or wander, sport or fight, buy or sell, comfortably, without an oak stick in his fist. If he travels, he will beg, borrow, or steal a shillelagh … if he fights, as fight he must, at market or at fair, the cudgel is brandished on high … "Leather away with your oak sticks!" is still the privilege, the glory, and the practice of Irishmen.'[15]

The word shillelagh has been explained as being derived from the Irish *sail éille*, 'thonged stick', referencing the habit some faction fighters had of tying a strap to their baton so that their weapon could not be fully knocked away from their hands in the heat of a fight.[16] (A writer in *The Tralee Chronicle* remembered 'great care and much taste being displayed in the beauty and strength of the thong which passed through a hole in the stick about eight inches from the top'.)[17] Alternatively, the term is often linked with the oak forest of Shillelagh, Co. Wicklow, which was renowned for the quality of its timber. In 1802, for example, it was said that the word represented 'an oak stick, supposed to be cut from the famous wood of Shilala'.[18]

A Kerryman tucks a cleith ailpín *under his arm, 1842. Drawn by J. Hastings. (Courtesy of the National Library of Ireland)*

There were a variety of fighting sticks, and Irish and English language terms to describe them. Among those that appeared in a Kerry context were *ailpín,* which translates as 'little knobbed stick'; *bata draighin*: 'blackthorn stick'; *buailteán* ('boulthaun'): 'flail'; *cipín* ('kippeen'): 'little stick'; and *cleith ailpín*: 'knob stick'. Further English language terms for different sticks included cudgel, wattle, sucker, and ash plant (or merely plant).[19]

According to Irish-born writers Samuel Carter Hall and his wife Anna Maria, who published a description of the country for English readers in 1841, the shillelagh was 'generally about three feet long', whereas the *cipín* and *cleith ailpín* were smaller weapons. In contrast, the wattle was a remarkable eight or ten feet long.[20] A modern enthusiast of the Irish fighting stick, John W. Hurley, has noted of the *cipín*: 'as a weapon, it is much easier to carry and conceal, especially under the large, native Irish frieze coats'.[21]

A sucker, meanwhile, referred to a stick that had been cut from the growing base of an ash tree, 'to make it have more weight at the striking end than the end which you hold in the hand'.[22] Other weapons used in Kerry were straight-edged lengths of wood, which appear to have come from the carpenter's yard or the sawmill rather than the hedgerow.[23]

Sometimes fighters would use two sticks at once. Limerick man Richard Denihan, whose father had been a faction fighter in Kerry, told folklorist Kevin Danaher that some men 'used to fight with two sticks. The *buailteán* was about four feet long … The other stick was a short one about a foot and a half long and 'twas very stout. The purpose of this stick was to stop the blow.'[24] Denis Casey, the leader of a Glenflesk faction, who appears to have fought in the late 1700s and early 1800s, 'could whirl two sticks on occasion'.[25] Scottish fencing master Archibald MacGregor, writing in 1791, noted that 'a number of the Irish are very good at fighting with two sticks … a short one in their left hand to guard with, and a long one in their right, which they manage with amazing dexterity.'[26]

A very different order of weapon was what was called the 'loaden butt', a stick which had its top filled with a piece of molten lead or fitted with a piece of iron (a ferule) to make it more devastating as a weapon. As Richard Denihan commented: 'A blow from that would smash a bone.'[27]

So fond were some fighters of their favourite sticks that they gave them nicknames. Tadhg Kennedy of Annascaul 'carried a huge blackthorn stick with long pointed knobs. He called this stick "*Bás gan Saggart*". This name meant that if anyone got a blow of this stick he would be killed on the spot before a priest or doctor would reach him alive.'[28] Paud Brien, who fought in Askeaton, Co. Limerick, also carried a stick with the same title, and another he nicknamed *Leagadh gan eiri* ('Down and out').[29] A historian of Irish fairs, Patrick Logan, recalled a former fighter and a subsequent maker of fighting sticks naming two of his creations 'Rid the Lane' and 'Dead with One Stroke'.[30]

'The Darling Ould Stick' could also be praised in song. A ballad set in Co. Meath related: 'If that stick had a tongue, it could tell you some tales/How it battered the countenances of the O'Neils'. The ballad continued:

It made bits of skull fly about in the air
And it's been the promoter of fun at each fair
For I swear by the toe-nail of Moses!
It has often broke bridges of noses
Of the faction that dared to oppose us –
It's the darling kippeen of a stick.[31]

The fighting stick was seasoned in order to make it as hard as possible. 'Sometimes it was tempered in a dung-heap, at others in slack lime, but the more usual mode was to rub it over repeatedly with butter, and place it "up the chimney", where it would be left for a period of several months,' noted the Halls.[32] 'The smoke and the heat from the fire beneath resulted in a very lasting and hardwearing instrument,' recalled a man who, as a young boy, had witnessed one of the last fights in the district of East Kerry known as Sliabh Luachra.[33] The Kerry poet Murroghoh O'Connor observed:

No Scymeter can pierce that hardened Wood,
Which many a Fight at Fairs and Patrons [with]stood;
A broken Scull ensues at ev'ry St[r]oak,
They'll bend with Blows, but never can be broke.[34]

Naturally, participants regularly received blows to the head from the hard sticks. In 1864, when the skull of a still-living Tipperary man was examined, 'it was found to be covered like a chessboard with scars and seams' from former fights between the Caravats and the Shanavests.[35] Seán Dobbs, a man from Abbeyfeale, Co. Limerick, was later remembered as having 'carried a silver plate on his head through life, because of some intermeddling in a faction fight'.[36] The first surviving record of a fatality at a Kerry faction fight that was the result of a stroke to the head with a stick was in Ardfert in 1762.[37] There was no recovery from the most serious blows; if men who were dealt fractured skulls did not die on the spot, they lingered in bed, finally expiring weeks after a fight. For the rest of the family, if the man was a tenant farmer, his incapacitation or death was a devastating outcome economically as well as personally, as they faced eviction, homelessness and poverty following the loss of the breadwinner.

The consequences for the families of those men who were convicted of killing others were also grim. In 1832 a gentleman boarded a Tralee coach that was also carrying convicts sentenced to transportation. 'No sooner had the coach stopped than it was surrounded by two or three hundred women, with their innumerable progeny, all joining in one wild howl, expressive of deep sorrow and implacable resentment, bewailing in Irish the fate of those who were leaving their native shores for ever.' Sitting into the carriage, the gentleman talked with a few prisoners. 'The second, an exceedingly fine young man, humble in manner, yet resolute in mien, of the better class … had killed a man in a faction-fight,' he related. The man could have been sentenced to death, 'but through the kindness of a gentleman at Listowel, life was spared'.[38]

CAUSES AND MOTIVATIONS

Some faction feuds, perhaps most of them, originally derived from particular root causes, and functioned as ways of venting and renewing grudges and grievances. The lengthy antipathy between the Fitzgeralds and the O'Keefes of East Kerry, for example, was said to be sparked by the abduction (or elopement) of a woman from one of the families.[39] In 1824 the conflict between the Bootashees and the Tubbers of Co. Cork was traced to an argument between two boys from around 1794 over a game of marbles, in which adults became involved.[40] The officer who witnessed the boys of Ballingarry in 1827 asked the faction leader afterwards for the reason behind the quarrel between the parties:

> 'Och, it was only some words between mysel and Tim Oulaghan, about a girl I wouldn't marry; an' he brought his faction agin' us, an' we fought it out, and beat them like min.'
>
> 'And why would you not marry the girl?'

> 'Sure, hadn't she a pearl on her eye like a biled cockle whin I seen her afore the Priest?'[41]
>
> 'You don't mean to say it was then first you discerned her blindness?'
>
> 'Whin else, your honour? Devil a stem of her I ever seen till then?'
>
> 'And were you going to marry a woman the first time ever you saw her?'
>
> 'Troth and that same's the custom among huz always. When a girl takes on to be married, her father or mother, or the like, goes match-making, and spakes to any boy they fancy, and if he's agreeable, and they offer fortin' according to his expictations, the priesht is invited, and the first thing the girl hears of the match being settled, or who is the man that's to own her, is whin the frinds arrive to eat the wedding dinner; and late in the evening, when all is hearty, in comes the boy, and thin they see each other for the first time.'[42]

At Ardfert, in 1892, two parties named Bowler and Gurnett fought with 'stones and shillelaghs':

> [I]t appeared that the germinal point of the antipathy might be correctly traced back to the venerable ancestors of the contending sides. Faction fights were not then infrequent, and the embittered feeling, intensified by imaginary wrongs, was preserved by mutual broils down to a few years ago … the Bowlers … continued working for a gentleman [nearby], which action, because the other side and a few [others] regarded the gentleman in question from an obnoxious stand point, the other side considered objectionable. Subsequently, they thought they were right in calling the Bowler family 'croobeens' and 'lick-plates'. This state of petty anarchy was comparatively available in its phases down to the present day … culminating in a serious riot a few months ago.[43]

Nevertheless, the original cause of a long-standing feud often appeared to have been forgotten by later generations, who simply continued to fight on regardless. The Rev. Horatio Townsend of Co. Cork observed a simple perpetuating dynamic at work as fights continued: 'Grounds of contention can never be wanting among people, in whose memory is carefully deposited the disgrace of a former defeat, and the dear hope of future vengeance.'[44]

Many commentators felt that men engaged in faction fights for the sheer love of fighting: the observant French traveller Alexis de Tocqueville felt that factions fought 'for the sole pleasure of the excitement that a fight gives'.[45] William Carleton, whose life's work consisted of revealing the world of the Irish peasant, wrote of 'the agreeable recreation of fighting … To be sure, skulls and bones are broken, and lives lost; but they are lost in pleasant fighting – they are the consequences of the sport, the beauty of which consists in breaking as many heads and necks as you can.'[46] Faction fights were thus partly examples of what modern scholars term 'recreational violence'. In her analysis of Irish faction fighting, historian Carolyn Conley commented that the goal of recreational violence 'was not to injure or kill but rather to participate in a mutual display of skill and strength … Rather than men bent on violence, the characters who emerge from the criminal records are more often people who enjoyed fighting as a sometimes lethal, but rarely malicious, form of entertainment.'[47]

Fighting served emotional and psychological needs too. While another observer explained that factions engaged 'merely for the diversion of fighting, or settling some point under dispute,' he added that 'the leading men in those factions do it from a spirit of pride and vanity'.[48] A Limerick clergyman, explaining that factions fought on the basis of 'honour or revenge', commented of the former motive: 'I can hardly define what a person in such a situation of life as they were in would mean by honour; but I should think it would be better expressed by pride; they wished to be superior to the opposite party.'[49]

Faction fighting was not only a matter for the participants, but also for those spectators who enjoyed watching a good fight. In 1812 the Rev. James Hall, a Scotsman, viewed a fierce cudgel fight in Limerick city: 'To the disgrace of the inhabitants, many of them shouted and applauded those that were most active, calling them by name from their windows, "Bravo! well done!" while they hissed those disposed to be quiet.'[50] By this public means, some fighters could gain for themselves favourable reputations within their communities and be praised in contemporary story, song or verse. In Kerry, stories about Seón Burns of the Cooleens and songs about 'Big Mick' Foley from Killorglin remained part of the folklore of their districts for a hundred years after they flourished their sticks.

An element of the fights that remains opaque, however, is how members of factions identified each other so that they only attacked the rival party during their battles, particularly in view of the fact that they sometimes amassed in very large numbers and that some fighters were recruited from so far afield that they cannot have recognised their opponents by sight. Up to 1,600 men took part in a violent faction fight in Tipperary town one day in May 1825, and in Kerry up to 2,000 men and women turned up for the Cooleen versus Mulvihill battle on Ballyeagh strand in June 1834.[51] A witness at a House of Commons inquiry, noting the large numbers engaged in fights at fairs, commented that he was 'almost astonished how they know those of each other's party … but I do not know that they wear any public emblem'.[52] It is possible that a scarf, neckerchief, shirt or other item of clothing of a particular colour was worn. In Kerry, celebrated strongman Seón Burns always wore a red handkerchief, while faction leader Peter Hurley of Listowel wore an exotic blue scarf.[53]

Some Irish factions may indeed have identified themselves by wearing recognised colours: in a modern analysis of the earliest years of the Gaelic Athletic Association (GAA), it was said that 'local allegiances … survived and were replicated within the G.A.A., with some teams allegedly taking on the colours that had been used by faction fighters in the preceding decades'.[54]

RITUALS OF FACTION FIGHTING

A faction fight was often begun with one or more ritualistic devices. Men of one gang would stroll up a town or village street shouting out the name of the rival gang or announcing that they themselves were present and ready for action. This might be accompanied by the practice of 'wheeling':

> I have seen many a faction fight, every one of which began in the same way, which was thus: one man 'wheeled', as they call it, for his party; that is, he marched up and down, flourishing his blackthorn, and shouting the battle-cry of his faction, 'Here is a Coffey aboo against Reaskawallahs; here is a Coffey aboo – who dar strike a Coffey?'

> 'I dar', shouted one of the other party; 'here's Reaskawallah aboo', at the same instant making a whack with his shillelagh at his opponent's head. In an instant hundreds of sticks were up, hundreds of heads were broken. In vain the parish priest and his curate ride through the crowd, striking right and left with their whips; in vain a few policemen try to quell the riot; on it goes till one or other of the faction is beaten and flies.[55]

In a prelude to a faction fight at Listowel in 1828, a journalist observed men 'performing many *graceful* and masterly evolutions usual on such occasions – such as uttering savage and diabolical yells, making frightful grimaces, wheeling cudgels, and stamping most gallantly in the mire'.[56] A policeman, in an encounter somewhere in Leinster, was challenged by a faction leader to a bout of single combat, which the latter prefaced 'by three jumps in the air and a war whoop that might have startled a Red Indian, twirling his cudgel at the same time'.[57] Another common practice was for a fight starter to take off his coat and trail it along the ground, demanding, 'Who will tread on the tails of my coat?'[58]

'THIS ANCIENT CUSTOM'

Fighting between various clans, in a more explicitly war-like manner, had been an ancient Irish practice. *The Annals of the Four Masters* catalogued countless fights, battles and territorial incursions in the history of Ireland from 1171 to 1616. Kerry lawyer and politician Daniel O'Connell once complained of these records: 'They are little more than a bare record of faction or clan fights.'[59]

Describing the world encountered by the Jesuit Counter-

Reformation mission to Ireland, a historian stated: 'There can surely be little doubt that the Ireland to which it came was a society dominated by kinship relations and articulated by feud. Anyone consulting the reports of the Jesuit mission in Ireland about 1600 will be impressed by the reporters' conviction of the prime importance of feud among the people they were dealing with.'[60] In Kerry, Murroghoh O'Connor linked stick fighting with the O'Connor clan, who had ruled a large tract of the north of the county until the early 1600s:

Here great O'Conner Monarch of the West,
Sway'd uncontroul'd, with Peace and Plenty blest;
If lawless Subjects mutter'd at his Laws,
Then green Oak Cudgels did decide the Cause;
No Pike nor military Art was us'd,
To conquer those that wholesome Laws refus'd;
But well dry'd Saplins ended the Debate,
From those whole Thousands met untimely Fate …[61]

He may have had reason to know this, as he claimed to be related to these O'Connors ('You know I can my Lineage justly trace, Sprung from that brave and bold Milesian Race') and he lived as a tenant on their former territory after it had been confiscated by Trinity College Dublin.[62]

Some subsequent rural factions did have links with the old clan system. One party of O'Donoghues, who fought on the streets of Killarney towards the end of the eighteenth century, was commanded by their titular leader, the O'Donoghue of the Glens, while the O'Keefes of Sliabh Luachra, who fought from the 1820s as the Daithínigh, had, in late medieval times, been chiefs of the area.[63] Kerry judge Robert Day told a House of Commons committee in 1825 that factions represented 'a remnant of the old barbarous Irish system of clanship, which still continues'.[64] In 1831 the assistant barrister for Kerry, condemning 'those disgraceful and unmeaning party feuds', commented that the time had come 'when this spawn of a feudal aristocracy should expire. It has lived long enough, Heaven knows.'[65]

Other factions, however, may have drawn upon a much more fanciful sense of status or identity based upon a spurious claim of an ancient lineage or of once having had some local historical importance. Something of the latter spirit appeared in a short story set in South Kerry published in 1842, in which 'the richest farmer in the parish' tells his son, 'I'm a rale descindant of Daniel McCarthy, who was kilt at the battle of Callara, fighting with the Fitzgeralds', and asserting that he has a claim to the castle of Dunkerron, 'instead of living in a thatched cabin'.[66] Perhaps, as Murroghoh O'Connor had observed in his verse portrait of Kerry, 'Here ev'ry Man's a Monarch in his Mind.'[67]

The wielding of sticks was noted in fact and depicted in fiction from the middle of the seventeenth century. In the course of a series of sectarian attacks in 1642, a man murdered at Carrickfergus, Co. Antrim, was stated in 1653 to have been struck on the head 'with a knotted Cudgell or staffe', also described as a 'Crabtree Cudgell'.[68] In the second part of a satire, *Pairlement Chloinne Tomáis*, written some time between 1662 and 1665, a clan meeting is guarded by '*tríochad do lucht cliubaoidh* [*agus*] *tríochad do lucht smístínidhe*' (thirty men carrying clubs and thirty carrying cudgels).[69] In 1695 the Irish parliament passed the

Sunday Observance Act, which prohibited 'cudgels, wrestling or any other games, pastimes or sports' on the holy day.[70]

Faction fights were first mentioned later in the century. Fr James White in his manuscript history of Limerick was said to have recorded 'a fracas between members of certain trade guilds' in 1669.[71] A traveller who journeyed in Ireland between 1675 and 1680 wrote that the fair of Quin, Co. Clare, was famous for quarrels between two rival families, the Malounys and the MacNamaras.[72] In 1705 Seán O'Neachtain wrote a comic poem in Irish that depicted an imaginary battle between two groups of men, in which 'Patrick Fitzsimon gave Eoin a blow with a big cudgel on the top of his skull which made him howl ... This is the time that the crowd of enemies attacked each other knocking each other over, fiercely, stoutly and strongly.'[73] In the early 1700s O'Connor portrayed faction fighting in Kerry as the continuation of an old tradition, calling it 'this ancient Custom'.[74]

Although the activity was to become best known as a rural one, many of its manifestations before the nineteenth century appeared as a feature of urban environments. What rural and urban factions shared was their being predicated on a strong sense of a particular shared identity. A 'desperate skirmish' took place in Cork city in 1729 between the butchers and weavers of the city, during which many of the rioters were crippled and several others later died of their wounds.[75] It was also in Cork that the Blackpool Boys, the Blarney Lane Boys and the Fair Lane Boys fought with one another between the 1750s and 1770s. In September 1765:

> the Fair-lane and Blareney-lane People to the Number of two Thousand and upwards assembled in the Fields back of the Cattle-market, when above one hundred Heroes at each Side, armed with Ribbing-Knives, Swords, Sticks, &c. began a desperate Engagement, in which several were maimed, and two Ringleaders of the Fair-lane Party, it is said, are mortally wounded.[76]

Combat between the Fair Lane and Blackpool gangs was described as taking place 'according to weekly custom'.[77] Similarly, in Limerick city, during the 1770s and 1780s, 'The County of Limerick Boys' regularly battled 'The County Clare Boys' at Thomond Gate.[78]

It was as a feature of rural life, however, that faction fighting would become most noted. An illustration depicting the activity as if it was a typical country pastime appeared in a Kildare estate map drawn up by John Rocque and decorated by Hugh Douglas Hamilton in 1760, later described as including 'imaginative pictures of farm and village life: one shows what looks like an Irish "faction fight" in which cherubic figures are seen beating each other with sticks'.[79] In August 1782, in Co. Sligo, it was observed that a gang had recently formed, 'in number not less than two hundred, who call themselves the regiment of cudgeliers', and that at the fair of Beltra, 'above one hundred of them assembled, with oak boughs, and armed with cudgels and other weapons, striking and desperately wounding several people as they passed along … we hear that they frequently assemble at fairs and on Sundays, have entered into resolutions, and are sworn to one another'.[80] In the same year Bishop Troy of Ossory, a diocese centred in Kilkenny, lamented that people often assembled at public gatherings 'with the anti-Christian intention of raising a quarrel, or revenging a real or imaginary insult offered to their relations, friends and partisans'.[81] By 1786 a member of the Irish parliament could conclude that 'our country people can seldom part at fairs or patrons without broken heads'.[82] Incidents may have become more frequent over time simply as a result of increasing opportunities to meet and fight: in 1684 there were 503 fairs held in Ireland, by 1780 about 3,000.[83]

On 16 June 1808 a correspondent from Kerry informed readers of *The Freeman's Journal* about 'village factions':

> The ordinary seats of war, selected by these village-campaigners, are Fair-places; and the time of their choosing, for the proof of each other's strength, Fair-days. This very selection of time and place is, in itself, a serious evil; the buyers and sellers at those meetings must, in consequence of a disturbance of the peace, lose their market; and of course, the internal commerce of the country must be very materially injured. We have witnessed a few days ago in a neighbouring village, Ardfert, an example of this kind at the Fair of that place.

By then factions and stick fighting in Kerry were likely well established, as there is evidence of the phenomenon having existed from the earliest years of the eighteenth century, and possibly beforehand.

I

EARLY FACTION FIGHTING IN KERRY

> 'John Connor, with an oak stick or cudgell, of the value of sixpence ... then and there held in his right hand ... gave the said John Jemmyson, with the cudgell aforesaid, in and upon the right side of the head ... a mortal wound of the depth of three inches and the breadth of one inch.'
>
> Indictment for assault at a fair in Ardfert in 1762[1]

Fighting at fairs may have been a feature of Kerry life as early as the 1600s. Richard O'Connell, the vicar of the Diocese of Kerry from about 1611, who died in 1653, 'regularly attended fairs and public gatherings in all the towns of his diocese, especially Killarney, Castlemaine, Tralee and Ardfert ... to try to curb drinking and fighting'.[2] Whether those incidents involved factions, as such, is unknown, however. Firmer hints of factions and stick fighters appear in the first decades of the 1700s. In the year 1714 it was reported that the O'Donoghue of Killarney, the leader of his clan, 'often brags that he has 500 men at his command', and that a George Eager 'having committed an affray' in the town, threatened a local justice that 'he would beat him with a great cudgel he brandished in his hand as long as his stick would last'.[3] The Eagers were remembered by Daniel

O'Connell, who told a story involving their fights with the Lynes at Killarney fair, where one of the latter raised 'the war-whoop of "Five pounds for the head of an Eager!"'[4]

Several references to faction fighting as a contemporary practice of the early 1700s were made in O'Connor's poem 'A Description of the County of Kerry', published in 1726:

Off go the Hats and Coats, the Fight begins,
Some strike the Heads whilst others strike the Shins;
The winding Cudgels round their Foreheads play,
They need no Leaders to begin the Fray.[5]

The governor of Ross Castle, near Killarney, complained in 1729 of bands of men in the area who were 'continually in riots', all of whom were 'protected by different clans here'.[6] In Castleisland, established factions were said to have been active from the mid-1700s.[7] In May 1762 John Jemmyson was hit with a cudgel in the fatal attack at the fair of Ardfert, and later that year there was a riot (as faction fights were sometimes termed) at a place called Gurtanane (probably Gortinane, Lixnaw), 'in which near 20 people were dangerously wounded', following which six ringleaders were apprehended and lodged in Tralee jail.[8]

By the late 1700s there flourished a number of stick fighters who garnered long-lasting reputations. A young man from the O'Connell estates of the Iveragh peninsula known as Tadhg *na Sceall*, 'Tim of the hard blows', was renowned for the damage he could inflict with his stick.[9] There was also Denis Casey of Glenflesk, 'a man of Herculean size' who was 'the leader of the

Glenflesk clans in their faction fights, which were very common in his youth at all the fairs of the county'.[10] Daniel O'Donoghue, known as the O'Donoghue of the Glens, led parties of men from Glenflesk into battle on Killarney's streets: '[He] was a man of gigantic size, and truly barbarian spirit, somewhat tinctured with insanity', it was related in 1832.

> He generally marched at the head of his sept on those occasions; and you will readily believe that his enormous strength, along with the respect that clung to his rank, and his large property, contributed a good deal to their ascendancy. … Many persons who saw Daniel in his old age have described him to us; and it is plain he would have been … a formidable antagonist. Though of course much fallen then, he was still a huge skeleton, far above the ordinary size of these degenerate days. 'His jaws,' said a gentleman to us, 'resembled a horse's, and the children of Killarney used to break themselves in buying apples for him to eat. It was the greatest delight to see the huge working of his jaws; and Daniel would easily devour a basket full; so that he had always a crowd of urchins after him through the streets. But this never gave him any annoyance: he was as simple as one of themselves. At a large pattern once, he was attacked by the faction of the Agars [Eagers], and got a great beating, but no man could knock him down; at last, he became completely roused; he ran to an old cabin, and laid about him with one of the rafters, until he cleared the field. In short, he was a giant. You could put a young child into his shoe; and his voice was so deep and hollow that one would think it came out of the bowels of the earth.'[11]

The most famous factions of the county, the Cooleens and the Lawlors of North Kerry, were reported to have been established from about 1784.[12]

A man with his cudgel raised greets his friend at a fair. Engraved by W. Ridley from an original miniature; printed for J. Parsons, 21 Paternoster Row, March 1794. (Courtesy of the National Library of Ireland)

In 1790 a French visitor noted of Kerry men: 'On Sundays they attend patterns, almost all of them dressed in blue – each man with a baton in his hand. These sticks are held in the middle in order to strike an opponent on the head and their owners use them with heartfelt joy to attack each other at fairs. At one time there were special teachers to teach this cudgel game; perhaps such people are still to be found.'[13] In 1794 a John Day, who was sentenced to death after shooting a man in a personal quarrel in the neighbourhood of Tralee, asked to be buried with his wooden leg, 'which together with his cudgel, he requested to have laid beside him in his coffin'.[14] In August 1798 it was reported that at a 'skirmish at a Fair in the County of Kerry' three yeomen, members of a local defence force, generally Protestant farmers, who were sometimes deployed for policing duties, were killed; the incident had been 'attributed to rebellious principles among the peasantry of that quarter; whereas, by several letters from that County … it appears to have been merely one of those factious broils between two contending parties, or Feudal Clans, not uncommon in the most peaceable times in many parts of this kingdom'.[15]

In 1803 there was a fight at Clogher church, near Ballymacelligott, then an old thatched building. Details were provided by a folklore source in modern times of what was called 'the Battle of Clogher'. It stemmed from the contemporary phenomenon of the abduction of well-off single women, who were forced into a marriage ceremony by which the man who kidnapped them could access their money or land:

> A Carmody woman was taken by force for marriage by Spillane from Killarney. But he was caught before he got home, dispossessed of the young lady and warned never to come to the parish again. The Slatterys of O'Brennan brought him in again to dare the Carmodys. Hence the fight. The priest said that the man who gave the 1st blow would regret it. It was a Slattery who gave it and he was killed in the fight. Against the Slatterys were the Carmodys, Learys, Butlers and Leens. The Protestants came to help the Cloghermen, but were late for the fight. As the old church was desecrated by the fight it was abandoned and a new one was built at Ballydwyer.[16]

The Slatterys already had a feud going with the Leens (or Leanes), which had started near Tralee, 'when a Leane man tipped the can off the head of a Slattery woman from Baile Uí Dhubhuidhir'.[17]

In August 1803 seventeen people were arrested at Tralee fair, when 'a serious riot took place between some country people'. In the course of the affray, one man came up behind High Sheriff Robert Twiss and 'gave him a violent blow of a stick on the head, by which he received a wound two inches long'.[18]

In 1805 an unnamed 'gentleman in the county of Kerry' complained that 'frequent riots take place amongst the lower class of people in that country, which sometimes require the utmost exertions of the civil power to suppress', and he felt that it was 'the party spirit of clanship which has given rise to their proceedings'.[19] In the same year, an English traveller to Killarney encountered 'a powerful, good-humoured-looking fellow, who told us he had got three large wounds in his head at the last fair. At these meetings the people frequently divide themselves into what are called factions, and fight for *love* when the whisky mounts high into the brain.'[20] In June 1806 Thomas Stack of Irremore was struck dead by a blow of a stone while 'endeavouring to separate and reconcile two contending parties' in the town of Listowel.[21] In August, at the Tralee assizes, in what may have been the resulting court case, eleven men found guilty of rioting were sentenced to be whipped publicly through the town.[22] In February 1807 it was reported that 'a desperate affray took place between two parties at the fair of Kilgobnet, Co. Kerry, in which several persons received severe wounds, and different lives are despaired of'.[23]

The village of Ardfert was, from the earliest times, associated with faction fighting (and subsequently featured as one of the established battlegrounds of the Cooleens and the Lawlors). At a fair there in June 1808, Darby Carroll of Clogher, 'the reputed ringleader of a numerous gang in the neighbourhood of Ardfert', put himself 'at the head of an unruly mob … proceeded to acts of violence, and actually assaulted John Segerson, Esq., a Magistrate who (assisted by the Rev. Mr Kerin and Lieut. Bonynge, with a party of the Royal Longford Militia) was in the discharge of his duty, dispersing the mob commanded by Carroll'.[24] An eyewitness reported: 'A motley collection from an adjacent hamlet, commanded by a very notorious leader, thought, early in the day, to parade and sweep the fair-place. However the career was soon retarded by a better disciplined force, a party of the Longford Regiment … The leader was obliged to capitulate and lay down his arms, the *shillaleagh*.'[25]

On 27 December 1809, at a Ballylongford fair day:

> upwards of five hundred persons, of opposite clans, were engaged during the greater part of the day in deciding with cudgels and other weapons the differences which existed among them; a great number were wounded, and we are informed that many remain without hope of recovery. This mode of adjusting the disputes which daily arise between the different clans or factions in that county, by taking what they conceive to be the means of redress into their own hands, and which invariably hurls destruction and ruin on the heads of those engaged in such illegal practices, has been long viewed with the keenest regret; various efforts have been tried to curb this party spirit, but without effect.[26]

In March 1810 the Rev. Adam Averell, a Methodist preacher from Co. Tyrone, visited Killarney. 'On my arrival … I witnessed a dreadful scene,' he wrote:

> It was as if McCarty More and O'Donaghue had come back to earth, and were restored to all their feudal licentiousness. It was market-day; two powerful factions were arrayed against each other in deadly combat, and seemed to threaten the whole town with destruction. Nor was it until a fight of some hours the conflict terminated, by the weaker party being obliged to seek safety in a hasty flight from their more powerful opponents. Popery seems to have its throne here; and the effects are fully manifested in the ignorance, superstition, and barbarity of the great mass of the people.[27]

One Sunday in June, in the same year, reported *The Freeman's Journal*, two men agreed to fight each other after Mass in the chapel of the village of Ballingarry, Lixnaw. This is the first surviving case in which the use of a loaden butt was recorded:

> [A] friend of one of the combatants conceiving his champion had received an *unfair* blow from his antagonist, stept in to his assistance, and without ceremony laid on the other: this was the signal for battle, and in a short time upwards of two hundred were engaged promiscuously in the affray, beating each other with the most sanguinary and brutal ferocity; many dreadful blows were given on both sides; one man in particular, named John Kane, a blacksmith, received so severe a wound on the forehead, inflicted by a heavy oak stick, cased with iron, that no hopes are entertained for his recovery.[28]

In Listowel, one Sunday in October 1810, a fight took place 'between two numerous parties – their weapons were mostly stones, which did such dreadful execution as to inflict the severest wounds upon the parties'.[29] A man named Kirk was killed and others seriously injured. Judge Robert Day, writing in April 1811, complained that 'two tribes were drawn out with all the formality of two armies in the square of Listowel of a Sunday; to battle they proceeded, armed with stones, wattles, scythes and bayonets, and only one man was murdered, the rest of the wounded having recovered. This of a Sunday when three or four magistrates happened to be in the town, and a large military force.'[30]

In May 1811 Magistrate John Raymond wrote to the Irish administration in Dublin, explaining that the Listowel area had been 'disturbed for some time past by riots of a most serious nature & in which lives have been lost', and that, at a fair held on 13 May, 'two great factions who had assembled in multitudes from the most distant parts of this country commenced a most sanguinary conflict which threatened fatal consequences to many'.[31] In what may or may not be an account of this incident, a newspaper reported that one evening in May 'a desperate riot' took place in Listowel 'between two factions, the Mullownies and Dillanies, in which, after some severe fighting, a man of the name of Mathew Mullowney, was fired at from a loaded musket, and a ball driven through his skull, of which he died in a few minutes'.[32] A Darby Kelly was arrested for committing the deed and taken to Tralee jail.

In Tralee, one Saturday in June 1811, 'a desperate affray took place, between two parties of the populace ... stones flew in every direction, and while this lasted, a man named Thomas Enright, who ... is stated to have been merely a spectator, having retired from their range, was pursued by a ruffian named John Connor, and four or five assistants, by whom he was so beaten that he expired on Sunday'. A man named Shea, from Castlemaine, was also killed, and another man was expected to die of his wounds, while many others 'received cuts and contusions'.[33]

On 23 November 1812 two parties met at a busy fair in Castlemaine. Both of them:

> as it appears, for some days before, were preparing for the conflict, which commenced at an early hour of the day; but in a short time one Clan, by a pre-concerted plan, retreated precipitately while the other rapidly advanced, until they proceeded to some distance on the road to Anna [Anagh], when the retreating party filed off to the right and left … Their friends lay in ambush, who, being well armed, discharged a volley of small arms, loaded with ball, swan shot, & c. at their assailants, which did considerable execution.[34]

One man was killed by a shot in the chest, two others were badly wounded and a fourth had his skull fractured. 'There are many others who received injuries of a less dangerous nature, but whose faces, & c. are considerably disfigured.'[35] Patrick Lynch afterwards made a deposition to a court official in which he stated that he and others were 'surrounded and attacked' by a mob with 'Sticks or Cudgels[,] Swords and other offensive weapons,' and that when people fought back 'for the preservation of their lives', the mob pretended to retreat in order to draw them into the ambush.[36]

Another fight took place at Killorglin on 11 August 1813: 'A serious riot took place at the fair … we understand that the military were implicated, and that several shots were fired; one man named Connor was shot dead, and several others dangerously wounded, both from the firing and the showers of stones which flew in every direction.'[37] Killorglin and the August fair (soon afterwards called Puck Fair) were the stamping ground of the Foley faction, and particularly of Michael James Foley, known as 'Big Mick', who was 'a notorious rioter and leader of a faction'.[38] (Kilgobnet, not far from Killorglin, was also associated with the Foleys, and a reported affray between two parties which took place in 1807 may represent another appearance of theirs.)

By July 1814 Magistrate James Lawlor could write that at Killarney fairs 'at least 5000 of the peasantry crowd in, without an atom of fair business & for no other purpose than fun as it is called, but more properly speaking to partake of any mischief or riot that may go forward'. He noted that 'within the last four years I committed near 500 persons to the Bridewell of this town for riots and Affrays'.[39] Factions also appeared in Listowel on Sunday 1 May of that year, as another report explained:

> two parties of men entered the town … and commenced so furious an attack upon each other, that Lieutenant Proctor of the Waterford Militia was called out with his party by the magistrates, in hopes that the combatants might be intimidated by the appearance of the military. It proved the reverse: their rage increased to such a degree that the magistrates gave orders to fire over their heads. Finding none fall, they turned their fury on the soldiers, whom they attacked with sticks, stones … still advancing till the magistrates found it necessary to order the military to level low and fire. The misguided people then fled in all directions, leaving, however, behind them seven killed, and eight seriously wounded.[40]

Earlier in the year a man named Dowling was assaulted in the town by two men from Duagh: 'Fitzmaurice knocked him down with a cudgel, shot with iron.'[41]

The village and parish of Glin, Co. Limerick, near the Kerry county bounds, was later described as having been 'very disturbed' by 1816. The men from Glin used to fight others returning from the fair of Ballylongford. 'Faction fights were numerous and many people were seriously injured in these encounters,' it was said.[42] This may have been a consequence of the fact that a master there named Séamus Ó Síoda 'had a school where he taught the art of stick-fighting and what he called the "seven guards"'.[43]

West Kerry, like the north and south of the county, also had its factions. The gang of note on the Dingle peninsula was the Kennedys, who plied their sticks predominantly at Ballinclare fair, near Annascaul. In 1817, however, they met in Dingle for battle with a party composed of men from west of the town, when over 200 fighters 'continued trouncing each other with sticks then until evening time'.[44]

An enormous number of men assembled in Killorglin on Sunday 9 January 1820. Two unnamed factions were 'to decide by battle, an unaccountable enmity which they bore each other, and for which the infatuated wretches could assign no ostensible cause'. One of these gangs was most likely the Foley faction. The town's parish priest, Fr James Looney, addressed people from the altar beforehand, warning them of the consequences of their actions, but 'some hundreds were already assembled, and many more crowding in from every quarter, making an aggregate of from six to seven thousand, armed with guns, pistols, swords and sticks'. The priest informed local magistrates, who in turn arrived with a party of militia; they succeeded in dispersing and disarming the men and surrounding a house where 'some of the chiefs of one of the parties were, they made them prisoners. On the suggestion, however, of Fr Looney, they were sworn to keep the peace.'[45]

By the 1820s faction fighting had become a permanent feature of country life in Kerry, as indicated by the following conversation. John Houlahan was questioned in court about a fight he attended in Lisselton, in the north of the county, on St Patrick's Day 1825, in which a man named Hennessey had been killed. He was examined by Daniel O'Connell:

You went to the fair by appointment?
I did.

Now, what business had you there?
To fight, to be sure. What other business would I have there?

Why did you make an appointment on that particular day?
Because the parties had agreed on the Sunday before to meet, in order to have a fight, and would you have me be absent on such an occasion?

How many fights have you been in?
For how long?

For your whole life?
Oh! You are not serious; how could I tell?

Could you even give a guess?

I could not, indeed.

Could you tell me how many battles you have been in for the last three years?

I could not, without taking a great deal of time to calculate.

Now, Houlahan, by virtue of your oath, did you ever see a fight that your teeth did not water to be in the middle of it?

Why, sure, one could not see two dogs fighting without wishing to take part with one or other of them.[46]

From the incident at Ardfert in 1782, when John Jemmyson was struck dead, to this fight at Lisselton in 1825, and including the incidents at Listowel, it is clear that North Kerry featured heavily in the annals of faction fighting in the county. Several factions flourished there, the most notable of which, the Cooleens and the Lawlors, carried on their enmity for a very long period of time and engaged in the single most remarkable faction fight in Kerry, the Battle of Ballyeagh.

2

THE COOLEENS AND THE LAWLORS

> 'In Tipperary the individual who merely whispered the word "caravat", had his head immediately broken by the bludgeon of a "shanavest"; a four year old in Limerick was the deadly enemy of a three year old; and in Kerry, at least in the northern part of it, the cry of "Here is a Cooleen!" [at] a fair or any public place of meeting, was promptly answered by "hurroo, here is a Lawlor for ever!"'
>
> *The Tralee Chronicle*, 11 September 1868

Of all the districts of the county, North Kerry had the greatest reputation for faction activity. There, fighting at fairs, pattern days and races was endemic. Firm evidence of the activities of specific factions is not always possible to substantiate, however, as gangs were often left unidentified in press reports. In 1829, for example, a Dublin newspaper wrote only that a fight between 'two well-known factions' occurred at Ballylongford; similarly, in 1859 a Kerry newspaper noted a great fight in Ardfert, which arose 'in consequence of an old faction spleen', but it provided no details of the parties involved.[1] Equally, in official reports to government, it was only stated that, in the Listowel area, disturbances of the peace in 1814 comprised occasional riots at fairs by people 'amongst themselves', or that in 1825 a detachment of the military was called out to prevent 'two parties or factions of Country People' from fighting in the streets.[2]

Nevertheless, as will be seen, many of the fights in this wide area were carried out by the two most famous gangs of North Kerry, the Cooleens and the Lawlors (although there were also other factions at work, such as the Dillanes at Duagh and the Ballymacks at Ballylongford).[3] After the Cooleen and Lawlor–Mulvihill battle at Ballyeagh strand in June 1834, *The Kerry Evening Post* commented:

> The great extent of country which is at present disturbed by those murderous hostile clans is well worthy of the serious consideration of the governing authorities of the land – from Tarbert to the Cashion, and thence to Ardfert and Ballyhigue, the country is kept in a state of fearful agitation ... the peaceable and well disposed must be terrified from attending either fair or market through the entire of two large baronies, and for an extent of country of upwards of thirty miles.[4]

During the 1830s it was stated that the Cooleens and the Lawlors had been feuding for 'above half a century', so perhaps since the 1780s.[5] The Lawlors fought in combination with their allies, the Mulvihills, also known as the 'Black Mulvihills'. The Lawlors and Mulvihills came chiefly from the northernmost barony of Kerry, Iraghticonnor, and their faction was sometimes known as the Iraghts, or the Iraght Men.[6] The Cooleens came mostly from Clanmaurice, the barony to the south. Their nickname was said to have derived from the fact that one of their original leaders, a man named Flaherty, was from a place called Coolagown.[7] It may also have been because some of the faction was drawn from Coolnaleen, a few miles south of Listowel, or because the faction fought their first battle against the Lawlors there.[8]

There were some anomalies when it came to the influence of geography upon faction loyalties, however. Coolagown, the home of Flaherty, the Cooleen leader, lay just inside Iraghticonnor, Lawlor–Mulvihill territory. Similarly, some of the Lawlors came from Maghera, an area that stretched from the mouth of the Cashen river to Ballyheigue and down to Ardfert in the barony of Clanmaurice, which was the Cooleen heartland. Other members of both factions were drawn from the West Limerick side of the Kerry county bounds. A writer in *The Tralee Chronicle* commented:

> It was a very general thing to see a man of the Lawlor faction married to a woman of the Cooleens, and *vice versa*; and, to the credit of the ladies … rarely have they abandoned the principles of their youth. Thus it was that many families were divided among themselves, and, in their eagerness to gain over the husband, the leaders did not hesitate to make the wife use that awful means of influence – a curtain lecture; and if she were unable to get him to fight for her party, to endeavor, at all events, to keep him at home the day of battle. It sometimes happened, too, that where the father of a family was not a fighting man the sons took different sides, according as their affection inclined towards the paternal or maternal relatives.[9]

Co. Limerick man Richard Denihan observed: 'There were laws too about servant-boys, as to whom they'd be with. Because very often a Black Mulvihill servant boy would be working with a Cúilín farmer.'[10] It was later observed that 'Sides were taken because of family connections and district affiliations but there was no specific territory completely sympathetic with either side.'[11] (Perhaps such anomalies are reflected in a fight of 1865 in which a number of men assaulted a man named Mulvihill, who, a policeman had to explain, 'instead of being a Mulvihill happened to be a *Cooleen*'.)[12] Despite their allegiances, both parties' antipathy did not necessarily spill over into daily life; apart from their 'dreadful fights', commented a contemporary, he had known the two opposing parties 'to meet and work at digging ground in the same field, converse together, and have no altercation whatever'.[13]

Different issues were later suggested to have lain at the foot of the factions' long-lived hostility towards each other. There was the story of an attempted sale of a horse to a Lawlor man in a forge in Coolnaleen:

> [T]he buyer of the horse demanded a minimum height in his prospective purchase but the horse in question was a half inch short … seemingly, the buyer in the course of the bargaining stalked from the forge in the traditional manner of all dealers, but later, on persuasion and in keeping with tradition, returned. At this stage the seller demanded that the animal be again measured and this time the horse's height measured up to all requirements. The astute buyer, however … had his eyes open and noticed a difference in the horse's shoes. The dexterous smith had in his absence changed the shoes for ones with advantageous 'cocking' that lifted the horse the required half inch. One can visualise the accusations and counter accusations and the fate of the strange buyer in strange territory.[14]

Alternatively, the conflict may have originated from an incident where 'a man named Lalor was beaten by some parties from a district named Cool … and gradually large numbers of young men were enrolled on both sides'.[15] Another tale related that the rivalry started with a row at a May fair in Listowel between some Coolnaleen men and some Lawlor men from Maghera 'over the comparative merits of potatoes grown in both districts'.[16] The argument:

> ended in a fight, where the Maghera men got off the worst, as they wouldn't have the backing in Listowel that the others had. At the Whit Monday fair in Ardfert the fight was renewed. Practically every man in North Kerry took one side or another, and for years after whenever people assembled at fair or market or Sunday after Mass, the fight was renewed.[17]

This story tallies with a comment made in 1869 that 'The evil had its birth in Ardfert.'[18]

A near-supernatural explanation was also suggested, possibly because later generations did not understand the source of the rivalry: 'How it originated is not very clear. One version is that it was a dispute as to the ownership of a small patch of land carried by the force of the River Feale from one side of the bank to the opposite side.'[19] To some observers' eyes, it was as if nature itself had brought about the rivalry.

Colourful as these stories are, the factions' great enmity may have had a more banal source. The Cooleens were Kerry natives, while the Lawlors and the Mulvihills were comparative outsiders. In the early 1600s the Lawlors (or Lalors) had been among seven strong families ('septs') transplanted from Queen's County where they had been regarded as too hostile to the English plantations established there; they were subsequently settled around Tarbert, in Iraghticonnor. Similarly, in the mid-1600s, the O'Briens, lords of Co. Clare, who owned the lordship of Tarbert, settled many Clare families in North Kerry, including the Mulvihills; this created resentment among several local families, and 'led to many bloody fights'.[20]

The Cooleen faction mostly comprised 'representatives of old Kerry families', chiefly the Flahertys, as well as the Ahernes, the Báni O'Connors and the Sheehys.[21] Another account also numbered the Houlihans, the O'Callaghans and the Roches in their ranks.[22] On the other side, the Lawlors and Black Mulvihills were supported by the Walshs, the Keanes, the O'Briens, the Sullivans and the Enrights.[23]

Writing about the great fight at Ballyeagh, a local historian later recorded (or rather, half-recorded) the names of the leaders of the parties at that time. 'The recognised leaders' of the Lawlors were 'in Clanmaurice, a farmer named S—s, and in Iraghticonnor two others named W—h, and M—h'.[24] The first appears to be Thomas Sells (or Selles), who was elsewhere described as 'heading the party of the Lawlors and Mulvahills' on the day of the Ballyeagh fight, and who seems to have been active since at least 1828.[25] The second appears to be one of the Walshs. The Cooleen leaders were 'H—, who was one of the strongest men in either faction, and F—'. These are most likely Paddy Hackett, a skilled fighter who led the Cooleens into battle at Ballyeagh on horseback, and one of the Flaherty family.

The Cooleens and the Lawlors often met at Listowel. Indeed

both groups were characterised in 1826 as 'Listowel factions'.[26] In January 1828 they arrived there shouting and roaring and wheeling their cudgels, 'and with *genuine whiskey courage*, driving men, women, children, pigs, cows, goats, and sheep before them in sad dismay'.[27] Afterwards, *The Kerry Evening Post* stated that the assistant barrister and local magistrates were determined:

> to suppress the horrible and demoralizing spirit of faction and outrage which has long been the curse and disgrace of this country, and which in almost every instance, proceeds from an immoderate use of whiskey: and to such a pitch has this savage spirit arisen in Listowel and its neighbourhood, that a very respectable Magistrate of that vicinity, declared it was impossible with safety to carry on the ordinary business or intercourse between man and his neighbour at fairs or markets.[28]

At Listowel bridge, in December 1831, Maurice Shea, a servant, was attacked by Patrick Sullivan, William Bourke and John Bourns. While returning from the town fair, Shea was 'hurraing for the Sheas, Cantys, and Coolheens', and in what may have been a sequel to a previous fight, he used his stick to hit a cart on which a sister of one of his assailants was sitting.[29] A fight ensued which finished when the woman held him down on the ground while Sullivan 'gave him the last fatal blow with a two-handed stick'.[30] After the inquest into his death, *The Kerry Evening Post* observed: 'It is very generally the consequence of faction and party feuds, among the lower orders of the people, that the defeated faction will seek every opportunity of waylaying and murdering individuals of the victorious party.'[31] Sullivan was very quickly apprehended, but Bourke and Bourns went on the run.[32] Sullivan was sentenced to transportation for seven years, while the other two men, who were eventually captured and later stood trial, were acquitted.[33]

In 1834 it was said that 'scarce a fair day passed at Listowel without a serious fight'.[34] In other episodes in Listowel, John Stokes, described by a policeman as 'one of those who did bad work in the country', was arrested with stones in his hands and 'in the act of calling out for Cooleens and factions' at the fair held in August 1836.[35] In February 1848 both parties fought at a fair in the town.[36] Ten years later, five men were sent to prison for violent assault and faction fighting in the Listowel area, 'arising out of the old Cooleen and Lawlor feud'.[37]

Their feud was not just centred in Listowel, however. Ardfert too 'was, for many years, the theatre of bloodshed between rival parties known as Cooleens and Lalors'.[38] It was a Cooleen stronghold and included an area called Cuil, which was remembered as 'the largest street in Old Ardfert, and the brigade headquarters of the old faction fighters' – it may have contributed to the faction nickname.[39] A fair there in June 1832 'was very much impeded by a fight between two well-known factions, the Lawlors and Cooleens', which was 'at length put down with difficulty by the persevering efforts of William Collis ... a magistrate of the County'.[40] At a fair a month later, there was a 'barbarous riot' in which a number of men were 'irrecoverably maimed and rendered for ever unable to earn support for themselves or their wretched families'.[41] At a fair in 1846 'skirmishes commenced between the old rival factions, the Cooleens and Lawlors', with their mobs on this occasion amounting 'to several thousands'. Among the participants was a woman 'who supported the assailants with stones from her apron during the assault'. During the event, after handcuffing a man, a policeman became separated from his fellows and was trapped and beaten by the crowd: 'Leahy [the policeman] was down in a saw pit and many assaulting him, still holding with a death grasp his manacled charge.' A farmer from the neighbourhood of Ballyheigue intervened and, 'with persevering exertions, and at great personal sacrifice warded off the foolish people'.[42] In 1857 magistrates meeting to decide the allocation of police to different districts still considered that 'the people of the neighbourhood were very much addicted to drinking in the public houses in the village, and to rioting and disorder'.[43]

Various other villages of North Kerry also provided platforms for the feuding parties. Fighting took place in Newtownsandes (later known as Moyvane):

> Long ago people used to fight with blackthorn sticks ... That fighting used to be going on in Newtownsandes between people called the Cooleens and the Black Mulvihills. They fought after Mass on Sundays, and when they met at fairs and markets they fought also. The parish priest of Newtownsandes often tried to stop the fighting but it was of no use. One Sunday they met ... to fight a terrible battle. They were fighting from about nine o'clock in the morning [until] about five o'clock in the evening, and at that time one of the Cooleens was dead.[44]

At Lisselton, on Christmas Day 1828, Maurice Flaherty was attacked by three men of the Mulvihills and a man named Fitzgerald, and 'cruelly beaten' with sticks and stones. 'It appeared that a drunken fellow[,] one Fitzgerald, infuriated with whiskey, brandished his cudgel and *halloed* for one faction[;] he was instantly replied to, and a most bloody affray soon commenced.'[45] It was asserted that Flaherty was killed 'under circumstances of the most shocking and unmerciful cruelty'. John Mahony Mulvahill, 'a young man', was convicted of manslaughter, and, seemingly based on the terrible nature of the killing, sentenced to transportation for life, 'amidst the deafening shrieks and lamentations of his male and female friends'.[46]

At Ballyheigue, on the evening of St Patrick's Day 1839, a crowd of about twenty people, whom a policeman believed to be Cooleens and Lawlors, struck each other 'as hard as they could pelt'.[47] At Beale, Ballybunion, the pattern day 'was usually marked out for a faction fight between the two great factions then in North Kerry – the Cooleens and the Mulvihills', said a later folklore interviewee.[48]

A recollection of Beale fair, which was held on 21 September, written in 1928, stated: 'It was the battle ground of the old faction fighters and next to Ballyeigh ranked as North Kerry's biggest event. Many and sanguinary were the fights that took place there between the rival factions that held sway in North Kerry and old men still tell tales of broken heads and bones.'[49] The two parties also met at the pattern days held annually in Knockanure on 15 August:

> In the earlier part of the nineteenth century this Pattern was the scene of many a faction-fight between what were known as the Couleens and the black Mulvihills; young and old assembled there to see the fight; the contending parties being armed with black-thorn sticks …

> Hard strokes were given and received, and many a young man was maimed for life. The fortunes of war varied from year to year, the defeated party always turning up the next year with fresh men, and attacked their opponents with renewed vigour.[50]

We must suspect that some of the earliest faction fights in North Kerry involved the Cooleens and the Lawlors–Black Mulvihills, even if there is no definitive proof. Perhaps they were the 'two contending parties' who fought in Listowel in 1806, or the two factions who entered the town and engaged in a furious attack on each other in 1814.[51]

Not surprisingly, at various times and places attempts were made to put a stop to the activities of the two gangs. This was often, though not exclusively, undertaken by the clergy, such as at Newtownsandes following the day-long fight which left a man dead: 'Every other Sunday after that the priest came out in the street after Mass, and ordered all the people to go home, and not to fight any more. The two sides were advised by him, and they never again fought.'[52] In December 1828, 'to reconcile contending factions', a priest had a large crowd of people from Ballylongford, Lisselton, Tarbert and the Galey walk, as a penance, from Tarbert to Tralee.[53] In 1832 there was an effort to persuade the two parties to cease fighting by a gentleman from Brandonwell, Ardfert, and it was reported that 'a cordial and sincere reconciliation has taken place between the factions of the Couleens and Lawlors. That honest and ardent patriot, Mr J O'Connor ... has been chiefly instrumental in effecting this good work.'[54]

Such reconciliations did not last.

FAMOUS FIGHTERS

Over the course of the two gangs' long existence several notable fighters stood out, and stories about them continued to be remembered among the people of North Kerry long after the factions had ceased to exist. By far the most famous of these men was John, known as Seón, Burns, who fought with the Cooleens.[55] He was 'a well-to-do farmer' from Coolaneelig, Duagh.[56] According to a folklore source from the Listowel area, he was 'a powerfully built man', standing 'about five feet eleven inches high with shoulders like a gint [giant] and weighing about 17 stone'.[57] It was from his mother that Burns got 'the terrible strength', said another. 'She was a Kenny from Castle Island known here as old mammy Kenny. Her people were known to be terrible strong.'[58]

One of the most popular stories about Seón related how one St Patrick's Day a drinking buddy, local magistrate Major Gallwey, persuaded him to pretend to be extremely drunk in the street in front of one Constable Molloy, 'an unusually strong man' only recently arrived in Abbeyfeale, just over the county bounds in West Limerick.[59] Versions of this story appear in many of the accounts to do with Burns which were collected for the Schools' Folklore Collection during the 1930s. Molloy grabbed Burns, but the latter shoved him away. When he caught him again:

> Burns seized him with one hand, lifted him over his head into the air and put him sitting in a cart … All the onlookers cheered and this roused the anger of the officer who again made for his prey, only to be again seized and put sitting in the middle of the street. Mr Gallwey … told Burns to put the officer to bed – Burns took hold of him and put him inside the barracks' door to end his bravery.[60]

On another occasion, when he was in Co. Limerick, he supposedly met a giant of a man, who challenged him to a fight, 'and to the surprise of those present Shone seized him with one hand and threw him over the seven foot wall nearby, thus ending his ambition to gain victory over the Kerry hero'.[61]

A folklore interviewee saw Burns fight in Listowel one day, when he was there alone: 'A number of men wanted to beat him and Seón had nobody with him. He saw there was too many of them against him and he had no way of saving himself. He faced a donkey's car and tore it asunder like a match box. He took one of the shafts out of it and cleared his men out of the town.'[62] Burns also fought in Newcastle West, Co. Limerick: 'Sean was often mixed up in a row at fairs in Newcastle but the police never attempted to arrest him for they knew they would not be able.'[63]

Burns, 'although a man of immense strength, was most inoffensive and of very placid demeanor', it was stated, yet his fighting career was not without fatal consequences:

> One evening when returning from a fair at Listowel 'Shown' was attacked some miles outside the town, and while defending himself against a number of assailants, lost his temper and striking one of them a deliberate blow of his fist – it unfortunately proved fatal. This accident was ever subsequently regretted by him. For months he was on the run in consequence and many interesting tales have been related – of striking incidents of strength displayed by him, until he surrendered to the law, which afterwards honourably acquitted him of any deliberate responsibility for the act which caused him so much pain.[64]

It is likely that this story represents a version of the incident in which Maurice Shea was killed at Listowel bridge in December 1831, and that Seón Burns was the 'John Bourns' who absconded from and was afterwards acquitted of the manslaughter.[65]

Seón appears to have died during the 1870s.[66] However, he continued to demonstrate his strength into old age. A story was collected about an English visitor to the Fitzmaurices, local landlords of Kilcara, Duagh. The man was 'a brave strong fellow, who did great feats in England and had a great opinion of himself'. One day 'the visitors were walking in the lawn where there was a great big stone, which Shone Burns used to lift. This famous English man had great looking at the stone, and Mr Fitzmaurice said, "you seem to [think] you could lift that".' The stranger disagreed, adding that there wasn't a man in Ireland who could do it. Fitzmaurice bet him £10 that he could 'get a man sixty years of age to lift it'. Fitzmaurice 'sent for Shone, and gave him a few pints of whiskey, then he told him what he wanted him for, "Oh said Shone I am too old to do these things now", whereupon the Englishman remarked, "there was never a day you could lift it".' This remark so annoyed Seón that he 'made one drive at it', and succeeded in raising the stone to his knees.[67]

Another Cooleen hero was Neanntanán Sheehy. '[He] was famed far and wide for his strength. There was only one person stronger than him and that was Seón Burns,' recalled Richard Denihan, whose father had been a member of the Cooleens:

> Neanntanán Sheehy was engaged in very many factions and he was never brought to his knees by any man, but he met his doom in the end and I'll tell you how he did because I was witness to it. We were

> living below in Athea at that time. Myself and my brother Tom were only garsúns about seven or eight at the time. We were sent to bed early in the night and the window of our room looked out in the street. About eleven o'clock we heard some skirmish in the street and faith we jumped up to the window. Who should be in the street but Neanntanán Sheehy – we knew his voice well – and two other men. My mother, God rest her, came down to us. 'Who are they, Mother?' says Tom. 'Oh,' says my mother, 'that's Neanntanán Sheehy and two men from over in Knockanare.' With that the fight started and one of them must have hit Neanntanán and knocked him for we heard one of the men saying to the other 'Hit him down on the head.' My mother told us to leave the window and she went away. Next morning Neanntanán was over inside the wall and he covered with blood. He died later on in the day. My mother warned us on our life not to cough a word as to what we saw or heard. 'For,' says she, 'we didn't see anyone, only heard them, and so we can't be sure.' … My mother the poor woman didn't want to come into any trouble if she could avoid it. The harm was done and she didn't want to bring the wrath of the others upon her. The place was full of police for a few days but they never took anyone for the murder, and it all passed away.[68]

The Lawlors and Black Mulvihills also had their champions. Gearóid Mulvihill was descended from the Mulvihills of Knockanira, Co. Clare, who 'had the reputation of being great fighters and men of splendid physique'. He 'led the Black Mulvihills in many a bloody contest. Gearóid used to stuff his hat with hay so as to lessen the impact of the blows on his head.' The following story about him also features 'a formidable fighter' for the Cooleens, Seán Sheehy, from Coolaneelig, who was known as the *Dailc* ('the hulk').

> Gearóid Mulvihill had many notable victories and was held in high esteem even by his enemies. At that time the champions of different factions used to challenge each other to fight in order to see who was the better man … Big Jim Hartnett of Abbeyfeale sent a challenge to Gearóid, which he accepted. He took none of his followers with him.
>
> It was a long hard fight which Gearóid eventually won. When the Abbeyfeale men saw their leader stretched on the ground they rushed at Gearóid and almost killed him. The Dailc and his followers, who were present, went to his rescue and beat back his attackers. The Dailc took him to his own home and got two doctors to attend him. After a long illness Gearóid recovered, but he fought no more.[69]

Daniel Keane was another strongman. 'It is told of him that he often took a sack of meal on his back from Duagh village to his home in Lybes nearly half a mile away.' He was 'Second only to Shone Burns … he often measured his strength against Shone.'[70] Another folklore interviewee remembered: 'One Sunday the Cooleens wanted to prevent the Mulvihills of going to Mass. Shone was not there that day. The Cooleens lined up at each side of the road and Daniel Keane led his party, and the Cooleens striking him at each side, his head was turning from side to side with the blows of blackthorn sticks, [but] he cleared the way and every man he struck fell to the ground.'[71]

Seán Doody, known as Shawn Láidir ('the strongman'), also fought for the Mulvihills. He was a man who 'shone out in deeds of strength', while the other men in his extended family, who numbered thirty-two, 'were courageous and warlike and their aid was eagerly sought at faction fights'. A tall tale was told to convey his strength: 'Beale strand was crowded with people as well as the usual tents & apple carts seen at a race meeting', reported a folklore interviewee of the local pattern day. 'Shawn Láidir[,] wishing to clear a space for the opposing parties [to] meet on, went over to an apple cart and took the donkey which was unharnessed by the side of the cart. Catching the donkey by the tail he raised him up & swung him around & flung him right over a tent and into the midst of the crowd scattering the people in all directions.'[72]

Edmond Walsh, from Newtownsandes, also called Eamon Kitough, was later described as a brave old war-horse of the Lawlor faction. 'That this old veteran died a natural death must be attributed to the fact that he was a man of fine physique, and, moreover, his head was bullet-proof … unquestionably he was the best-known exponent of the national pastime during the rough old days of the blackthorn.'[73]

Another imposing man, Peter Hurley (or Hurly), from Clievragh, near Listowel, fought in the feud, seemingly as a leader of the Mulvihills. In 1871 Peter was described as having been 'the "head centre" in the faction fights long, long ago', and as having taken part in the great fight at Ballyeagh in 1834:

> At the head of the celebrities of this village hamlet, chief among the 'braves', whose voice at the council fire is loudest … and who rules as despotic as any titular crowned head, stands … the celebrated, well-known, highly-valued, and justly esteemed Peter Hurly, a giant in stature; yet thin and lank of frame, a visage shrewd, which he varies by strange and grotesque contortions; his neck is swathed round in the voluminous folds of a comforter … containing on its

> azure ground the flags of all nations, and divers inscriptions in the Arabesque, a language that Peter favours.[74]

Women also took part in fighting for both these factions, but some of them had another role, that of *bainfhile*, partisan songwriters who could quickly conjure up verses to celebrate the heroes of their own faction or mock their rivals. Thomas Culhane collected some of these verses during the 1960s; he explained that on one occasion, as Gearóid Mulvihill was leading his party into a fight in Listowel, Kate Flavin, a poet of the Cooleens, shouted out: '*So chúinn Gearóid an buaileam sciath/agus coca féir ar bharr a chinn*' (Here comes Gearóid the show-off/and his hat stuffed with hay). In return, Nancy Keane, for the Mulvihills, addressed Seán Sheehy of Coolaneelig, as the Cooleens came up:

> *Cé hé an spriosán suarach críonna*
> *le scata dúradán 'na thimpeall?*
> *Nach é Seán salach ó Chúil an Aoiligh,*
> *Seán bundúnach an chinn mhóir mhíolaigh?*
>
> Who is that petty old waster
> with a band of weaklings around him?
> Is it not filthy Seán from the Dung Heap,
> silly Seán with his big head infested with lice?

Unfortunately for Sheehy, the name of his homeplace could be interpreted literally as 'the dung heap'. Keane then looked to the champion of her own party, in contrast:

Go mbuaidh Dia leat, a Ghearóid ghroí,
is tusa togha agus rogha den bhuín.
Níor staon tú riamh i mbrúion, a chroí.
Buail an diabhal is gach Cúilín.

May God raise you up, oh vigorous Gearóid,
you the multitude's chosen one.
Never did you fail in battle, my dear one.
Strike at the devil and all the Cooleens.[75]

The pride and the passion of the Cooleens, the Lawlors and the Mulvihills, so well demonstrated in these verses, was most fiercely and fatally expressed on the field of battle at Ballyeagh strand, near Ballybunion, on Tuesday 24 June 1834. There a huge number of men and women amassed for a conflict which transformed into a rout and left between eighteen and twenty-nine people dead, scandalised the local and national press, required two official inquiries, and resulted in transportation or imprisonment for a number of North Kerry men.

3

THE BATTLE OF BALLYEAGH, 1834

> 'Oh! shame on ye, shall it ever be said that the Cooleens feared to meet the Lawlors and Mulvihills and Walshes on such a day as this, after all the blustering preparations that have been made. Is there a man among ye that don't remember the fine trouncing ye gave them last year, and what reason is there why ye would not inflict a similar castigation to-day?'
>
> Part of a speech addressed to the Cooleens at Ballyeagh[1]

Horse races had long been held on St John's Day, at Ballyeagh strand (north of the Cashen river, which separates the baronies of Iraghticonnor and Clanmaurice from each other). Although some gentlemen of the county took part, these were rated as 'farmer's races'; sometimes there was a cash stake, but more often saddles formed the modest prizes.[2] And as long as the races had been run, fights had been staged between the Cooleens and the Lawlors on the occasion – a Listowel correspondent of the *Limerick Herald* called them 'the annual riots at Ballyeagh'.[3] In 1832 the day had passed off without incident: 'although there was a vast concourse of country people, the meeting was not disgraced by any appearance of riot'.[4] In 1833 the Cooleens defeated the Lawlors. As the races of 1834 approached, it became known to local observers such as Fr Jeremiah Mahony, parish priest of Listowel, that not only was a fight planned for the day, but that 'this fight was spoken of as one of an unusual complexion'.[5] John Francis Hewson, magistrate of the district and deputy lieutenant of Co. Kerry, also explained that it was conceived not as a regular fight, but as a 'great fight'.[6]

A local historian revealed over thirty years afterwards that 'the event which subsequently led to the great fight at Ballyeagh was the death of a prominent [C]ooleen at Causeway' (which, deep in Iraghticonnor, was Lawlor territory):

> He was killed under circumstances of peculiar barbarity. It was at a fair in Causeway, in 1832, or early in 1833. As he was sitting in a public house with his back towards the door two men entered, one of them struck him with some blunt instrument … the man F— died the following day. Nobody was punished for this crime, it was night, and the murderer easily escaped. It is believed it was not from party motives the man was killed, but for some private wrong, the details of which I have heard, but am not at liberty to give to the public. I have said that the man killed was a *Cooleen*. To avenge his death his friends prepared themselves for the ensuing races of Ballyeagh; and accordingly on the 24th of June, 1833, the Cooleens assembled in great numbers on the racecourse, and completely routed their opponents. Adopting the enemy's tactics, the Lawlors made vigorous preparations for 1834, but not so secretly that the Cooleens were not fully aware of their proceedings; so that both parties resolved to put forth their whole strength, and it became known on all sides that the coming contest would be a trial that would determine the supremacy of some one party, although neither of them could foresee the dreadful and horrific tragedy by which that supremacy was obtained.[7]

The Cooleen killed in April 1832 was Mathias Flaherty. A contemporary newspaper report noted that he had been at the fair, 'drinking in a public house with several others, with his back near the room door, when *somebody*, from the doorway struck him on the back of the head, with a weighty stick, from the fatal effects of which blow, he died'. As he was dying, Flaherty claimed that a man named Crowley 'gave the blow as he was his enemy, and had previously threatened to kill him. The evidence was deemed insufficient, and the prisoner was acquitted.'[8] Denied justice, as they believed, the Cooleens were keen to continue to extract it physically at Ballyeagh, but the Lawlors did not wish to be beaten as they had been in 1833, and were determined to win by appearing in huge numbers and applying some field tactics.

'The preparations for the fight at Ballyeagh were on a most extensive scale,' the historian related:

> For months before it came off messengers were [sent] by the leaders of both parties to all parts of the county, and even to the county Limerick. ... Friends either by blood or marriage were entreated by the honour of their name and family to stand by their party, and, where entreaties were not successful, threats of persecution were used in a most ingenious manner, and were actually carried into execution in many instances.[9]

Among non-participants, attitudes towards the two factions and their encounters at Ballyeagh varied. John Hilliard, a semi-retired army officer, stated that he regularly 'heard persons in the rank of gentlemen say it would be better to let them fight it out' or remark 'that it would be better to have one half hanged, and the other half slaughtered'.[10] He and a colleague, Maurice O'Halloran, were afterwards questioned at a court of inquiry as to why they went to the fight of 1834, seemingly with a view to suggesting that both had gone to enjoy watching a fight (rather than to prevent it, as would have been considered their duty). Hilliard had great difficulty genuinely condemning the fighters, while his colleague caused consternation in court when he remarked that he 'did not care if they fought until they beat each other well' and that 'unless murder was committed [he] would look on and see them *fight with pleasure*'.[11]

Others took action to try to prevent the fighting. For the coming event of 1834, David Pierse, the agent of the Staughton estate around the village of Ballyduff, went in advance to several churches and spoke to tenants after Mass, warning them that if he found them on the scene, 'they should feel the conscquence on the day after'.[12] William Sandes of Pyrmount said that his uncle 'made it a point with all his labourers to spend that day at Sallowglin, for the express purpose of preventing them from attending'.[13] Similarly, every parish priest in the neighbourhood read 'exhortations and cautions from their altars to prevent the fight, or even to appear on the strand', but, recalled Mr Hewson, 'the people were determined to fight and would not be prevented'.[14]

Magistrates had become aware of the scale of the long-intended conflict a month beforehand. Accordingly, Hewson requisitioned some troops from Tralee Barracks, and early in the morning of the races marshalled sixty soldiers and two officers of the 69th Regiment, along with twelve policemen under Captain William Brady of Listowel Station, and rendezvoused at Ballyduff. Following a rumour that the Cooleens might make use of firearms, they searched houses and gardens between there and the Cashen river, as these 'principally belonged to the Cooleen faction'.[15] They then crossed the river by ferry and arrived at the strand, but their forces were far too small to deal with the huge crowd of fighters.

There were about 150 tents on the beach. According to a later interviewee, who had the information through his grandfather, a Cooleen, these displayed 'plenty roast beef and fresh mutton'.[16] There were also whiskey, rum, ale and wine, he said, and, indeed, on the day, Captain Brady would see 'a great number of people under the influence of liquor there'.[17] By about 10.30 a.m. up to 200 of the Lawlor faction were estimated to be lodged at the tents, having occupied the ground from earlier in the day. Many more were hidden further from view, however, as 'a large portion of the Lawlor party were concealed behind the sand banks to the rear of the tents'.[18] It appears that they were planning to mount an ambush against the Cooleens after giving them a reduced sense of their true numbers.[19]

At one point the Lawlors shouted and cheered (perhaps rousing themselves in anticipation of battle), so Mr Hewson and Lieutenant Lossack went among them, confiscating their sticks, but – remarkably – handing them back on getting the men to promise that there would be no fighting. Hewson was confident that the mere appearance of the soldiers and the police on the beach 'had put an end to the intended fight'.[20]

The Lawlors held a collection for a prize, marked out a course in the sand and ran a horse race. There appeared to be some ruction among them at about two o'clock, and Hewson sent over the police, under Captain Brady, to quell it. When he arrived,

Brady came upon Magistrate Thomas Ponsonby of Crotto, who asked him where he was going. He explained what he was instructed to do, but Ponsonby told him to leave, as bringing the police along 'where no riot existed, might be the cause of serious consequences' and might serve to 'irritate the people'. Ponsonby also said that what had gone on was merely shouting at a horse having won a race and that it was not indicative of any impending fight. Brady pointed out that he was following Mr Hewson's orders, but Ponsonby replied, 'You are aware, Sir, that I am a magistrate of the County, and I will take the responsibility on myself, should Mr Hewson attach any blame to you; I now give you an order to retire, and inform Mr Hewson with my compliments that I do so.'[21]

Soon afterwards, Brady came upon Ponsonby again; now in the midst of a crowd of Lawlor men, he was brandishing a whip and 'using the most energetic language to persuade them to desist' (seemingly from ill-discipline among themselves).[22] Police Sergeant William Phillip saw 'sticks wheeling and heard much shouting'.[23]

Brady noticed that Ponsonby knew these men well and called them by their first names. 'Mr Ponsonby then said in these words, if my memory serves me right, but certainly to this effect: "There is your place, boys; move off there to the right", pointing with his hand to a hill to the right of the tents.'[24] This expression greatly surprised Brady at the time. What the magistrate may have been doing was later suggested by historian Patrick O'Donnell:

> [Ponsonby] managed to confuse the police and get them away from where the tents were pitched. He did not want them there because

> he was engaged in getting some of the Lawlor-Black Mulvihills out of the tents where they were drinking poteen and whiskey. He was concerned about having the fighting men ready in good time for the coming engagement. His task was apparently more difficult than he had anticipated and he used his crop to tap men on the shoulder and order them out. 'Come on now, boys', he urged. 'Tom, Mick, Pat, up there to your places'.[25]

Hewson later recalled that 'all remained quiet until about half after three in the afternoon'.[26] Indeed, up to that time, Fr Mahony thought there might not be any fight, and he noted that 'it was a subject of conversation that the other party would not appear'. Nevertheless, the Lawlors had some of their forces well organised among the tents, ready for action; according to another witness there were 'a number of persons arrayed and drawn up in regular order; they had the appearance of persons drawn up to oppose another party … they were ranged there for two hours'.[27]

The Cooleens crossed over the Cashen by boat at a point known as the new ferry. Oliver Mason, an elderly magistrate who lived close by, met them as they prepared to cross and warned them: 'ye are doing a very bad job, my boys; and ye may suffer for this'.[28] According to a later account, local priests at the scene:

> used all their influence, and threatened the leaders with the most terrible denunciations if they did not disband their followers, and go to their homes. One of the Priests was also present at Dirrerah, opposite Ballyeagh strand, endeavouring to prevent the people from crossing, and he even offered to pay the men employed in the lighters and fishing boats any reasonable sum if they would discontinue ferrying over the people.[29]

According to the same account, however, there was also an attorney there – characterised as a 'meddlesome pest' – who made a rousing speech to the assembled Cooleens, firing them up for battle and telling them not to be afraid of the soldiers and to ignore the priests.[30] We cannot now know who this man was, but it is worth considering that a lawyer called Daniel Supple Jr, who had family connections with Listowel, later led a group of shillelagh-wielding men – seemingly Cooleen faction fighters – who marched up and down Denny Street, Tralee, in an intimidating manner, in support of the O'Connellite candidates during the election campaign of 1841.[31]

What the actions and speeches by Ponsonby for the Lawlors and the unnamed attorney for the Cooleens suggest is that members of the local elite had a role in mustering these particular parties. That both men were ostensibly involved in upholding law and order makes their activities all the more remarkable. Yet such patronage may not have been unique in Kerry faction fighting. Over a century earlier Murroghoh O'Connor had written:

Oft have I seen two Landlords at a fair,
Where Tenants with their Sheep and Cows repair;
A Quarrel first betwixt themselves create,
Then urge their Clans to end the fierce Debate.[32]

Elsewhere in the country, too, it was claimed that 'The landlords used [to] have their own factions and enjoy seeing them fighting.'[33]

On the day of the battle, when the group from Clanmaurice arrived on the other side of the river, they joined up with a party of Iraghticonnor Cooleens who came along from the Rahoona road.[34] There may then have been between 600 and 1,000 Cooleens.[35] They carried along with them cartloads of stones, and the younger men and the women 'were ordered to take charge of the stones, and have them in the centre of the strand as a reserve in case a retreat became necessary. Loading themselves with stones they then advanced, about 300 of the best men forming the van [vanguard].'[36] According to a later account, two leaders of the Cooleens, Paddy Hackett and Sylvester Ahern, rode on horseback before the crowd.[37]

Some of the fighters involved for both parties were listed by Patrick O'Donnell. (For some reason, Seón Burns was not among them.) The Lawlors were headed by 'the mighty Michael Simon Mulvihill' from Lisselton, of whom little is known other than that he was jailed a couple of years afterwards for 'malicious assault'.[38] There was also a man called O'Sullivan Bird: 'In this fight he wielded a blackthorn with several prongs on the striking end, and whenever he got two enemies close together he is said to have struck both down with the one blow!'[39] Mike Horrigan was a leader of the Cooleens, while:

> William Quinlan, John Hayes, John and Patrick Lynch, Maurice Sheehy, Dan Boyle and John Wholihan were leading sections. Prominent in their ranks was Pat Sullivan, nicknamed 'Halloo' because this was a favourite greeting of his. A tall, tough man with bushy eyebrows and tanned, leathery face, he wielded the long handle of a spade with great effect. Pat Hackett was particularly good at knocking the sticks from the hands of his opponents. Maurice Sheehy was a two-handed fighter ... John Davis's gambit was to stagger an opponent with a stone-throw and then close in with his stick before his enemy could recover.[40]

Hayes would be arrested early in the fight, but by the end of the day Ahern, and his lieutenants, the Lynch brothers, Sheehy, Boyle and Wholihan, would be dead.

A horse race had just finished when the Cooleen faction arrived on the strand, between half and three-quarters of a mile away from the Lawlors, 'approaching in a large body … and coming along in a regular manner'. Despite their numbers, Hewson said that the Lawlors 'were still much the stronger party'.[41] The latter 'had assembled in full force before the Cooleens made their appearance … As they were defeated on the race day the year before, they were determined on the present occasion to secure victory at whatever sacrifice.'[42]

A roar went up from the Lawlors: '*They are coming!*'[43]

Upon arrival the Cooleens were ready to fight: their coats were thrown off and they were 'wheeling their sticks, hurraing, and approaching steadily across the strand'. Lieutenant William Moore observed that they were 'advancing in a kind of trot'.[44] Fr Mahony had gone to the races determined to prevent any breach of the peace by his parishioners and others, and he and Mr Hewson rode over to try and remonstrate with the approaching crowd, but they 'would not be heard'.[45]

On seeing the Cooleens advancing, the Lawlors 'immediately gave signal to commence fight, by wheeling sticks and yelling for the opposite party to come on'.[46] With women amongst them, they started running towards their enemies, stopping briefly near the centre of the strand to cast off their coats and shoes. The Cooleens, who carried stones and were further supplied with them by several women who held them in their aprons, started firing them at the Lawlors, as both factions, 'sticks flourishing in the air', collided violently with each other.[47]

The force of the Cooleens' onrush gave them the initial advantage and, still pelting stones, they drove the Lawlors, who abandoned their plan of ambush, back two miles along the strand.[48] At the same time, Sergeant William Phillip saw 'immense numbers of men, women, and children', who had simply been attending the day, 'running towards the military and police for protection'.[49]

As the fighting played out, Hewson saw ten or twelve men beating one man, and many men laid down 'as if dead'. Constable Gason of Ballyduff Station 'was knocked speechless by a blow of a stone', and he had to be carried away from the scene by two colleagues.[50] Many of the fighters used sticks that were weighted with iron ferules, which were described locally as being about four inches long.[51] Some of the Cooleens had succeeded in bringing firearms and a party of the Lawlors asked the police: 'Oh won't you take their guns?'[52] (There were no specific reports of weapons actually being fired.) The Lawlors, too, 'had a quantity of firearms concealed behind the tents, though they were not used'.[53]

Mr Hewson, Fr Mahony, Captain Brady and the police tangled with different clusters of rioters, managing to haul sixteen men and one woman away, and giving them over to the custody of the military. Many of these prisoners were 'either cut or wounded'.[54] The priest rode in among the rival factions, exposing himself to such danger that Captain Brady begged him 'for God's sake not to risk his life and keep out of the way'.[55] By this stage Hewson (whom Fr Mahony characterised as a 'brave old gentleman') had been hit by a stone as well as thrown from his horse.[56] Captain Brady had 'narrowly escaped being killed' and his horse was badly injured.[57] There were several bodies on the ground, 'bleeding copiously, as if dead'.[58]

The Cooleens 'utterly routed the Lawlors at the first onset, their leader being left for dead on the strand'.[59] Among the wounded was Tom Walsh of Ballydonoghue, great-grandfather of Maurice Walsh, author of *The Quiet Man*; he left the field suffering from a head wound, his shirt soaked with blood, and returned home temporarily, where his wife tended his injury. 'Give us a clean shirt,' he was said to have begged her as she tended his wound, 'and let me drown meself for there's divil the hope.'[60]

It looked like the Lawlors and Mulvihills were going to endure defeat for the second year running.

'BARBAROUS AND DISGRACEFUL RIOT'

Over time, however, the tide of battle changed. The Lawlors in retreat found themselves in fields north of the strand. 'Snatching up stones from the fields and gardens, they faced round and confronted the Cooleens once more. Although many of these had their pockets full of the missiles, yet as they kept up a running fire on the retreating forces, their ammunition was nigh exhausted when the Lawlors charged them in turn.'[61]

Richard Denihan, whose father, a Cooleen, was at Ballyeagh, gave an account of the fight, although he mistakenly reversed the roles and the fates of the two factions on the day; correcting this error here, it would seem that a champion of the Cooleens, 'was doing a great execution till a woman … threw a horse-shoe at him and hit him in the head. This blow laid him out' and the Cooleens 'began to lose courage at that' and the Mulvihills 'got their spirit and made a rush at them'.[62]

The Cooleens were forced back, 'and in the confusion which ensued a small number of them were able to reach the reserve of stones' which they had placed in the centre of the strand:

> The greater part of them made towards the river, where they expected to find fresh supplies. In this they were not disappointed, for as soon as the people at the Clanmaurice side (and many remained at that side for safety sake) saw the Cooleens flying, they sent several boat-loads of stones across; but this could not be done so quickly that the Lawlors had not time to overtake them.
>
> Meanwhile the skirmishing continued in the centre of the strand, and had spread even as far as the road leading out of it. Both parties, that is, such of them as were not at the water's edge, had betaken themselves to the more congenial and manly weapon – the stick. The Cooleens fought bravely, but they were outnumbered, and besides there was a general feeling that the Lawlors were at all times better men at the sticks. One Cooleen was pursued by three Lawlors, he attacked them separately … when he perceived them some distance asunder. The nearest to him he knocked down with one blow, and was making towards the second … when his right arm was severely hurt by a Lawlor woman, who had taken off her stocking, and filled it with stones.[63]

One group of Cooleens fled the strand where they had originally entered it, from Rahoona, while the party that had run back for the Cashen river attempted to pile into boats there and escape. 'On the opposite side of this river there were many tents of "the Cooleen" faction, and could they have got over, they would have escaped the fury of their assailants,' recalled Mr Hewson.[64] It was at that point that the day's grim work truly began:

> Their friends at the opposite side thought only of conveying stones across without sending any assistance to empty the boats. Thus when the Cooleens arrived, some of them had to go into the boats, and throw the stones out on the strand to the others; and before a tenth of these had armed themselves the Lawlors were on them! It was in vain that they attempted to make head against the overwhelming numbers that came pouring down on them – they rushed afrighted on all sides, some along the margin of the river – [some] into the water, having put off their coats and shoes – and others into the boats that were already half-laden with stones … One boat alone was able to move into the water, the others stuck fast, and scarcely was it afloat when the Lawlors redoubled their blows with sticks and stones … It sunk.[65]

Denis McAuliff had a view of what happened then. There were:

> about 30 or 40 trying to get into the boat, but all did not get in; they were getting in until the boat sunk; as soon as the boat went down, the Lawlors commenced throwing stones at these in the water, when the poor creatures were trying to make the strand; they were struck with sticks and stones … the Lawlors went above their knees in the water for the purpose of striking the drowning party.

McAuliff rescued one man, Paddy Brick from Lixnaw: 'this man was struck a blow on the head with a stick at the time he was being dragged out of the water', and he saw another man hit on the head by a stone who 'went down' and 'did not rise again'.[66]

While some gentlemen, such as George and Wilson Gun, David Pierse, Frederick Mason, Kerry Supple and others, were riding into the water in an effort to rescue those under attack, members of the Lawlor faction, according to Captain Brady, were shouting out that those in the water should 'not be let come ashore'. [67] Wilson Gun saw 'seventeen or eighteen people on the strand engaged in murdering the unfortunate strugglers in the water'.[68]

According to Richard Denihan, speaking in the 1960s, seemingly on the basis of the recollections of his father, a number of Lawlor men at the shore:

> had saddle-horses and hadn't up to this taken any part in the fray. So now they swam their horses out in the water and began to attack the boats. A number of the boats got capsized but mostly in shallow water. One boat with nine men in it was attacked by five or six horsemen and sunk. The men were thrown into the water and began to sink and every time a head came up the horsemen gave it the *buailteán* [a variety of fighting stick that he said was about four feet long].[69]

Another witness said that while several men were struggling to avoid drowning, 'he saw a tall man so busily employed in slaughtering them with a heavy hurley and with stones that he … was certain he must have killed six or seven human beings, who might probably otherwise have escaped'.[70] This man appears to have been Thomas Sells, who was afterwards tried for committing murder at the shore. Patrick Sheehy swore afterwards that Sells and Theade Canty struck his brother, Maurice, as he was trying to escape to a boat: 'that he was within 40 spades of his brother when he was struck by the prisoner with a stick, and by the other man with a stone, which killed him'.[71]

Another witness, James Maddegan, also saw Sells '*standing in the water*, and striking the people in the water with a *hurl*'.[72] John Fitzgerald said Sells struck John Lynch with a stick, at the edge of the water, knocking him down, and another man struck him on the forehead with a stone; afterwards Maddegan saw two men named Enright 'take the body and throw it into the water'.[73] After the Cooleens were killed, Sells rode away, sharing a horse with another man behind him and throwing Patrick Lynch and John Fitzgerald a 'desperate look' as he passed.[74] Among other Lawlor fighters much later said to have been involved at the shore were Pat Halloran, Richard McCarthy, Tom Fitzgerald and Ned Walsh, the last the celebrated faction fighter known as Eamon Kitough.[75]

Women also appear to have been involved in violence at the shore. It was stated in one account that 'the women helped the men to drown them', and in another that when three men 'tried to regain the river bank … a woman named Downey drowned them by striking them with a loaded stocking'.[76] Another folklore interviewee, whose mother had been at Ballyeagh on 'the day of the big fight', said that women 'took off their boots and put stones into their stockings and with the Mulvihills drove the Cooleens out into the [water] and followed them and turned their boats and drowned seventeen of them'.[77]

A story was later related about the killing of a young man from Dunferris:

> He was the finest athlete in North Kerry in his time. The poor chap got wounded early in the fight, and, being unable to continue the struggle, he bolted from the strand. Nearing the end of the strand

> at Rahoona, he weakened, and being overtaken by the enemy he was brutally killed. There were some women lolling about, whose business it was to try to act as a kind of rearguard to one of the sides, and one of these stuffed the dying man's mouth with slob sand to prevent his recovery.[78]

Captain Brady believed that 'the numbers assembled to oppose each other would not be less than one thousand of each party. I do not include the women who, in carrying sticks and stones, and otherwise mingling in the affray, nearly equalled the number of men.'[79]

When the violence had begun, people had run to Fr Mahony, who was elsewhere on the long strand, and alerted him to what was happening: 'Oh God! sir, won't you come down, and save some of them: they are driving them in crowds into the water,' they cried. He made his way to the shore as fast as he could, and when he got there he was 'horror-stricken' by what he saw.[80] Mr Hewson and the soldiers subsequently arrived, but the crowd had swollen, partly obscuring what was happening, and when Hewson and the soldiers came up, the former only saw in the distance three or four men 'struggling for life' who had swum over to the Clanmaurice side, while nearer by 'hats and sticks were floating in all directions'.[81]

Upon the appearance of the soldiers, some of the assembled men and women ran off. Hewson wanted the military to fire warning shots over the heads of those engaged in the violence, but Captain Richard Hooper told him, 'there is a special order that if the military fire, it should be at the persons of the rioters', and, rather than doing so, no shots were discharged at all. The wider crowd on the strand subsequently came to realise what had gone on at the shore, and 'the shrieks of the people were heart-rending,' remembered Hewson. Fr Mahony exclaimed to Captain Brady that 'the shocking monsters would not give relief to their sinking fellow-creatures and even prevented their landing'. Meanwhile, the party of Lawlors who had chased after the group of Cooleens who had left by the landward side of the strand returned, and were 'shouting and exulting' (either rejoicing at their chasing off the other portion of the Cooleens or at what had taken place in the water). After all the fighting was over and done, Captain Brady heard a woman's 'lament or keening', and 'there was rather an awful silence'.[82]

The day's affray lasted for about two hours in total. During that time, Hewson 'saw several persons struck and beaten severely', as well as one man who had his leg broken and another who had his eye knocked out.[83] Doctor Jeremiah Tuite later noted that the body of a man named Scanlan had 'a hole in his head that he might thrust his hand into'.[84] James O'Callaghan saw a man named Martin Flaherty being beaten with sticks by a crowd of men, and intervened to save his life. He 'put his hat on the man's head, he was bleeding copiously' and brought him into a house behind the strand. Flaherty was said to have recruited a group of men for the day to avenge the death of his brother, whom a witness believed was killed in a previous fight on the strand (although perhaps it was the man who had been killed in Causeway two years previously).[85]

A later folklore interviewee related how his grandfather was saved: his leg was broken, but 'as he lay prostrate in the strand a man from Lixnaw riding a grey steed galloped past him' whom 'he implored to take him up behind him'; the rider replied that 'he was only flying for his life' and that it was impossible for the man to mount the horse with a broken leg; he nevertheless managed to get up and had the rider deposit him at the mouth of the Cashen where he saw a man he knew who was operating a boat and got him safely across the water.[86]

Throughout the fight, several gentlemen tried to control the rioters, to make arrests and to save the injured: David Pierse captured a man he thought was named Cullinane ('he was covered with blood'), while a servant of his saved a man named Neil from being killed.[87]

At around five o'clock, Hewson ordered Captain Brady to read the Riot Act, a formal charge to the crowds to disperse in the name of the King. This was very late in the day's proceedings, but he later argued that he had been too involved in the heat of the conflict to have it done earlier. He ordered the tents taken down and the site cleared. The Lawlor faction may have felt that the non-intervention of the military had enabled their victory, as some of them shouted out to them: 'thank ye, gentlemen, we're obliged to ye, long life to ye'.[88] The police and military left at about half past six or seven, waiting until the evening tide almost covered the strand.

The bodies of twelve men killed at the waterside were washed ashore on the evening of the fight, reported the *Tralee Mercury*, 'and as we have been informed are still lying on the strand their friends being afraid to come near them, lest a similar fate may befall them, as in doing so, they should go to the Lawlor's side of the river'.[89] By the following day the death toll had risen to sixteen: Patrick Lynch, John Lynch, Maurice

Sheehy, Daniel Boyle, Thomas Fitzmaurice, Sylvester Ahern, Cornelius Gallivan, Richard Sturdy, Maurice Horgan, Michael Leary, Thomas Sullivan, Daniel Guerin, Darby Sullivan, John Houlihan (or Wholihan), and two men surnamed Danniher and Rahilly.[90] Michael Leary had been unconnected with the fight, having crossed by boat from the Clanmaurice side of the river, only to arrive when the Lawlors were driving the Cooleens into the water. Rahilly was a street pedlar from Tralee who had gone to the races to sell cakes.[91] Among the dead faction fighters, John Houlihan was said by Doctor Tuite to have had his neck broken by the blow of a blunt instrument;[92] Sylvester Ahern 'was got next day buried to his hips in the slab [slob] at the point of Rahonnah', and his lieutenants, Boyle and Sheehy, were also killed at the shore.[93]

By 7 July the number of dead totalled eighteen.[94] There may have been other deaths, however: 'It is generally supposed, by the country people, that upwards of twenty-five men and women were murdered in the river,' reported *The Kerry Evening Post*, 'amongst whom was a decent country woman and two fine boys, her children; six women's cloaks were found floating on the water. It is said that a well-dressed man, with a watch in his pocket, was found dead, and shockingly mangled, in a potato field, who has never since been claimed nor identified.'[95] (Captain Brady also saw 'a man apparently lifeless, lying in a field'.)[96] A much later report stated that twenty-nine Cooleens had been killed, while among the Lawlors twelve 'were carried home with broken jaws, hands and legs, almost beyond recognition'.[97]

Prisoners taken on the day, some of whom hailed from Co. Limerick, were lodged in Listowel Bridewell around nine o'clock.

All of them seem to have been seized long before the killings at the shore, including Michael Horrigan, who was recognised as 'the Captain of one faction'.[98] Lieutenant Lossack afterwards released the only female among them, telling Captain Brady: 'poor woman, I let her go'; one report claimed that he had done so 'in admiration of her prowess, and pity for her black eyes'.[99] Ten of those arrested were subsequently 'liberated for want of evidence'. Charges of rioting were presented against seven others, including Cooleen member John Hayes, who 'had his coat off, was wheeling a stick, and encouraging his party'. They were held until the afternoon of the following Sunday, 29 June. They were then due to be transferred to the county jail in Tralee, but Brady told Magistrate John Raymond that he did not think it was safe to do so (perhaps fearing their being rescued by their faction or being attacked by their enemies): 'at that hour, with so few men, I could not proceed; particularly under the circumstances, with men of such character'.[100] Accordingly, as only evidence of rioting, rather than murder, had been presented against them, they were bailed, bound to appear at the next assizes and released. 'Many others went on the run, but were never arrested,' it was much later stated.[101]

THE AFTERMATH

Between July 1834 and February 1835, nineteen individuals, including two women, were arrested, charged and remanded in custody in connection with the Ballyeagh fight.[102] They included Lawlor champion Edmond Walsh, and Edmond Stoughton, who had gone on the run since the fatal day and was captured in Tralee after putting up a hard struggle with a number of policemen.[103]

Another was Maurice Leehy (or Leahy) from the Causeway area, remembered in one account as 'a well-to-do farmer', and described in another as a thirty-seven-year-old man with five children, who worked as a farm servant.[104] Leehy had been going home in the evening after the fight when a man stepped out of a house on the way and asked him how the fight had gone. He replied firmly: 'What we didn't kill we drowned.' The remark resulted in someone reporting him to the police and he was arrested. He was tried in Tralee, in the new courthouse which had been completed in March 1835. 'He was the first prisoner to be tried and as being the first in the new Court house and according to custom he should be released but he was not,' it was later stated. 'He was put back a criminal and transported to Van Dieman's Land on perjured evidence.'[105]

Leehy was found guilty of manslaughter, after what a newspaper termed 'a long and patient investigation' (which it did not detail).[106] While he remained in Tralee jail, he tried to break out among a large party of prisoners. The attempt appears to have been well planned. On Sunday 3 May 1835, while the governor, Mr Murphy, was at Mass, prisoners overpowered wardens, and thirty of them, armed with the hammers they used to break limestone during punishments of hard labour, tried to break open the outer gate of the jail – on the other side of which a hundred people were waiting for them. The escape attempt was put down by the military. 'The convicts were ultimately secured, and are now heavily ironed, and safely locked up in their respective cells,' reported *The Kerry Evening Post*, describing Leehy as 'the most desperate' of the prisoners involved.[107] (It is unknown whether this was a general insurrection or one organised specifically by the imprisoned faction members.)

On 13 May, when he was due to be transferred with other prisoners to Cobh, for onward transportation to Australia, Leehy borrowed a penknife from another prisoner:

> as he alleged, for the purpose of pairing [paring] his nails: having got the knife he retired to a remote and secret part of the convict yard and stabbed himself, two or three times, in the abdomen. One of the wounds, inflicted a little below the navel, was rather deep and severe; but, on surgical investigation, not likely to produce fatal consequences; and the desperado was packed off with the other delinquents for his ultimate destination.[108]

Leehy was among 250 Irish prisoners shipped to Australia aboard the *Hive*, which departed Cork in August 1835.[109]

Lawlor faction leader Thomas Sells was tried in March for sixteen murders committed at the strand.[110] As he had previously evaded a party of police by brandishing 'a short gun or blunderbuss', the lord lieutenant had offered a reward of £100 for his capture; he eventually surrendered himself to Thomas Ponsonby.[111] The other men charged with the same offence declined to appear at the same trial (probably wary of being linked with Sells in the jury's mind). A number of Cooleens told the court that they saw Sells hitting men in the water with a hurley stick. Their evidence against him was firmly stated, but equally firmly contradicted by two gentlemen witnesses, Kerry Supple and Wilson Gun. After a direction by the judge, which was characterised as being long and precise (although no details were reported), Sells was acquitted.

In July 1835 sixteen men agreed to plead guilty to committing manslaughter at Ballyeagh. The prosecution had offered them this option, having failed to convict Sells of murder.[112] There were no newspaper reports of evidence presented against them at their trial – their guilty pleas to manslaughter may have obviated the need to present any. Afterwards, the judge addressed them for sentencing:

> Prisoners – You have all severally pleaded guilty to the charge of manslaughter, of an unusually extensive description, which has hurried no fewer than sixteen of your fellow creatures unprepared into eternity, under circumstances of more than ordinary horror; their brains having been beaten out while struggling in the deep waters of the River Cashion, in which their boat had been overset; and you have done all of this impelled by none of the motives which lead to the commission of homicides in other countries, but have slaughtered your own neighbours, merely because they bore certain surnames, at which you take offence, as indicating that they belong to families and factions, between whom and your own families and factions, unmeaning, but hereditary animosities, have existed from generation to generation.
>
> This fact, alike melancholy and extraordinary, might hardly be credited in other nations. It is the peculiar character and disgrace of our own country; a character however which I am happy to say is gradually disappearing, under the influence of extending civilization, and the administration of wholesome laws. I lament to find that it has not as yet disappeared in this county.
>
> Prisoners – You are much indebted to the lenity of the Crown Counsel, who have been your prosecutors, who have intimated to the court their strong wish that upon your acknowledgement of

> your offence by pleading guilty, your punishment should not be carried to the extent of transportation. It would not become a judge to decline compliance with such a desire so expressed; but I wish it distinctly to be understood, that had it not been for this interference, on the part of the prosecutors, the Crown Counsel who represent the Attorney-General on this Circuit, the Court would not feel that it discharged its duty, if it did not transport you for life.
>
> Your sentence must therefore be imprisonment for a considerable period. The duration of which I have endeavoured to adjust in some proportion to the different periods for which you have already been respectively confined, so as to equalise the entire period of the confinement, pretty nearly in respect to all – your sentence therefore – Timothy Lawlor, Thomas Howard, Garrett Moore, Patrick Molyneaux, Patrick Leahy, and Charles McElligott, is that you be imprisoned for two years from the present period – yours, Thomas Griffin, that you be imprisoned [for] one year and nine months – and yours Michael Dunne, Garret Nash, James Enright, Tailor, James Enright, Yeoman, John Enright, John Bunnyan, Garrett Stack, John Meehane, and Patrick Connor, that you be imprisoned for one year and a half, and that you all be kept to hard labour, during the alternate months of your imprisonment.[113]

Despite the intensity of the violence at Ballyeagh and the judge's personal desire to impose the most serious penalty, the convicted men did not spend long in prison. They were afterwards pardoned by Lord Lieutenant of Ireland Constantine Phipps, Lord Mulgrave, in April 1836, having served about nine months of their sentences.[114] Mulgrave was keen to demonstrate a benevolent policy in Ireland and the Ballyeagh men appear to have benefited from his approach.

But what of Leehy, transported to Australia? A story was later told about a government medical officer who was inspecting the settlement of Freemantle, and who ended up walking some distance away from his horse:

> [H]e asked the governor to send one of the convicts to bring the horse to him. When the convict had unloosed the horse and sent him going in the direction of the inspector, he put his hands on the horse's loins and sprung on his back. When he came up to the officers, the inspector complimented him on his agility, and remarked that he saw that feat performed only once before, and that was in Ireland. 'Perhaps in Kerry', said the convict. 'Yes', said the inspector. 'And perhaps in Causeway', said the convict. 'Yes', said the inspector. The doctor had been a poor scholar in Causeway, at the common school of Mr Charles Church … and used to stay frequently at the paternal home of Leahy, and Leahy was the man whom he had seen perform the feat previously. He used his influence with the government on Leahy's behalf, as the result of which he was released on parole, and got a parcel of land to work for himself, after which he brought all his family out to Australia.[115]

In November 1848 Leehy was among several convicts who received a conditional pardon, 'on condition that they do not return to the countries or colonies from which they were respectively transported'.[116]

The Ballyeagh races were discontinued for a few years after the fight. They were reintroduced in 1840 and ran without incident until 1856.[117] In that year, the feature race of the second day was won by Johnny O'Connell of Rathmorrell, riding his own horse, May Morning:

> In a thrilling finish O'Connell on 'May Morning' defeated 'Bay Jane' and 'Timekeeper' owned by two of the landlord class, Messrs Hurley and Sandes respectively. Immediately after the race, Sandes, who had plunged heavily on his own horse, struck O'Connell across the face with a riding crop. O'Connell retaliated, and a row ensued in which both groups of supporters joined.[118]

Thereafter, the races were moved to Listowel, becoming the successful and long-running meeting there.

The Cooleen–Lawlor fights did not quieten after the Ballyeagh riot. The two factions fought later in the same year, in November, at Listowel and at Ballylongford. At the latter encounter, from 150 to 200 on each side 'commenced attacking each other with sticks and stones to such a savage degree as became terrific in the extreme'.[119] In 1836 it was feared that both parties would engage at Ballyeagh pattern, held on 8 and 9 September, and a strong force of police was dispatched there, although there are no reports of any fight taking place.[120]

Nevertheless, by 1839 a speaker at a political meeting in support of Daniel O'Connell and the administration of Ireland by Lord Mulgrave could declare that the legal calendar showed that the Listowel district, 'the former hot-bed of foolish party squabbles', had become a relative ocean of calm:

> We stand this moment within view of Ballyeagh, where … fourteen horrible murders were committed to satisfy the foolish feelings of your 'Cooleens and Lalors' … Thank God we live to see a better state of things brought about (hear, hear) – when the people have learned under an auspicious government to appreciate

> the blessings they enjoy, and to avoid foolish feuds and faction fights.[121]

Some men certainly gave up the feud. In 1841 Mr and Mrs Samuel Carter Hall visited the rooms of the celebrated Fr Mathew, the leader of the Irish temperance movement:

> [T]here were men and women of all ages, waiting to take the pledge: among them was a sturdy mountaineer from Kerry – a fine athletic fellow who had led his 'faction' for a quarter of a century, whose head was scarred in at least a dozen places, and who had been renowned throughout the country for his prowess at every fair within twenty miles of his home. He had long been a member of this society, and had brought a few of his 'friends' to follow his example. He described to us, with natural and forcible eloquence, the effect of temperance in producing peace between man and man, in his own immediate neighbourhood – in terminating the brutal fights between two notorious and numerous factions, the Cooleens and the Lawlors, whose names had figured in every criminal calendar for a century back. 'No matter what was doing, it was left undone', he said, 'if any one of either party chose to call up the rest. They'd leave the hay half cut, or the oats to be shelled by the four winds of heaven; and, taking the hay-fork, the reaping-hook, and the scythe in their hands, they'd rush out to massacre each other. Tubs of potheen [*poitín*] would be drunk hot from the mountain stills; and then, whooping and hollowing like wild Indians, they'd mingle in the unnatural war of Irishman against Irishman. I've known them fight so on the sea-shore, that the sea has come in and drowned those that had fallen drunk in the fray. How is it now? At the last fair at Tralee, there wasn't a stick lifted. There was peace between the factions, and the Cooleens and the Lawlors met, for

> the first time in the memory of man, without laving a dead boy to be carried home to the widow's cabin.'[122]

Others continued to fight in subsequent years, however, and the old faction cries could still lead to trouble as late as 1867. In that year Timothy McCarthy and three men named Quilter were drinking in a public house in Listowel when three McElligotts entered; one of the Quilters shouted out 'Here's a Cooleen against a McElligott', whereupon a fight started 'in which sticks were freely used'.[123]

Eventually the fighting petered out, but memories of the events of 1834, and of the great factions who took part in them, continued to form part of local lore. 'For three-quarters of a century afterwards the people in this district and in North Kerry generally recorded events from "the year the boat was drowned" or from "the night of the big wind"', recalled a man from Causeway in 1934. 'Up to recent years whenever men met they enquired of each other whether they were Culeens or Lawlors. Even yet some old people take pride in the fact that their ancestors took one side or another.'[124]

4

ELECTION RIOTS AND FACTION FIGHTS

> 'He would beg of them to take warning, and bring no branches or badges of any sort, though there was no law to prevent Irishmen bringing their shillelagh.'
>
> Report of a speech by John O'Connell during the county election campaign of 1841[1]

Fighting sticks were regularly flourished in Tralee during the first half of the nineteenth century, primarily by the supporters of different election candidates. Kerry freeholders (those men eligible to vote on the basis of the value of their land holdings) had to travel to the county capital to cast their votes, and there they often encountered, and fought against, freeholders, as well as the non-voting supporters, allied to rival candidates.

Since 1793 these voters had included Catholics as well as Protestants, and by 1825 the number of freeholders in Kerry amounted to 6,716 men, 5,537 of whom belonged to the poorest class of eligible voters, tenants who were known as the forty-shilling freeholders.[2] 'Unlike in England where the lower orders were widely disenfranchised, in Ireland more than 100,000 40-shilling freeholders had the vote,' it was later observed.[3] Nevertheless, regardless of what personal opinions these men may have held, they generally voted in accordance with the wishes of their landlords, some of whom might themselves be candidates, or relatives, followers or friends of the men standing for election. There were consequences for doing otherwise. Magistrate H. J. Brownrigg stated that if a Kerry tenant voted against his landlord, 'it goes to ruin him decidedly; there is no question about it'.[4] An election campaign in Carlow furnishes an example of what the consequences could be; there, a landlord, accompanied by a magistrate and some policemen, dragged a tenant out of his house and demanded that he vote for particular candidates in the town and county constituencies; when the man continued to refuse, his landlord told him: 'I will eject you on Monday morning after the election, and scud you and your family to the road.'[5]

Voting was done in public in each county courthouse in the country, which made it difficult to go against the landlords' wishes. During the Kerry election of 1831, attorney Daniel Supple Jr became concerned when David Peter Thompson, agent for Lord Ventry's estates on the Dingle peninsula, sat opposite men as they came to the ballot and took a note of how they voted.[6]

Landlords, agents or candidates in Kerry and elsewhere did not necessarily have to resort to intimidation: they could encourage the eligible tenantry to go to the poll and vote in the desired fashion by gathering them together and travelling with them, and supplying accommodation in the houses of supporters, who treated them royally to food and drink for a number of days. Moreover, the relationship between landlord and tenant was not always one of domination by the former, and some tenants felt a bond of loyalty to their landlords; Irish MP Jonah Barrington observed that a well-regarded landlord 'reigned despotic in the ardent affections of the tenantry, their pride and pleasure being to obey and to support him'.[7]

Violence was not just an issue in Kerry; fights and riots at elections had a countrywide panorama. 'Sticks, stones, and horsewhips [were] in active requisition' in Co. Armagh in 1826.[8] In Limerick, during the election of 1832, the streets were:

> crowded with the partizans of the candidates exhibiting most violent feelings. The Court-house presented an extraordinary scene. The yelling, screeching, and uproar, was indescribable. The centre gallery was in the possession of men with shillelaghs, who were well able and knew well how to use them. The front of the dock and every prominent place in the Court were occupied by men with large sticks. These were wielded with wild zeal, accompanying each twirl with a shout, or rather shriek, for their respective favourites.[9]

In Kerry, in the general election of 1826, several bouts of fighting took place in and around Tralee, which ultimately ended in tragedy. Three men were standing for the two Co. Kerry seats available. Maurice Fitzgerald MP of Listowel, who was also known as the Knight of Kerry; Colonel James Crosbie MP of Ballyheigue Castle; and a new, young candidate, William Hare, whose grandfather, Viscount Ennismore of Cork, owned an estate near Listowel. All of the candidates, including Fitzgerald, who was a Tory, sympathised publicly with the growing cause of Catholic Emancipation (the removal of various prohibitions against Irish Catholics), although Hare was distrusted because his father, Richard, was well known to have anti-Catholic views.

On Sunday 25 June voters from the estates of William Mullins, 2nd Baron Ventry, assembled in Tralee, where they intended lodging overnight before voting the following day. Unfortunately for them, Mullins had withdrawn his previous allegiance to Colonel Crosbie and wished his freeholders to transfer their votes to Mr Hare, and this became the spur to the violence that subsequently flowed from Crosbie's supporters.

At about two o'clock, a mob loyal to Crosbie attacked a building beside Tralee courthouse because it believed that a large number of Ventry's freeholders were lodging there, and 'proceeded to such acts of outrage that a party of the rifle brigade were obliged to be sent into town from the barracks'.[10] Afterwards, at about three o'clock, a very large crowd, all armed with sticks, came up 'in a very riotous manner' to the corner of Nelson Street (later Ashe Street) and pelted the military with stones.[11] It then dispersed, but at about four o'clock 'a parcel of infuriated fellows, probably in a state of intoxication' set out for the nearby village of Blennerville in order to intercept freeholders for Hare coming in from Lord Ventry's estates on the Dingle peninsula, and some fighting took place there.[12]

Around seven o'clock, freeholders from Crosbie's Ardfert estate arrived in Tralee, 'with drums beating and banners flying'.[13] They were surrounded in the streets 'by multitudes of the populace, who proceeded with them to Col. Crosbie's committee-room'.[14] A number of gentlemen urged the Ardfert electors to retire to their town lodgings, but soon afterwards between 100 and 200 of Ventry's freeholders came along from the Dingle peninsula, some on horseback, some on carts and others walking, and on their arrival at the end of Nelson Street:

> they were met by the mob who assembled about the Ardfert freeholders, and an immediate attack, with stones and other missiles, commenced on the Corkaguiny men, many of whom were very badly used, and they were compelled to fly in all directions for safety. A scene of riot and confusion here ensued, which it is impossible adequately to describe.[15]

One witness later said that he 'never saw two factions fight with such fury as the mob on Sunday, except the Listowel factions' (meaning the Cooleens and the Lawlors).[16] Ventry's tenants then proceeded up The Mall protected behind a number of policemen, while 300–400 of their opponents assembled opposite Devine's Hotel, Castle Street. When Ventry's tenants arrived at Nelson Street 'the mob from Devine's rushed towards them hurraing [and] attacked the freeholders in a furious manner'.[17] Another witness reported that the mob 'commenced on both sides of the freeholders beating them with sticks and throwing stones at them' and he saw one man 'receive a blow of a stone on his head, which knocked him off his horse; while hanging to the horse another came up and gave him a blow on the head with a stick'.[18]

Following this intense violence, Crosbie's supporters gathered outside the courthouse and were faced with soldiers, who were ordered to fire shots. The mob scattered, but someone shouted 'boys, they are blanks', and they made a fatal decision to return to the scene.[19] Firing commenced from the soldiers for five or six minutes, killing five people and wounding thirteen others. One of those killed was Eugene Sullivan, a labourer aged seventeen, who had carried a hare hanging from the end of a pole in a procession a couple of days beforehand as a pointed gesture directed against

Mr Hare.[20] The young man may have been targeted deliberately; a witness later said that he heard a voice in command call out, 'There is the fellow who carried the hare. Level him!'[21]

As a result of these events, voting in the election was postponed until the following Monday. When a large crowd of Lord Ventry's voters entered Tralee for the postponed poll, however, they were again 'assailed by shouting and yells, and … stones were thrown', and two men were attacked at The Mall 'by a man who struck them with a heavy cudgel and cut them'.[22]

As a result of the commotion largely brought about by his own supporters, Crosbie withdrew from the contest, leaving victory to the Knight of Kerry and Mr Hare.

After Catholic Emancipation was achieved in 1829, Daniel O'Connell began a campaign for the repeal of the Act of Union, which had abolished the separate Irish parliament in 1800 and amalgamated it with Westminster. In pursuit of that aim, in 1831 he stood a Repeal candidate for the Kerry constituency against his former ally, the Knight of Kerry. By this time, however, the forty-shilling freeholders had been disenfranchised as voters for county seats by the Parliamentary Elections (Ireland) Act of 1829, which had been brought in partly as a trade-off to reduce the impact of politicised Catholic voters following Emancipation ('the attempted political neutralising of plebeian trouble-makers', as it was later described).[23] Accordingly, 'the total number of 543 who voted in the County Kerry election in 1830 was a pale shadow of the several thousand who voted at the general election in that county in 1826'.[24]

With such small numbers of voters, in subsequent elections it was even more important for different candidates and their supporters to bring as many of their voters to the poll as possible while at the same time intimidating as many of their rivals' voters away from it. During the 1831 general election campaign, Tralee 'was disgraced by one of those scenes in which our populace are so fond of shewing their fitness to be entrusted with extended political functions', complained *The Kerry Evening Post*. 'Some of the lowest of the low amused themselves after night-fall, with parading an effigy, purporting to represent the Knight of Kerry, which with all the ceremonies of mob-justice, was duly hanged, burned ...'[25] A printed ballad was also circulated (and presumably sung out on the street) titled 'A New Song in Praise of Our Favourite Candidates, of Tralee', which included the lines 'Men of Tralee, come forward crush the Tory faction,/Let each elector boldly cry "we're all prepared for action"'.[26]

In the county election of 1835, violence against freeholders who supported the Knight of Kerry committed by factions supporting the O'Connellite candidates, Morgan John O'Connell (Daniel's nephew) and Frederick William Mullins, was rife in various parts of the county. The contest was destined to be hard fought because Daniel O'Connell, seeing Whig parliamentary support as the only vehicle for his own policies, could not countenance the election of as prominent a Tory as Fitzgerald in his home county.[27] Accordingly, he viewed the exertion of pressure on voters as being vitally important during the campaign. Afterwards, almost 100 freeholders who had supported the Knight complained that Catholic voters had been intimidated from voting for him and said that:

Daniel O'Connell, in pursuance of such threats, proceeded to the

> county of Kerry, addressing assemblages of people in various places with inflammatory and threatening language respecting the votes they should give at the election … at Tralee he perambulated the town at the head of canvassing factions, the principals of whom threatened several shopkeepers with exclusive dealing [boycott], and ruin to their property, in case they should dare to vote against the nominees of the said Daniel O'Connell; and from a balcony or platform in front of the Commercial Reading-room in the Mainstreet of Tralee, he addressed a crowd of voters and others, to the effect that 'there was not a demon in hell more base than the Catholic who should vote for the Knight of Kerry', adding, 'I will have a death's head and cross-bones painted or printed on a placard, and posted on the door of any Catholic who votes for him.'[28]

In the course of the campaign, physical violence was dealt out to Fitzgerald's supporters around the county, and freeholders stated how 'persons were dragged forcibly from cars and carriages' and 'the coaches carrying freeholders were attacked by mobs'.[29] A witness at a later inquiry into events during the election explained that prosecutions of offenders did not follow on: 'at other times, as well as at election times, many persons put up with a beating rather than prosecute, because they would probably get more again at another time'.[30]

Voters for the Knight were also insulted by a lurid notice that was attached to the chapel in Listowel, entitled 'The Patriot's Curse':

> I declare at once that whatever creature clothed in human nature, whatever base wretch, political renegade or hireling ruffian (oh, the weakness of human language to describe him!) should be found so

> vile, treacherous and corrupt as to vote for the knight of Kerry … should never be seen in public, but as a loathsome object at which the slow, unmoving finger of scorn shall be pointed … Amen.
>
> May his conscience prove the worm, ever gnawing upon his vitals … Amen.
>
> May his wife, if he have one, prove incontinent, being found oftener in the brothel than by the home fireside, and may he nightly repose himself in sheets contaminated and adulterous. Amen.
>
> May his children prove ungrateful and disobedient, and should he need a crutch, may they pluck it from their old, limping sire, and with it beat out his brains. Amen.
>
> May his daughters turn to general filth, becoming lewd, lustful and lecherous in their teens, nay in their green virginity; may they do't in their parents' eyes. Amen.[31]

In the campaign for the borough of Tralee, a shopkeeper named Legett stated afterwards that different groups of men came into town 'with their hats covered or ornamented with old ribbons, and pieces of old silk and calico or cotton rags, and many of them with their persons half covered with green boughs [and] leaves, shouting in a frightful manner', and that deputations came to his house to persuade him to vote for their candidate, Maurice O'Connell (Daniel O'Connell's son), while after the election mobs passed by his house, 'shouting and brandishing cudgels' and threatening to drive him out of business.[32] (O'Connell ultimately won the contest against the Conservative candidate William Denny.)

At the election for the town borough held in August 1837, John Bateman of Oakpark contested Maurice O'Connell. The election officer, Mr Hickson, had to decide on the validity of a number of votes cast on either side, disallowing more of O'Connell's than his rival's, after which 'a rabble mob, urged on by blundering agents', burned him in effigy.[33] On a Sunday night afterwards, a number of people had their windows broken 'by an infuriated mob of blackguards and prostitutes'. According to *The Kerry Evening Post*:

> The exhibition of that unlawful assemblage on Sunday night last, was truly disgraceful; the peaceable inhabitants of the town exposed, during the whole night, to the destructive violence of yelling outrageous miscreants … The rabble carrying torches among the thatched houses at the extremities of the town, appeared as if they intended to burn it down.[34]

The county election campaign of 1841 was also tumultuous. Arthur Blennerhassett stood for the Conservative interest, with Morgan John O'Connell and William Browne representing the O'Connellite party. John O'Connell (Daniel's brother) and Daniel Supple (as Browne's election agent) engaged in what *The Kerry Evening Post* reported to be 'inflammatory harangues at Listowel, Abbeydorney, and elsewhere' in which they 'desired their freeholders not to "forget their shillelahs"'.[35] O'Connell's remark about there being no law against bringing a shillelagh may have been as jocular as it was threatening (it was greeted with laughter on the occasion).[36] Nevertheless, on 13 July Supple led a procession of several thousand men up and down Denny Street for almost an hour, 'each individual armed, according to Mr John O'Connell's advice, with a short stick, which each brandished in a most menacing manner'.[37]

Some of these men may have been associated with the Cooleen or Lawlor factions. Members of the North Kerry factions – referred to on this occasion by *The Kerry Evening Post* as 'the Ballyeagh men' – appear to have been mobilised against Conservative voters travelling from the Listowel area.[38] (It is a little more likely that they were Cooleens rather than Lawlors, seeing as the latter appear to have enjoyed a kind of alliance with landlord and magistrate Thomas Ponsonby, who was a Conservative.)[39] This suggests that faction fighters of the traditional type may have been more active in fights of the political kind that occurred in Tralee and elsewhere than the bare facts of these melees indicated. Such men were certainly employed around Killorglin during the general election, when, in that instance, the local Foley faction was recruited to protect Tory voters from attack.[40] It is also notable that a court reporter wrote in 1836 that the Brosnahan faction of Castleisland called themselves 'the Wigs', perhaps his misspelling of Whigs, signalling an allegiance to the party associated with O'Connell.[41]

Politically motivated faction fights returned to the streets of Tralee for a final time during the 1880 election campaign for the town constituency. The candidates were Daniel O'Donoghue ('The O'Donoghue'), who was the popular man seeking re-election, and Samuel Murray Hussey, a local landlord and land agent who was greatly disliked. At nine o'clock on the night of 23 March, however, 300–400 men entered Tralee, marching along, armed with sticks and cheering for Hussey. 'They were met by The O'Donoghueites, and an alarming encounter ensued. Volleys of stones were fired by the rival parties, and, after a good battle, the Husseyites were forced to beat a retreat.' Later that night

O'Donoghue declared that it was laughable that Hussey had to 'bring a party of hirelings from the neighbourhood in order to prove that he had the sympathy of the people of Tralee. Had he come in the broad daylight, they would soon make mince meat of himself and his backers.'[42]

NON-POLITICAL FIGHTS IN TRALEE

Non-political faction fights in Tralee were not as significant as they were elsewhere in the county. Some faction fighting was said to have been practised by visiting parties at the fair that was held in Rock Street, although we are not informed in what years this took place. According to Jeremiah O'Keefe of Pembroke Street, writing in 1917:

> The faction fighters of North Kerry usually finished the year's programme in Tralee on the 13th December – Rock St. fair day (*Aonac-na-Carraige*) on which date the stalwarts of Ballymacelligott and Castleisland were invited by leaders of the two factions to cross black-thorns … The matrons were bound to be there also with a pair of 7lb 'diamonds' encased by each in the long black stocking, which proved a more deadly weapon of destruction than the prickle-edged blackthorn. The combatants face to face were afforded means of defence, but from behind chance of avoidance there was none unless some friendly spectator intervened and stopped the amazon's hand … I often learned from the lips of old men that the Rock Street battle was the fiercest of the whole fighting season. A description of the day's proceedings given by old men of forty years ago was well worth listening to.[43]

Fights took place at the Rock at other times of the year, too.

On a Sunday evening in October 1833, 'a most violent riot and affray occurred at the Rock in this town between two notorious factions', most likely visitors to the town.[44] More significantly, one day in July 1809, at about five o'clock in the evening:

> a mob of near 300 persons sallied through the principal streets, 100 of whom were armed with stones which they pelted at a man about fifty yards in advance, in consequence of some crime it was alleged he had committed against the Rock – they continued to pursue him until he arrived within his own precincts at Boherbue, when his party in their turn became the assailants and a similar pursuit took place.[45]

These districts appear to have considered themselves as opponents generally: when bonfires were lit to celebrate St John's Eve, 'great was the rivalry between the different streets as to the size of their fires'.[46]

At Boherbee, a fight between unnamed groups was prevented in February 1836, when the police 'immediately repaired to the proposed scene of action, "the cross of Boherbee", where both factions had assembled and shouldered their *Halpeens*'. Captain Brownrigg, JP, 'proceeded to the several public houses in that part of the town to secure the ringleaders', while another man addressed the crowd, attempting to talk up the benefits 'arising out of peace and temperance'. As the chief of police appeared to the crowd to be preparing to read out the Riot Act, '[the] cry of "run boys run it's the Riot Act, the Riot Act", was immediately raised by the mob, who, conceiving safety depended in flight, took to their bipeds in all directions'.[47]

Elsewhere in the town, in November 1822, a resident of Tralee named John Dunn, a felt-hat maker, 'having at the fair of Castlemain, been with his party' was 'severely beaten by people of the name of Leary (also residents of this town) and their faction':

> The Dunns and their friends, after being sufficiently primed and charged with whiskey to the gullet, about 9 o'clock on the night of Thursday last, determined on retaliation, proceeded with shouts of 'five pounds for a Learys head', to Brogue maker's lane, where the Learys (who are tobacco twisters) reside; here as may be expected, a murderous conflict ensued, in which the wretched man John Dunn, received a stab of a bayonet in the belly, the point of the weapon passing out at his back ... he expired at half past 9 o'clock last night, in excruciating torture, leaving a wife and six helpless children to beggary and ruin ... We understand the quarrel originally commenced at a cock-fight in this town.[48]

The streets of Tralee also formed the stage for the established factions of the Sullivans and the Riordans of Castlemaine, who were happy to fight each other across a wide geographical range, meeting also at Currans, Castleisland and Firies. One evening in January 1846 some men belonging to the Sullivan faction, 'who had been shouting for the Riordans, were arrested and lodged in bridewell'.[49] In January 1831 a man named Riordan attacked a shopkeeper in his Castle Street premises after boasting 'of his amazing prowess and dexterity in the noble art of *cudgeling*', reported *The Kerry Evening Post*, and 'that he never saw a man *from over the Hill* that he was not able to *smash*'.[50] His surname and the reference to 'over the hill' imply that he was a member of the faction who fought the Sullivans from Castlemaine, which was separated from the Tralee area by the Slieve Mish mountains.

The Sullivans featured in the final incident of faction fighting in its traditional form that took place in the town. On the evening of 15 August 1856, there was 'a sharp fight' in Castle Street.[51] It was 'like a pitched battle between some hundreds of the drunken champions of two ruffianly factions, between whom there was no real cause of quarrel, except bad temper and worse whiskey'.[52]

> [T]he fight which was one in which farmers, named Sullivan on the one side [and] Hussey on the other, were principals, commenced near the Chapel when Head-Constable Burchell and Constable Addis arrested [Eugene] Creagh, who appeared to them to be one of the principal originators and actors in the affray. At the end of Castle-street, near Denny-street a large crowd was then collected and the striking with sticks and fists went on as fast as possible and most furiously. Several of the parties were severely cut and others had their eyes well blackened. The fight was instantaneous and lasted about a quarter of an hour, when, owing to the great exertions of Mr. Ireland [sub-inspector of police], who received some strokes himself, and the police, order was again restored, and seven of the ringleaders safely lodged in Bridewell.[53]

The Tralee Chronicle was pleased that 'the parties engaged in this barbarous proceeding were strangers, residing far from Tralee, and no inhabitant of this town … participated in this detestable proceeding'.[54] However, the fact of the fight having taken place on the Feast of the Assumption was something of an irritant to Dr David Moriarty, the bishop of Kerry. On Sunday 24 August the bishop, it was reported, addressed his congregation from the floor of the church, 'to condemn in strong terms the inefficiency of the local Magistracy in preserving the peace … The reverend Bishop went on to say that as the Magistrates did not do their duty, the people should, under such circumstances, unite and maintain the peace of the town themselves.' Magistrate John H. Shiel, who was in the church when the bishop made his remarks, wrote to him defending the conduct of the magistrates. He afterwards read out these letters in court, while two of his fellow judges 'spoke strongly in condemnation of the injustice of Dr Moriarty's charges, which they said were totally unwarranted, and only to be treated with contempt'.[55]

Ten men concerned in the fighting ('very respectable looking farmers') were charged with rioting or with obstructing the police. The case came before the courts amid a tense atmosphere, still more so as it was in the court before the trial that Shiel read out his to-and-fro correspondence with the bishop. Mr Collis, defending, commented that the case:

> had excited a great deal of feeling, and in dealing with the parties he knew their worships would not be influenced by what had just taken place [Court – no, no]. They admitted what had occurred, for which they were exceedingly sorry, and they were now on as good terms as ever. They did not seek to justify their conduct, but would appeal to the merciful consideration of the court.[56]

Mr Morphy, appearing for others of the defendants, instead flattered Shiel, as he 'begged to bear his testimony to the efficient manner in which [he] has always discharged his duties'. Those being tried were caught in the crossfire of a dispute among the establishment. Even though Eugene Creagh 'alleged his total innocence, saying that he was only trying to make peace between the parties', he and seven other men were sentenced to two months' imprisonment with hard labour, 'the Bench refusing to substitute a pecuniary fine in any case'.[57] Pierce Chute, the chairman of the court, perhaps conscious of the bishop's attention, 'declared in the strongest terms the intention of the Magistrates to put down, by the severest measures the practice of faction fighting, which had lately begun to show itself again in the country'.[58]

The sentences and the publicity attached to the case may have proved to be a final disincentive to faction fighting in Tralee, and it certainly appears that faction fighting in its commonplace form, which had never been particularly strong in the town, no longer occurred afterwards. There were other parts of the county, however, where the practice flourished.

5

THE GEARALTAIGH AND THE DAITHÍNIGH

> 'Some of these feuds are of very ancient date. The grudge between the Castleisland folk is of 80 or 100 years standing – so long is the memory of those quarrels treasured up.'
>
> *The Nation*, 10 January 1846

The remark above by *The Nation* newspaper suggests that the factions of Castleisland sprang up around the 1740s or 1760s. If that is true, it would make the gangs who gathered in the town among the oldest in the county. Faction fights may have been older still: the poet Aodhagán O'Rahilly witnessed one at a fair there some time before 1726.[1]

Information about the events of these early days has not survived, and it is not until 1820 that two parties are reported: the Brosnahans (or Bresnehans, Brosnans) and the Connors (or O'Connors), who assembled at a fair in October, 'to the number of upwards of two hundred a side'. These factions had 'publicly been preparing for some months for this combat', and armed with a variety of dangerous weapons, as well as sticks and stones, they 'commenced their operations at an early hour, beating and wounding each other desperately, and in this manner the entire day was spent'.[2]

A later folklore source observed that when the fair days came around 'the people gathered at the fair, mainly the Brosnahans and the Connors and they fought between themselves because they liked fighting between themselves. They fought at every Fair in Castleisland.'[3] A local man, Uileog Ó Céirín (1791–1863) wrote a poem in Irish advising them to desist. He lamented 'Neighbours and friends in disagreement with each other/And no one knowing the cause of the dispute', and he hoped that 'if they come to fight on the day of the fair … those of them who survive thrashing each other … would concede that it would be better to leave each other alone.'[4]

In 1836 two of the Brosnahan brothers were involved in a fight at the fair of Abbeyfeale, West Limerick. During the fray a man named Hartnett, whom a policeman characterised as 'a great rioter', came to their aid.[5] This may have been Big Jim Hartnett of Abbeyfeale, better known as a champion of his own faction, or Patrick Hartnett of Killaculleen, about whom a song was composed ('On street or green on the day of battle you never flinched').[6] A witness saw the Brosnahans 'at the door of a house getting sticks', after which they called out for the Herlihy faction and wheeled their weapons. Another man saw Hartnett and the two Brosnahans 'wheeling and hallooing' for the Herlihys and 'the Boccaghs' ('the Beggarmen'). John Herlihy announced, 'there's a Herlihy here' and was then struck by one of the Brosnahans, after which he hit Timothy Brosnahan with a stick 'several times on different parts of his body'. Herlihy ended up cut three or four times on the head, 'and his breast [was] full of blood'. A man named Walsh went over and 'desired Bresnahan to be quiet and he sulkily said "he would not, that he should keep the town'". There was then a second battle, in which the Walshes became involved, with the result that 'there were 100 men there rattling each other through the fair'.[7]

Later that year there was 'a violent riot ... between two factions' at another Castleisland fair, which may represent another appearance by the Brosnahans, although there were also other parties fighting in the area.[8] On 19 January 1840, for example, two factions comprising several hundred people gathered in town for a battle, in which the Leynes and Reidys faced the Sullivans but were dispersed by the police and a detachment of soldiers from Tralee.[9]

Fights between groups that were left unnamed in newspaper accounts were prevented from taking place by the police on New Year's Day 1845 and went on at the June fair of 1848, but little more was reported from the town, and by the 1850s fights in Castleisland were dismissed as 'of the olden times, and of but rare occurrence in late years'.[10] A single late outlier almost went off in 1853, when 'two very respectable men', Maurice Reidy and a Mr Pembroke, fell out over who had the right to the tolls from Castleisland's many fairs and markets; both assembled men on either side:

> and it was expected that one of the most dreadful faction fights that ever disturbed this county would have taken place, as combatants were being collected from all quarters round about. The authorities got a hint, and at once the night before some half a dozen of the supposed ringleaders were arrested and bound over to keep the peace; and yesterday morning early a company of the 57th regiment and a force of police were marched into the town. The presence of

> so large a force and the precautions taken the evening before had the effect of putting a stop to the anticipated hostilities.[11]

In later years some individuals from the Castleisland area who were involved in stick fighting were remembered. There were two men from Gortacloghane – Mat Sheehy, known as Mat the Herder, and Seán O'Leary – who both lived 'in the beginning of the nineteenth century', according to a later folklore interviewee. Mat 'was a stout firm man and had great arms'.[12] The pair used to bring firkins of butter to sell in Cork city, where 'there was a great fighting man. One day the Buffer of Cork challenged any man to fight him.[13] Mat came up to Leary and said it wouldn't take such a great man to beat him.'[14] O'Leary advised him to keep quiet, but the Cork man had heard him. He challenged Mat to fight and handed him a blackthorn stick, 'so they took at it. The Buffer was giving him great strokes in the head but they were … taking no effect out of him. In the finish Leary said to Mat in Irish … to take him low. At that Mat struck him across the ribs and … brought him to the ground.'[15] The Cork man told Mat that he was a good man and that he had never been beaten before. 'The Cork people said they would give him his hat full of gold if he shout as a Cork man but he said he would not, saying, "I am a Kerry man and I'll shout for no other County but Kerry".'[16]

On another occasion, 'a great man from County Limerick heard about Mat so he said he would have a trial out of him' (a 'trial' meaning a bout of single combat):[17]

> He picked two good sticks … for himself and another for Mat. As

> soon as Mat saw him he got in dread of him so he said he was not Mat the Herder at all but he'd carry him to Mat's house … Mat was in dread to attack him alone without Leary with him for Leary was a better man than himself. If he beat him himself Leary would have another chance and if Leary beat him Mat would still hold his good name. When they landed at Leary's house Mat had a private talk with him and Leary said to him not to be in dread. Then they started fighting and no one of um was getting the upper hand for a half an hour. It was getting very hot then and Mat was getting too much of it. Then Leary told him in Irish not to draw at all but to keep up his guards and that he would get tired. Mat did so and stroke by stroke the other fellow was [failing]. Then all of a sudden Mat struck him across the ribs and brought him to the ground so Mat held his good name and gave up fighting at the age of fifty.[18]

'Several fights' were held at Currans fair, near Castleisland, another folklore account related.[19] In 1830 a letter writer to the *Tralee Mercury* described scenes he witnessed there at the May fair, when men 'with fiendish yells' attacked each other 'with clubs and bludgeons', and he was appalled to see 'the great incisions in human flesh, that human hands, with deadly weapons and deadly intent, inflicted'.[20]

Currans was stated in 1838 to be the home of the Moynihan faction.[21] Twenty years later, they may still have been at work: at the May fair of 1860, a policeman found John Moynihan, one of the leaders of his party, fully engaged in a riot; another officer helped to capture Moynihan and 'just as we went into the yard he put his foot before me and knocked me down, and then he said he was satisfied, as he had the pleasure of throwing me down'.[22]

SLIABH LUACHRA

Various stick fights occurred, were scheduled to occur or were suppressed in the area beyond Castleisland, stretching east and further south of the town, known as Sliabh Luachra. This area is generally thought of as including Kerry districts such as Ballymacelligott, Brosna, Knocknagoshel, Barraduff, Gneeveguilla, Scartaglin and Rathmore, as well as areas of Limerick such as Athea and Abbeyfeale, and parts of Cork such as Ballydesmond and Knocknagree.

At Clogher, near Ballymacelligott, fights took place involving the Slatterys. In 1803 the Slatterys of the parish of O'Brennan fought the Carmodys outside the old Clogher church, where the former were also opposed by the Learys, Butlers and Leens.[23] They also featured in 'one of the last and greatest of the faction fights known locally as the "Battle of Clogher"':

> This battle was caused by a remark about character made it is said by a man named Slattery, about a woman named O'Connor. As the latter was going into Mass this disparaging remark was passed and ere long the ire of all her name was thoroughly aroused. Around went word and those who bore the name of O'Connor rallied to defend the maiden, while the Slatterys called the members of their tribe to stand as one man in defence of their clansmen.
>
> One family took no part because the heads were an O'Connor [and] Slattery joined in wedlock. The parish priest heard of the approaching faction fight and banned it. In fact it is said that harm would befall the man who would raise his hand first. Still the fight went on. The Connors gained the day, but death came early to their leader and the 'Priest's' curse fell.
>
> All the Slatterys from Carrignafeela and friends from outlying

> districts were in the fight, while the Connors of Clogher parish were there to a man, helped by others who were not cousins of the insulted lady, but bore the same name.[24]

A few Kerry factions, in addition to the aforementioned Brosnahans, fought in and around Abbeyfeale. Bouts were held between the Collins family 'of the bounds of Kerry' and the Macks of Grogeen, Caherlane, Abbeyfeale. 'Scarcely a fair day – race day – or pattern day would pass that these two parties would not have a fight,' reported a folklore interviewee, adding that there were as many as a hundred people on each side.[25] Until around 1875 there used to be a fair at Portenard (often referred to as 'Port'), Abbeyfeale, and this was 'the scene of many a bloody battle in the days of the Faction Fights when the two rival parties of North Kerry (the Cooleens and the Black Mulvihills) used to cross swords for supremacy,' reported a local national school teacher.[26] The business of the fair would go on until, 'towards evening, a shout "Here's a Cooleen" rent the air. The response was "Here's a Black Mulvihill" and at once all business was over and on goes the walloping and shouting.'[27] In one of these fights a man was shot by the military and one of the women combatants, meeting a female rival, 'called out viciously, "See Joan, is that your gander that's down?" Joan replied, "See Bess, lest it be your own gander!" Bess got calm and on inquiry found to her grief 'twas her own husband that was killed.'[28]

But faction fighting was not limited to Abbeyfeale; in fact, it was common throughout Sliabh Luachra. The races at Knocknagoshel were the occasion for a fight in October 1895:

> Both sides entered into the fray with the greatest ferocity. Sticks, stones, and other weapons were used unsparingly by the combatants on one another with shocking results. Bleeding heads, gaping wounds, and disfigured faces were speedily in evidence, and the fight waxed hot and furious until the arrival of a posse of police, who set about quelling the disturbance. Following the custom usual in such cases, the rival factions ceased belabouring one another, and turned on the police, whom they severely maltreated.[29]

Similarly, at a spot between Knocknagoshel and Brosna, a pattern day used to be held every 15 August, but 'faction fights were a feature of every gathering, and the fights at this pattern became so fierce and so dangerous that the local clergy decided that no further anniversary masses would be offered at this place'.[30] As late as 1900 there was 'a faction fight … on the evening of the 15th of August between parties returning from the Knocknagoshel "pattern"' in which some of the combatants were 'savagely treated'.[31]

Several battles were waged in the parish of Brosna. The assistant barrister of the county complained in 1832 that 'in the neighbourhood of Castleisland, particularly in the parish of Brosna … factious rioting and daring outrage has been carried to such an excess as to render life and property quite insecure, upwards of one hundred fellows being frequently at one and the same time, engaged in tumultuous and murderous conflicts'. The parish priest believed that the fights were due 'to the inordinate and immoderate use of spirituous liquors, supplied by improper persons (who are themselves perhaps, leaders of factious clans)'.[32]

In January 1833:

> upwards of sixty gladiators of two riotous factions – the Leahys and the Curtins, from the parish of Brosna … were indicted for several murderous conflicts … these were regular premeditated battles on which the whole force of two hostile clans and their auxiliaries, were drawn out in the noonday, regularly officered, and brought to the charge by their leaders.[33]

Afterwards, in court, their leaders were selected, 'as the most criminal, for exemplary punishment', and were given prison sentences with hard labour and bound to keep the peace for seven years. *The Kerry Evening Post* commented: 'Many of these leaders of factious turbulence had all the appearance of comfortable farmers, and so numerous were the forces under their command – that we have heard it asserted on good authority, that eight or more gallons of whiskey have been swallowed at one council of war!!!'[34]

In a different conflict, a folklore source reported that long ago in Brosna there was a faction fight between the Curtins of the village and the Lanes of Caherlane, Abbeyfeale. There was a woman of the Lanes and:

> she was the strongest woman in the parish and she was six feet tall, and she was nicknamed Máire Mór na Muinge.[35] Herself and her husband and her nine sons took part in the fight. They fought with sticks and stones. There was a hole in the stick with a thong running through it[,] this thong was twisted around the wrist to prevent the stick from falling when they got a stroke in the hand.

> Máire was all day drawing stones to the Lanes, and in the evening she took off one of her stockings[,] filled it with stones to beat the Curtains, [and in the fight] she knocked out two or three of them with the stocking.[36]

The Curtins were driven out of the village and across the Clydagh river nearby. 'In the evening they [members of the Lanes' faction] took Máire on their shoulders through the village, for she was the best help they had in the fight.'[37]

Further south lay Glenflesk. The district was more important for supplying faction fighters than as a location for fights. During the 1770s the Glenflegians formed the cudgel-wielding army led by their chieftain, the O'Donoghue of the Glens, who marched on the streets of Killarney.[38] In the late 1700s a well-built man named Denis Casey was 'the leader of the Glenflesk clans in their faction fights'; this may have been the Denis Casey who 'could whirl two sticks on occasion' and who took part in a fight at Kilgobnet, near Killorglin, sometime in the first two decades of the 1800s.[39] Hand-picked men from Glenflesk were also recruited in 1845 for the Sullivan versus Riordan battles of Castlemaine, about twenty miles away.[40]

In Gneeveguilla, several families of the Traveller community, the Sheridans, the Harringtons and the Coffeys, fought each other one-against-one. These bouts included elements drawn from the faction fighting tradition. 'In those tribes there were strong, able, powerful men who enjoyed fighting ... The older tribes always fought with the fists. But later on the younger tribes adopted ash-plants as weapons.'[41] When Traveller women such as Mágeen Ginger and a woman known as 'the Wolf' prepared to fight, they 'used to drag their shawls after them, and cry out, "Who shall dare tred [tread] on the tail of my shawl". If any one did so, it would be the cause of a fight.'[42]

Factions also met at Scartaglin and environs. At a fair in 1829, reported *The Kerry Evening Post*, 'nothing could be more barbarous or sanguinary than the riot which took place there: numbers of the vanquished faction were left bleeding and prostrate on the road without a human being to afford them succour or protection from the fury of their merciless pursuers'. The newspaper commented that it was 'a melancholy reflection that nothing can check the cursed propensity to riot and disorder among the lower class of our countrymen'.[43]

No more is known of factions in this district, yet they may have been long-standing: as late as 1893 what were described as 'two old factions' from the neighbourhood of Scartaglin engaged in a series of fights in the streets of Castleisland following a race meeting.[44] Furthermore, at the crossroads of Cordal nearby, it was recalled in a 'Song of Cordal' that 'many a faction fight was fought of old'.[45]

GEARALTAIGH AND DAITHÍNIGH

By far the most celebrated factions of Sliabh Luachra were the Gearaltaigh (the Fitzgeralds) and the Daithínigh (the followers of Daithí, or David, O'Keefe).[46] Both gangs included several Kerry families, although many of their fights took place in Knocknagree, Co. Cork, just beyond the Kerry county bounds; they also met at Cullen, further east, on the holy day of Latiaran Sunday held at the end of July each year in honour of the local saint.[47] The former party had their headquarters at the east end of Knocknagree, while the latter went to the west end. The Gearaltaigh were remembered as having been led at one period by Andy Sheehan from Kilcummin, while the Daithínigh were captained by Darby Moynihan from Gneeveguilla.[48]

The parties sprang to life around 1825.[49] As with some other feuds, the enmity had its origin in a dispute over a woman, although there are two contrasting accounts. Apparently, from the Gearaltaighs' perspective, an affront was committed by an O'Keefe against a Fitzgerald:

> David O'Keefe of Cullen had arranged to elope with Ellen Fitzgerald … but her brothers heard of it and attacked David O'Keefe after Mass either in Cullen village or in the vicinity of it. From that little brawl the fight grew. Every Sunday the parties met and their numbers gradually grew until it attained huge proportions in 1859 or 60.[50]

According to a different story, however, a man named Daithín 'had a lovely daughter and another farmer wanted to take her as a bride. They were making the match and the fortune at that time was not money but cattle. This man's name was "Gearaltach" and being a wealthy farmer his fortune was seven cows.' However, Daithín was not satisfied with Gearaltach, 'so he said he would not leave his daughter marry him on any account'.[51]

> [Gearaltach] said he would take her by force and so he did, but a large gathering and Daithín followed him and they had what was called a faction fight. After that the people were talking about the matter – some in favour of Daithín and others against him.

> In this way the people were arguing and out of the arguing came the faction. Usually at fairs and markets they fought and often at Church Gates.[52]

The Fitzgeralds and the O'Keefes were both described as 'long-tailed' families (families with multiple connections, branches and relations) and it was explained that the Fitzgeralds could thus draw to their ranks the Moynihans, the Dalys, the Sheehans and the Hickeys; while the O'Keefes could gather the Caseys, the Mahonys, the O'Riordans and the Murphys.[53] In August 1834, at the fair of Dromagh, beyond Rathmore, on the Cork side of the county bounds, the Kellehers and the Driscolls, both families seemingly from East Kerry and allies of the Gearaltaigh, fought 'the Davies', as a newspaper termed the Daithínigh. In a most violent encounter, three men were killed and two women, 'assailed while endeavouring to escape', were so badly injured that they were not expected to survive.[54] The fights 'so regularly held at this fair, are conducted in general by Kerry people', commented the Tralee newspaper *Chute's Western Herald*.[55]

'Their weapons were called "three-quarter ash" which was made in the form of the spoke of a wheel,' it was later explained, in a detail which has not been noted elsewhere. 'There was a hole in one end where a leather thong was attached and it was twisted around the wrist of the hand in order that the ash-plant would not slip from their hands when fighting.' Neither party fought with stones, it was stated:

> The time between fair and fair was spent preparing the 'three-quarter' ash or *cláirín* or *cleath-ailpín*.[56] As the fair day drew near,

> messengers were despatched to summon the rival gangs. Often the business of the fair went late, especially when say in October the fairs were large. In such circumstances the fight was postponed and took place the following day.[57]

At the start of battle, one side 'used call out, "Here is a Daitheenigh" and the other party used call out, "Here is a Gearaltaigh"'.[58] For several days before the fair of Knocknagree, 'the opposing factions prepared their three-quarter ash sticks and after the business of the fair was completed each faction would assemble in the fair field'. Then:

> A bugle was sounded as a signal to tent owners etc. to pack up their wares and move to safer quarters. Prior to the bugle-call each faction filled the 'shebeens' in the village … They often drank as much as four gallons of whiskey before the fight. At the bugle-call they lined up and one would take off his coat and drag it after him across the fair-field towards the opposing faction shouting, 'Who dares to tread on the tail of my coat'. An opponent would do so and then [the] melee started. The onlookers would line the fences – only a very few houses were in the village in those days. The fight finished when one faction retreated before the other. Often men from opposing sides drank together when the fight was over … The fight was fought with a clean manly spirit and only those whose skulls were able to withstand a strong blow took part in the fray.[59]

The use of a bugle to signal the start of combat may have been more common than the single source here suggests. Cork artist Daniel MacDonald painted a scene in 1843 that features a fighter in a half-stripped shirt, gripping a stick and accompanied

'Who dares to tread on the tails of my coat?' Postcard by Lawrence Publishers, Dublin, c. 1900. (Author's Collection)

by a man blowing a bugle, as a crowd of stick-wielding men assemble in the near distance.[60]

Andy Sheehan, who bore the nickname 'the Russian', was among the most prominent of the Gearaltaigh.[61] (Such a name was also attached to a Tipperary faction fighter, Michael 'The Russian' Buckley, 'so called from his great physique'; it can be assumed that Sheehan received the nickname for similar reasons.)[62] Stories about him survived, especially among his enemies. For example, as he and another man were going home one night they passed a wake at the house of a man named Herlihy, whose family was allied with the Daithínigh (and probably of the party who fought the Brosnahans in Abbeyfeale in 1836): 'The other man told him to shut up that there was a wake here. He said he did not care if all the Herlihys in Farrankeal were dead. Three Daitheenigh jumped out over the fence and beat him. He was unconscious. He was in a neighbour's house for two months before he could be taken home.'[63]

In what appears to have been a separate altercation, as Sheehan was going home from Knocknagree fair, he was again met by some of the opposite party, who beat him badly. A song was composed about this incident:

The 'Russian' can remember the 23rd September,
When he was made surrender by the Davie boys alone,
The Russian was not able to go to the Kerry stable,
So they laid him in Daly's table,
With a plaster to his nose.[64]

Another story related that Conny the Blare Murphy of Gneeveguilla, who 'was able to beat every enemy that attacked him … hit the "Russian" and the latter had to go to hospital'.[65] For all his notoriety and purported strength, it seems that Sheehan made a habit of being bested by his enemies.

Others involved in the long-running feud included Donncadh *Beag* O'Keefe, who was known as the *Gaiscidheach*, and who 'started the fight each day'.[66] (The nickname signified someone who tried to outdo others in deeds or feats.)[67] There were also, for the Daithínigh, Tadg Betty Murphy, 'who cleared all the

Geraltaigh out of the fair', Jack Casey, 'who beat seven men at Knocknagree', and Donnchadha *Dubh* O'Riordan, 'about whom a song was composed'.[68]

On the Gearaltaigh side, Bill MacCarthy was 'a notorious man', who travelled from Killarney as an ally:

> He was about six feet in height and had a broken hip. He was never beaten till he came to Knocknagree.
>
> One fairday about sixty years ago [*c.* 1877] he came with the Daly clan from Kilsorcon and being unable to get any man to fight him he started punching a big horse. Every fighting man in the place ran from him he looked so terrible with his yellow baffety shirt and corduroy trousers.[69] He was a 'baitín' boy by the Dalys and would kill a person for two pints of porter.[70] One day he paid for his fighting. Con Totely the famous Shanballa highway-man struck him with his stirrup-iron and broke all the teeth in the front of his mouth.[71]

Con 'Toatly' Mahony, from Shanbally, Knocknagree, was a member of the Daithínigh.[72]

Another man, named Casey, who sided with the Gearaltaigh, one fair day in Knocknagree spotted one of the Daithínigh, a man 'around 50 years of age and the people were mocking him because he wasn't married'.[73] Casey called out a verse, after which battle commenced:

> *Out in India among the Tawneys,*
> *Where there is neither rule or law,*
> *When one is acclimatized already,*
> *He perhaps might find a squaw.*[74]

Among the women who took part in the fights, 'the most outstanding woman must have been Moll Casey of New Quarter [County Kerry], as her name is still mentioned … Moll used a stocking filled or partly filled, with stones and, of course, nobody "would strike a woman"[;] consequently Moll often "cleared" her corner of the fair'.[75]

As was sometimes claimed of some other factions, such as the Cooleens and the Lawlors, some local landlords or gentlemen were said to favour one or other of the parties. Daniel Cronin Coltsman, a Catholic landlord, was, according to one account, 'a tyrant'.[76] A folklore interviewee said that he 'was friendly with the Gearaltaigh'.[77] During the course of one fight he 'came riding on horse-back and he wore a red-coat … he hit one of the Daitheenigh with a whip across the face and the man Dan O'Connell by name said that if he would strike him again he would bring him off the horse. Cronin Coltsman hit him again and Dan hit him with his plant.' Alas, there was a sequel to the conflict: 'Dan [O'Connell]'s mother was a widow and Cronin would leave her in the land if she sent Dan away. She refused and they were evicted.'[78]

A local priest was also said to favour one faction; his surname may have necessitated a certain allegiance. During the 1840s, 'Fr Edward Fitzgerald … was styled *Sagart a' bhata* and was a noted Gearaltach (*ní nárbh iongnadh!*) [no wonder!] He is reputed to have used his blackthorn with [good] effect on several occasions – but always on the Daithíneach boys.'[79]

The long-running feud was at its height in 1859 or 1860, reported folklore collector Díarmuid Ó Múimhneacháin.[80] Certainly, those with whom he shared his surname, the Moynihans (followers of the Gearaltaigh), had a fierce encounter with the Murphys (followers of the Daithínigh) on the fair day in Barraduff, then known as Six Mile Bridge, in September 1859. A policeman described the scene at about seven o'clock in the evening, as opponents Frank Tim Moynihan and Jeremiah Murphy stalked up and down the fair, eager to fight. Murphy 'was very violent' and could not be controlled by others or by the police:

> at the end of the fair about twenty persons formed a square and commenced to fight with sticks; they used no stones ... They were divided into two factions, the Murphys and Moynihans; there was only six police there and they were in dread to interfere. They were fighting about a quarter of an hour, and the Murphys then had to retire. Some of the rioters could not but be injured. It is said they will fight again on next Sunday. We called upon the publicans to close their shops but one or two refused. There was a great crowd of people about the rioters.[81]

Among the men charged later was one Thomas Daly, who carried a stick with a small ferule attached to it, which was described as 'about 5 or 6 feet long and about 2½ inches in diameter'.[82]

Ó Múimhneacháin explained that the Gearaltaigh and Daithínigh battles ended 'when eighteen men from each side were sent to the Cork County jail on Hard Labour for four months. The last big faction fight was in October 1860.'[83] After that date, 'the fight amongst groups of families waned and only individual families kept up the ... Gearaltach and Daitheenach war-cry'.[84]

Among those who continued were the Moynihans, who came out for a fight in 1869:

> It appears that a hostile feeling existed between two parties named respectively Moynihans and Cullitys on account of one of the latter as was alleged, stated that one of the Moynihan's had to hide himself in a house in Killarney some time since, fearing that he would have been attacked by the Cullitys. To remove this imputation Moynihan himself challenged the party who circulated the statement concerning him, immediately after last Mass at Glenflesk, on Sunday week last. Both parties having their anger aroused, a dangerous row would have occurred but for the interference of the Parish Priest, the Rev Mr. Shanahan, and Mr. McCartie, J.P., both of whom succeeded in suppressing the threatened *melee*. The enmity however was not forgotten at either side, especially on the part of the Moynihans, as they appeared to have made elaborate preparations to renew the quarrel at the [Barraduff] fair last Monday, where both factions mustered in considerable numbers. However, thanks to the police force from Killarney, Rathmore, and Glenflesk … the parties made no attempt to renew the encounter, and the day passed off without any disturbance.[85]

At Barraduff, on Sunday 9 June 1873, the Moynihans again gathered for a fight, this time against some Dohertys:

> [S]hortly before the commencement of Mass, an immense crowd had assembled in the chapel grounds, a large portion of whom were 'bent on mischief'. Mass being over, the hostile clans, with their adherents, mustered in the chapel grounds for the purpose of carrying out their evil designs, but on witnessing the large *posse* of police, and being unable to procure drink in either of the two public houses, they manifested a chopfallen [crestfallen] appearance. It was not, however, until Mr D. McCarthy, the respected magistrate residing in that locality, exercised his influence on the leaders, that

they abandoned their intentions, and quietly left for their respective homes early in the evening.[86]

Ó Múimhneacháin explained that the fighting that had continued 'died down when the Land war became hot'.[87] The war, waged by farmers under the leadership of Charles Stewart Parnell and the Irish National Land League, was a campaign to redress the balance of power between tenants and landlords. It demanded fair rents and fixity of tenure for the former and it used the power of boycott against both landlords and non-compliant farmers. The campaign began in 1879, becoming strongest in Munster between 1886 and 1891.

The old faction enmity resurfaced in the area afterwards, in a different context – in the form of attachments to different political parties. Locally, 'the supporters of the All for Ireland League and the Irish Party were mainly the old Gearaltach & Daithíneach brigades'.[88] In Knocknagree, during a general election contest in January 1910 between Patrick Guiney of the AFIL and Michael Barry of the IPP, 'the political factions were powerful and determined on each side. And indeed much of the political spite could be traced to the old faction fighting days (the Gearaltach and Daithíneach)'.[89] The supporters of the rival candidates lined up on the western and the eastern sides of Knocknagree respectively (perhaps mirroring the locations of the factions' old headquarters in the village). Some carried revolvers, and others had 'sticks and pockets filled with stones'.[90] They were only prevented from attacking each other when a priest repeatedly drove his horse and trap between the two groups.

Faction and feud was kept up for a very long time in the

area of East Kerry. Yet while recollections of the North Kerry gangs such as the Cooleens and the Lawlors continued in their locality, and a plaque commemorating the Ballyeagh fight was even unveiled at the end of the twentieth century, only the rough verses and the accounts of the Gearaltaigh and Daithínigh collected during the 1930s survive as testaments to their former glory.

An actor represents an Irishman with his fighting stick, in Joseph Reed's play The Register Office, 1806, drawn by Samuel De Wilde. (Courtesy of the National Library of Ireland)

6

'THE SAVAGE CONFLICTS OF BARBAROUS MOBS'

> 'Perhaps the most numerous Faction Feuds that I heard of when in Ireland were what took place in the Neighbourhood of Killarney … I was told there were from Two to Three thousand sometimes engaged in them.'
>
> Colonel James Shaw Kennedy, inspector-General of the Royal Irish Constabulary from 1836 to 1838[1]

Fighting at Killarney fairs had been noted from the 1600s, and during the early 1700s there were further indications that different parties had been involved in stick fighting in the area.[2] Among the earliest factions of the district were the O'Donoghues, who were praised as faction fighters by the poet Murroghoh O'Connor in 1726:

Where e'er the brave O'Donaghoos engage,
Well known with Cudgels such brave Fights to wage;
All must submit unto their stff'ning Blows,
Unless th' O'Sulivans their Sticks oppose.[3]

The O'Sullivans may have been members of the family of O'Sullivan Mór, the last of whom died at Tomies Wood,

Killarney, in 1762. The O'Donoghues may have been one or other of the two branches of the family of chieftains, one of which was known as the O'Donoghues of Lough Leane, Killarney, and the other as the O'Donoghues of the Glens.

During the late 1700s Daniel O'Donoghue (the leader of the latter branch) regularly brought his faction into Killarney from Glenflesk, where he had an estate. Glenflesk was then:

> inhabited by a fine race of people, stout, tall, hardy mountaineers; and … these fellows, under the countenance of their chieftain … rode rough-shod over the town of Killarney. On every fair and market day they marched through it, shouting, hallooing, and offering five pounds for the head of any man that would dare oppose them ...
>
> At last the people of Killarney … became quite indignant at the tyranny of the Glenflegians, and determined to throw off the yoke. The fair day of Killarney was fixed for that purpose, and both parties prepared themselves accordingly. When it came, the stout wealthy farmers … poured in; and the town itself furnished an excellent force.
>
> The Glenflegians in a large body marched as usual through the streets, 'dancing out of their skins', shouting and hurraing. O'Donoghue, in a gold-laced hat and coat, was at their head. As they passed through Hen Street [afterwards Plunkett Street], the first opposition appeared. A smith, Hearty Cronin, had got his head shaved the day before; he knew that he must get many cuts, and was resolved to save the apothecary the trouble of cutting off his hair. Having placed a table before his door, he mounted it; and the first of the Glenflegians that reached him he struck. In a twinkling, the judiciousness of his precautions was seen. He was dismounted … and right well cut, under several blows. But the battle began. The townsmen and their friends fell in, and the row became general.

> At first men shunned O'Donoghue. His clan were attacked with right good will; but no one forgot the old respect entertained for him, until a miner, Larry *Plukh*[4] … a man of great strength and courage, coming up to O'Donoghue with a fine black-thorn stick, exclaimed, 'By G[od] I'll never go to the feet, while I've the head'; struck him, and sent his gold-laced hat whistling up into the air. It will give you a notion of O'Donoghue; he struck Larry in return with his open hand, and felled him to the earth; where he remained for a long time spouting blood through his mouth and ears. But after that O'Donoghue and his Glenflegians were attacked without distinction. At length numbers prevailed, and the Glenflegians were wholly defeated. They were chased a mile out of the town.[5]

After they suffered this defeat, 'the Glenflegians never since raised their head as a faction in the town'.[6]

Another faction, the Flemings, may have operated from around 1805. In an incident in December 1828, they assaulted a man named Sullivan because he was 'a distant relation of the Cummins, a party opposed to the Flemings', reported *The Kerry Evening Post*. As he was returning from Killarney fair the man was badly beaten by five others, 'each armed with a heavy bludgeon'. The men from the Fleming faction were sentenced to twelve months' solitary confinement, fined and bound to keep the peace. 'You shall be separated from your families and friends for a time, and while others are enjoying the blessings and comforts of the passing seasons, you shall be estranged from them,' declared the judge. The sentence, said the court reporter, 'was approved of by a crowded court, and the prisoners on being removed from the dock to the bridewell, wept bitterly'.[7]

Other members of the party continued, assaulting members

of the Crimeens at Fossa, Killarney, in July 1829. 'It appears in evidence that these abominable feuds are in existence during the last twenty-five years,' commented the judge, who condemned 'these brutish factions'.[8]

Meanwhile, other O'Donoghues carried on the practice of fighting in Killarney. 'Two clans, the Moynihans and the O'Donaghues, had been in a state of perpetual feud for half a century,' wrote Fürst Hermann von Pückler-Muskau, the German prince who visited the town in 1828. 'Wherever they met in any considerable numbers, a shillelah battle was sure to take place, and many lives were usually lost.'[9]

These parties engaged in Killarney and nearby, at Cloghereen fair, Muckross. In January 1824 'there was much rioting in the town of Killarney between two factions, one named Moynehan and the other Donoghue … the leaders have been taken into custody and held to bail'.[10] At Cloghereen, three men named Donoghue were among seven men implicated in October 1827, following 'a savage fight between two factions' in which a man was killed after he received 'two blows of a heavy cudgel on the bare head'.[11] Folklorist Thomas Crofton Croker wrote an account of the fair and a meeting between the groups whom he barely disguised as 'The Minehans' and 'The Donoghues'. Although published in 1829, his description was based upon research from a slightly earlier time, carried out in the Killarney area by Adolphus Lynch, a semi-retired army officer whose manuscripts he had bought. Croker's style was to present such material parcelled up in the form of a story or a tale, rather than in a straightforward manner. The following excerpts have been stripped of storytelling elements and amalgamated to present an impression not just of a fight, but of the wider context of the fairs in which fights most often took place:

> The fair ground consisted of two gentle slopes on the public road ... The road was lined with the tables or stands of dealers in dillisk (a dried seaweed of a pink colour, and no bad relish it is to a bit of bread and butter), fruits, frize, flannel, croobeens[12] ... and, in short, everything necessary for rustic economy and enjoyment; while the common ground was occupied by horses, cows, and pigs, with their buyers and sellers.
>
> Here were to be seen groups of giggling girls, with their riband-adorned caps and blue cloaks; and there whispering matrons with their shawled heads: here were men occupied in shrewd bargains, with their frize loodies (large loose coats), corduroy breeches, and well seasoned sticks – sticks not destined long to remain inactive; there a half gentleman – a squireen, known by his body coat with brass buttons, Caroline hat, and polished boots armed with but one spur[;] here leaders of opposing factions scowled defiance at each other; and there may be seen the joyous recognition of long-parted gossips.[13]
>
> Under the trees which skirted the entrance to the village were several tents, or rather apologies for tents, constructed by means of long wattles bent to a semicircle, both ends of which were stuck in the ground, and this frame-work was covered over with patchwork quilts and sheets. At one end stood the porter and whisky barrels, on whose heads were placed in most tempting array, jugs and tumblers, bread and butter, salmon, and mutton pies.
>
> Towns-people and country-people were mingled together, some of whom had business at the fair, and others who had no business, save and excepting what they considered the very pleasant business of getting drunk.

> 'Hurroo here's a Minehan, here's a Donoghue,' resounded through the fair. This was followed by the immediate clashing of sticks, mingled with the wild shouts of the combatants. In a moment the tent was emptied, and we among the rest ran out to take a view of the fray, which did not promise to be very dangerous to those engaged, as they were so thickly wedged together, that stick waved over stick, and met with a world of noise and clatter; but few received, or could possibly receive, a single blow.
>
> Presently the mounted police dashed up and dispersed the combatants, while the magistrate, aided by a body of the foot police, triumphantly seized on their shillelaghs.[14]

Twenty years later an English visitor published an anonymous recollection of his former experiences in Ireland, which included a description of a faction fight at Killarney. 'It was no uncommon thing to see columns, of many hundreds strong, march into Killarney from opposite points, for the sole purpose of fighting on a market-day. Why they fought nobody could tell – they did not know themselves,' he wrote.

> 'Sure, it's a Moynehan!' was repeated by fifty voices in a row at Killarney, where all who could come near enough were employed in hitting, with their long blackthorn sticks, at an unfortunate wretch lying prostrate and disabled amongst them. Fortunately, the eagerness of his enemies proved the salvation of the man, for they crowded so furiously together that their blows fell upon each other, and scarcely any reached their intended victim on the ground. It was ridiculous to see the wild way in which they hit one another; but so infuriated were they, that no heed was taken of the blows ... The screams, and yells, and savage fury of the combatants would have done credit to an onslaught of Blackfeet or New Zealanders, whilst

> the dancing madness was peculiarly their own. But in spite of the vocal efforts of the combatants, and the constant accompaniment of the sticks, you could hear the dull *thud* which told when a blackthorn fell upon an undefended skull.[15]

By 1828 both parties may have retired. Von Pückler-Muskau explained that since the formation of the Catholic Association, 'it has become the interest of the priests to establish peace and concord in their flocks':

> Accordingly, after the fight which took place last year, they enjoined as penance that the Moynihans should march twelve miles to the north and the O'Donaghues an equal distance to the south, and both pronounce certain prayers at their journey's end; that all the lookers-on should make a pilgrimage of six miles in some other direction; and in case of a repetition of the offence, the penance to be doubled. All this was executed with religious exactness, and ever since the war is at an end.[16]

Cloghereen later hosted other parties, such as the 'Poul-na-mucks' (named after a townland on the outskirts of the town just beyond Flesk bridge, on the road towards Muckross). In June 1830, after they met at the fair there without incident, a man from the barony of Magunihy knocked down one of the Poul-na-mucks in Killarney. 'A challenge was sent to decide the matter between two champions, one from each body, which was accepted, and … O'Brien of the Poul-na-mucks took up the glove of Ahern, the chosen of Magonihy', with their sticks to be laid aside in favour of their fists.

'Sunday morning was appointed, and *Cournamalavogue* was to be the field of honour; as early as three o'clock, the Magonihians began to muster – a few of the Poul-na-mucks were also at the post; but their champion was not forthcoming, and taunts were freely thrown.'[17] O'Brien arrived late, explaining that he had been bound over to keep the peace, but the fight was aborted when he was arrested and Ahern, too, had to flee from the same prospect.

The Poul-na-mucks faction came to notice again one Saturday evening in June 1833, when they fought a party from Philadown, Glenflesk (as Glenflesk lay in the barony of Magunihy, the latter party may have been the same 'Magonihians' they had faced in 1830). In this incident:

> a gang of ruffians about 50 in number, rushed from the vicinity of the Court house, uttering the most savage and horrible yells against the objects of their vengeance … as they indiscriminately knocked down all who were not of their party. They proceeded down the new street and between the police and military barracks they met with opposition from some persons who particularly appeared to be objects of their murderous attacks.[18]

The fighting was only quelled when a detachment of the 76th Regiment assisted police in arresting the ringleaders. *The Kerry Evening Post*, which was somewhat the champion of law and order in the county, bemoaned 'such acts of savage barbarity and atrocity' in which men 'seek the lives of their fellow-creatures, for no reason but one bears a different name from the other, thus keeping alive that demoralising system which gives to Irishmen all over civilised Europe, the character of barbarians'.[19]

Its rival newspaper, the *Tralee Mercury*, played down the event, however:

> [S]ome drunken countrymen ... for want of other employment, introduced a system of Gymnastics hitherto forgotten in this part of the country: we mean that of wheeling clubs. The noise occasioned in consequence, attracted the attention of our active and efficient Sub-Sheriff, who, perceiving that some of the performers designedly let fall their clubs on the nobs of others ... put an end to the performance by securing four of the greatest proficients.[20]

The newspaper printed a comic poem that had been forwarded by a local man, in which 'the Philas fled like flocks of geese,/And the Poulas cheered and started'.

> *June twenty-two, in Killarney town,*
> *There was a dreadful battle,*
> *'Twixt Poulnamuck and Philadown,*
> *With black and thorny wattle.*
> *With savage yells they rushed along,*
> *'Quest the objects of their fury,*
> *But the Barrister, he'll change their song*
> *When they come before the Jury.*[21]

The barrister mentioned in the poem was Assistant County Barrister William Deane Freeman, who, from the beginning of his appointment in 1829, strongly condemned and punished faction fighters throughout Kerry.[22]

In a different incident at Cloghereen, in December 1832, a

man named Downey was 'twisting his stick, hallooing' and 'saying he'd beat Cloghereen fair'. As he was crossing Torc bridge, on the old Kenmare road, he was overtaken by a number of men and 'on getting to the middle [they] all *walloped* away with their sticks at him, without saying anything'. He believed that some of the men had a grudge against him because he had married a relative of theirs but 'did not take with her' and had sent her home.[23]

THE BARRYS, LEARYS AND HORGANS (AND THE CLIFFORDS, MARAS AND CRONINS)

Beginning from the late 1820s, flourishing in the 1830s and continuing for decades, a significant number of factions, both named and unnamed, fought at Killarney. Chief among them were the Barrys, Learys, Horgans, Cliffords, Maras and Cronins.

In January 1829 numbers of Barrys, Learys and Horgans were convicted of assault and riotous assembly in Killarney.[24] A Richard Barry had been convicted of the same activity in October of the previous year, and the strong sentence imposed on him may represent official censure of an already recognised faction, as he was given not only six months' imprisonment, with hard labour, but was heavily fined to keep the peace into the future.[25] Thomas Crofton Croker portrayed the Barrys and the Learys, again in semi-fictional style:

> Scarcely had we entered the town, when our ears were assailed by a most tremendous uproar. – 'Here's a Barry' – 'Here's a Leary' – 'Five pounds for a Barry's head' – 'Ten pounds for a Leary' – 'Here's up-street for Barry' – 'Here's down-street for a Leary' – resounded through the town.

> 'Spillane, what's all this uproar about? the stag-hunt whiskey seems to be stirring among the good people of Killarney.'
>
> 'O sir, it's only a bit of a skirmish between up-street and down-street, and the faction of the Barrys and Learys; it's nothing to what they used to have long ago, when one part of the town fought against the other, with old scythes and swords and stones; and the women used to come behind a man, with a parcel of stones in an old stocking, and knock him as dead as a herring.'
>
> Presently there came a cry of 'The Peelers' – 'The Peelers' – and immediately three or four green-coated, black-belted horsemen, with a fiery magistrate at their head, dashed into the thick of the crowd; and after some time, succeeded in putting an end to the fray.[26]

A major battle was prevented on 25 March 1830, when mounted police charged at unnamed groups of fighters in the crowded streets and 'prevented these heroes from showing off in their usual style'.[27] A related search of a house in New Street yielded a remarkable 200 cudgels. On 12 April 1830 an affray took place between two rival factions, and on 28 December 1831, at a fair held at the same time as criminal court sessions were taking place in the town, 'two hostile factions had the audacity to come to action and engage in mortal combat in the streets'.[28] These episodes may represent further appearances by the Barrys and the Learys, but it is fair to say that they shared the stage of Killarney's streets with other gangs.

In 1832, in almost the same circumstances, 'several new factions', as they were called, fought on St Stephen's Day, and kept up a continuous clamour during the night:

> to the great annoyance of the peaceable and respectable inhabitants; and yesterday being the first day of the Sessions, and a new fair day, the same demoniac spirit prevailed, in the very teeth of a Court of Justice – various hordes of these wretched beings commenced those dreadful affrays, which disgrace this unfortunate county – the engagement was so frightful that the shopkeepers were obliged to shut up their doors, and suspend their ordinary business.[29]

At the end of December 1833, a fight took place 'between two factions from Glanflesk … severely beating each other through the streets up to the new Court-house'.[30] Towards the end of January 1834, two days of fighting took place in Killarney 'between the numerous riotous factions that infest that town':

> [F]rom an early hour on Saturday evening last, every shop in Henn-Street was obliged to be cleared up[;] so furious was the conflict on both sides that the shopkeepers in that part of the town would not risk the safety of their persons and properties by keeping their doors open; one wretched man, we are informed, now lies in a very precarious state, from the effects of a violent blow of a spade, inflicted on his head by a *woman*!
>
> On the following day, notwithstanding its being the sabbath, the war-whoop was again raised, at the sound of which hundreds of infatuated beings assembled and commenced their murderous work, bludgeons and stones being the implements of destruction … the frightful state of things which at present exists in Killarney cannot longer be endured, some decisive measures must be immediately resorted to, the shopkeepers and middle classes are the sufferers to this nefarious system, and nothing but the utmost rigour of the law, we are convinced, will bring those deluded wretches to a sense of their error.[31]

Later that year, barrister Freeman (whose legal role was as a judge) lamented that although he had passed severe sentences on all of the rioters who had been convicted before him, 'it was to no purpose'.[32] A report of a fight in the town shortly after his remarks cited the Maras and the Cliffords as well as the Learys and other parties unnamed, and 'their disgraceful propensity to rioting', as being the factions involved.[33] (The Maras and the Cliffords may thus have formed some of the 'new factions' noted in 1832.)

The same collection of gangs, and others, engaged in a particularly violent bout at the Killarney summer fair held on 4 July 1834. At some point a fight began, after which two of the ringleaders were arrested, and shortly afterwards a general riot took place in which hundreds of men became involved. 'During the entire night, the town was a scene of the utmost confusion,' recorded *The Kerry Evening Post* afterwards. 'Three men are at this moment lying in a most precarious state, no hopes being entertained of their recovery by their medical attendants – quantities of blood was seen the next morning in the channels and a cart which stood in Hen street was literally covered with it.'[34]

In July 1835 what *The Kerry Evening Post* characterised as 'the well known faction shouts of "The Cliffords, Maras, Learys, Cronins, Barrys, and Horgans", rung through the town'. Then 'a forest of sticks was instantly raised up, and a general engagement immediately ensued, which continued without intermission for some hours to the great terror and annoyance of the shopkeepers and other inhabitants'.[35] A magistrate and the police arrested twenty-six men, seventeen of whom were subsequently convicted, including John Meara and John Cronin.

Some of the same gangs are likely to have been among those who had gathered in June, at the fair of Droumirourk (as Cloghereen was also known) where:

> strong symptoms of rioting were exhibited by several rival factions; however they deferred carrying their malicious and deadly designs into execution until their arrival in Killarney, where a dreadful and alarming riot took place, in the evening … The Magistrates, gentry, and police, were beat off with showers of stones flung at them by the combatants, and after having received several cuts and contusions, some of them knocked down and kicked in the most brutal and savage manner while on the ground, were obliged to retreat. The rioting, we are informed, continued until a very late hour in the night.[36]

The year 1835 represented a high-water mark for these gangs, with *The Kerry Evening Post* complaining of 'the savage conflicts of barbarous mobs at fairs, and at every public meeting in that town'.[37] At the August fair, the Barrys and the Mearas fought again.[38] One man had his arm 'dreadfully lacerated', and another, John Brosnahan, was killed.[39] At the inquest into Brosnahan's death, the jury expressed its opinion that:

> in consequence of the increasing riotous disposition of the peasantry of this neighbourhood, our town being in a continual state of disturbance, and our trade materially injured by such riots, the Coroner and Magistrates acting with him on the present occasion should make immediate application to the Lord Lieutenant for a strong military force, to be permanently quartered in Killarney.[40]

In response, it was later planned that the number of policemen at the Killarney station be augmented by an additional sixteen men.[41]

In December 1835 *The Kerry Evening Post* observed:

> The town of Killarney, many years proverbial as the seat of the most dreadful riots and disturbances, but which by the well-timed punishments inflicted on the various offenders convicted before Mr Freeman, had been for some time past in a comparative state of peace and tranquillity, has, we are informed, since the rumour of that excellent functionary's removal has been confirmed, resumed its former aspect … Night after night, for several weeks past, the entire of that town has been in a state of riot and confusion, utterly impossible for us to describe – the war cry of the wretches engaged in these inhuman riots, has been swelled with rejoicings at the removal of our late Chairman, and an impression is abroad, that the very heavy recognizances in which it was his practice to bind those unruly disturbers of the public peace, are, by his removal cancelled.[42]

It is worth noting that most of the gangs of the 1830s may not have originated in Killarney, nor in its immediate environs, but in more outlying areas. In 1835 a newspaper commented that, 'from the vast numbers of country people who flocked into town it soon became evident that a most sanguinary conflict was contemplated'.[43] The Learys were later described as being from Barraduff, and the Cronins from Headford, both districts roughly six miles east of Killarney town.[44] A later folklore interviewee also explained that a bout was once arranged between men from Rathmore and men from 'the West of Killarney', to be held in College Street. 'The men from the West had a great name as fighters and the Rathmore men were in dread enough of them.

But they thought of a plan.' A man among them, Dan T. Long, from Kilquane, about a mile east of Barraduff, was seven feet four inches tall, but he was 'as quiet as a child and never in a row in his life'. His companions 'prepared a huge club and induced Dan T to hold the club over his head and march in front of their band. Although he never struck a man in his life, his appearance frightened the men from the West and they ran away.'[45]

How numerous membership of the parties around Killarney was during the mid-1830s may be gauged from Colonel James Shaw Kennedy's remark that up to 3,000 people may have taken part in total.[46] After that period, however, organised faction fighting seems to have disappeared from Killarney for ten years, although the use of the stick did not. In 1839 a German traveller mentioned to a local boatman a man who was a problem in his homeland, to which the zealous guide exclaimed, 'If I could reach him with my shillelagh I'd strike him dead without batting an eyelid, dead as a doornail, stone dead, Your Honour, for he is surely an abominable fellow!'[47] In December 1840 an English visitor to Killarney came upon some country people on the road to Muckross who had been drinking *poitín*, and he was told by his guide that they would soon be 'wielding the shelilah "merely for the love to each other"'. A man approached him, 'armed certainly with a formidable looking stick', who told him that 'no Father Matthew should deprive him of his drop of the creatur'.[48]

Factions re-emerged in Killarney during the 1840s. In August 1844 there was 'a riot … between two factions' after the Killarney races.[49] In March 1845 there was 'a desperate riot', and factioneering was described as 'again becoming prevalent'.[50]

When factions returned, the Maras and the Cliffords were in the vanguard. On St Stephen's Day 1845, the Maras prepared to engage with a group named as the 'Sullivans Brack':[51] 'At three o'clock the town was crowded, and a casual observer might perceive the general indications of a row being about to commence, from the different groups of peasants exchanging their new coats and hats for old jackets and caubeens, and securing their sticks around their wrist bands with leathern thongs.'[52] The arrival of heavy rain, along with 'the imposing display of force that patrolled the town under Sub-Inspector Bannon' ultimately prevented the fight from starting.[53]

The Cliffords reappeared at the Killarney races in July 1846, which became 'the scene of the most desperate faction fighting' between themselves and the Maras. 'On each occasion, we understand that the peasantry did not exhibit any signs of their combative intentions until after the police had left the course, when they had the place all to themselves.'[54] It was afterwards declared by a writer in *The Cork Examiner* that 'It is deplorable that these people will not learn sense enough to let each other alone. The affair was thought to be drying off, but was revived on the first and second evening of the Races.'[55]

English novelist William Makepeace Thackeray viewed the races in 1842 and was impressed by 'one of the most beautiful spots that ever was seen; the lake and the mountains lying along two sides of it … The grand stand was already full; along the hedges sate thousands of the people, sitting at their ease doing nothing, and happy as kings.'[56] There, too, he saw tents selling tea rather than alcohol (following the influence of Fr Mathew), pipers and dancers, gamblers and gaming tables. Thackeray did not report faction fights, but he attended the first day only; much later 'Small' Ger O'Leary of Main Street, Killarney, commented:

> Before my time they used to have the races out where the golf links are now. That was a hundred years or so ago. There'd be fun then. Those races were the scene of the famous Faction Fights. When the horses came in after the last race the second day, you picked up your bones and went fast. If you didn't you could be in trouble. The faction fights would start at Mahony's Point, and if you were around you weren't asked what your name was.[57]

Others of the long-standing gangs reappeared in the early 1860s. The Barrys and Cronins fought against the Learys and Horgans in a brief battle in High Street on Stephen's Day 1860.[58] On the same holiday, three years later, it was reported that 'a faction feud has broken out into overt acts in that neighbourhood, between the "Barrys and Cronins" on one side, and the "Learys and Horgans" on the other.' On the night of St Stephen's Day, small parties of these rivals also met a few minutes' walk outside the town and commenced to beat each other with sticks and stones, during which 'faction cries were called out'.[59]

During the late 1880s, the Learys, Horgans, Barrys and Cronins briefly renewed their feud. In June 1887 an episode occurred that *The Kerry Evening Post* described as representing a revival of faction fighting in Killarney, 'which in former years was remarkably prevalent in this part of Kerry'.

> The day having been the monthly cattle fair day in Killarney the farmers after disposing of their stock indulged pretty freely in the

> whiskey and porter. About six o'clock two men of this class, armed with heavy sticks, came down High Street shouting, 'Here is a Leary and a Horgan.' The two heroes were met opposite the Town Hall at the Market Square by two other men, ardent champions of the opposite faction, called the 'Barrys and Cronins'. This party has ever been the most powerful of any faction gang in this locality and often figured in a bloody fight. The latter two came to their antagonists, and, without much ado besmeared them with gutter in the faces, and then gave them a severe beating with sticks on the head. The former made as good a fight as they could, but they were not able for the latter; and they had to beat a retreat towards their way home by the Cathedral.[60]

On 6 January 1888 the Learys and Cronins 'had á semi-intoxicated dispute in the Fair Hill and in the course of the encounter, in which the "black thorns" and the "hazels" were freely used, one of the [members of the] former faction had had his cranium so severely fractured as to render his removal to hospital necessary … The leaders of the two sections were well pummelled on the occasion.'[61] After this, no more was heard of them or their fellow gangs.

A single late incident went off in the election year of 1910 between supporters of rival candidates.[62] That bout represented the end of faction fighting in Killarney, which had been run along its streets and in the districts nearby for over 150 years.

7

'THE WILD IVERAGH DEVILS' AND OTHERS

> 'The Derreen and Lauragh men had been gathering whilst Teague was speaking, and the best men from Glentrasna to Coomeengira were now at his back, and stood listening to their spokesman and leader with angry and determined looks. When he had finished, they gave a loud cheer or rather yell of defiance, and wheeled their sticks over their heads.'
>
> William Steuart Trench, *Ierne: A Tale*[1]

This scene was set at Kilmackillogue pattern day, and there and elsewhere along that portion of the Beara peninsula that forms the southernmost part of Kerry, as well as in the several towns and villages of the Iveragh peninsula, factions played their rough games. The battles in these districts were as often associated with religious pattern days as with fairs. This was unusual as most of those types of events which were riotous elsewhere throughout the county and country had long since been cleaned up or prohibited by the Catholic clergy. They had been condemned from the 1700s; Bishop Troy of Ossory, for example, complained in 1782 that visitors to patterns 'finish the day by the perpetration of the grossest impurities, by shedding their neighbour's blood, by murder, and the transgression of every law'.[2] In Kerry, as long previously as 1747, Bishop William O'Meara had advised his priests to try to reverse the situation whereby the secular amusements of these events had become more important than the religious observances.[3]

Cahersiveen was visited in 1822 by Royal Navy man Thomas Reid, who saw fighting at the fair in which a woman felled a man with a stone she swung around in her apron. Asenath Nicholson, a Protestant missionary from New York, was there in March 1845. '"A fight! a fight!" was now the cry,' at the fair she observed, and sticks 'were flourishing in the air':

> One old woman rushed into the crowd to rescue her Paddy, and she was dragged along regardless of age or sex, her cloak was torn from her, her cap set awry, (bonnet she had none), and while one pulled one way, another seized the other side, till the sight from the ludicrous became painful, lest she should be 'pulled in pieces'. The priest was called, but they heeded not the threats of denunciations from the altar, which he assured them they should have on the morrow … he was obliged to leave them as he found them, to rattle their sticks, as they did till midnight, though it was next day reported that no dead or wounded were carried from the field that night.[4]

Fights appear to have taken place at a Cahersiveen pattern day, and on one occasion these were suppressed 'with a heavy stick' by Fr O'Sullivan.[5] This may have been the pattern held at Carhan, near the town, on 29 September. Daniel O'Connell was fond of attending the day, but complained in 1813, '[a]s I left this place early, the fellows availed themselves of the opportunity to flog each other *elegantly*. I do not believe there ever were so many broken heads and bloody faces in the country before.'[6] At what appears to have been the same event the following year, he said, 'I spent the rest of the day in deciding wrangles, preventing riots.'[7]

Stick fighters from Cahersiveen were summoned by their allies to engage at Kilmackillogue pattern, and at Ballinclare fair on the Dingle peninsula, but little is known of their activities in their own neighbourhood, despite the fact that the town hosted several fairs every year, which must have represented plenty of opportunities to fight.[8] They may have appeared in connection with others when the 'wild Iveragh devils and their neighbours of Glenbeigh' were condemned for the level of their violence at a faction fight at Kilgobnet which appears to have taken place sometime in the early 1800s.[9]

On Valentia island, the pattern day of St Darerca, held on 22 March, was 'a great day of sport, music and dancing, and a great day for feuding as well', it was later related in an Irish-language account. 'There was a tribe of the Maitheamhnaig [Mahonys] all around Iveragh. They were a bad sort. No one respected them because they committed a lot of bad deeds.'[10] There was a feud between those of them who lived on Valentia and the O'Neills, and on one particular day they met at the pattern. The O'Neills gathered many of their party from the mainland and the Mahonys also amassed in large numbers:

> On the morning of the pattern day they came into Baile na Mánach [Ballymanagh], all of the Maitheamhnaig in boats and pulled in on the high tide. They went up to the Patron, which used to be held at the side of a hill. When everybody saw the Maitheamhnaig coming they knew there would be a big day of fighting ahead.

> The leader of the Maitheamhnaig took off his coat and pulled it after him to see who would tramp on it, as that was the way they used to begin a fight at that time. The leader of the Ó Néills tramped on it and then battle commenced …
>
> They weren't long fighting before some of them were stretched out bleeding. They continued fighting and in the end there was neither a man nor a woman who was not involved in the fight, as there was no one there who wasn't either related or connected to either tribe involved. In the end the Maitheamhnaig were beaten and they fled down to the boats on the shore.[11]

Their defeat marked the end of the affair, and the pattern, too, was subsequently discontinued as a result of the incident.

Further along the mainland was Ballinskelligs. In modern times Michael Kirby related a story he had heard about Donal McCarthy, a former faction fighter of the village. As he indicated that McCarthy had lived through the Famine, its aftermath and 'the years of recovery', the story may date from the 1860s. This old man was 'expert in the use of the cudgel in self-defence'. A coastguard, Tommy Adams, wanted to test McCarthy's skill and challenged him to a fight, to take place in Paddy Haren's tavern. 'The winner was to be the contestant who first made bodily contact three times. He would receive a half bottle of ship's rum, the loser a quart of ale. Each man was to have the approved shillelagh of equal design.' Before the fight began, Donal:

> performed a short ritual dance, twirling his shillelagh like some Zulu warrior. The coastguard explained very sincerely to the old man that he only wanted to ascertain the truth of whether the Irish

> stick-wielders were skilled in the art of fencing. McCarthy replied, '*B'fhearr dhuit ciall a bheith agat*', meaning, 'Better for you to be sensible.' … Old Donal danced like a paper doll and it was soon evident that he was under pressure from a very skilled adversary, a product of naval training. As yet an opening for a touch had not presented itself. Old McCarthy was backed into a corner. Then it happened: the knob of Donal's shillelagh made contact over the coastguard's left ear. Tommy Adams winced under the sudden stinging impact, only to receive two more resounding taps in quick succession, directly in line over the left ear.
>
> Paddy Haren stepped in, declaring the contest over. Adams shook the old man's hand, who remarked, '*Ná dúirt mé leat ciall a bheith agat*', meaning, 'I told you have sense.' Three lumps like thrush's eggs began to grow over Tommy's ear, to which he applied cold water … The above account I heard from my cousin, old John Fitzgerald of Horse Island.[12]

Perhaps the old man was a veteran of the pattern days that used to be held at St Michael's Well, Dungeagan, near Ballinskelligs, every 29 September. These were a three-day spree. 'It was common to see blood flowing freely from skulls due to blackthorn sticks – mayhem, murder and noise! The second pattern day was even worse than the first,' related storyteller Seán Chormaic Ó Sé.[13] Earlier, in the mid-1750s, visiting antiquarian Charles Smith had also noted that 'when their penance is performed, the day is ended with drinking and revelling'.[14] In 1838 a small party of policemen attended Dungeagan:

> a spot well known as being the most lawless part of the county of Kerry, for the purpose of assisting in keeping the peace at a

Stick fighting outside a tavern, c. 1805. Drawn by Charles Mackenzie. (Courtesy of the National Library of Ireland)

'pattern'. A row having commenced at a late hour in the evening, the police interfered, and arrested some of the parties, but were immediately assailed by an immense mob of, we understand, at least 1000 persons, who made every effort to rescue the prisoners, but not succeeding in this, they threw vollies of stones at the police, by which the head-constable and several of the men were struck, and some of them severely hurt; the attack continued for upwards of an hour, during which the police had several times to charge their adversaries, and it was at the point of the bayonet alone they retained their prisoners and escaped with their lives.[15]

There were also battles at St Finnan's (or Fíonán's) Well, Mastergeehy, on the day before St Patrick's Day, said Ó Sé; fellow storyteller Seán O'Conaill said that 'there were fights and strife. A man was killed there, and that put an end to the Patron.'[16] This may be the incident recorded for 16 March 1834 at 'Tubberfinaune', when 'a dreadful riot occurred between two factions – the Sullivans' and the Sheas' – in which a man, named John Shea was killed'.[17]

NA CASÚRAIGH

The famous party of Mastergeehy was comprised of a branch of the O'Sullivans who carried the nickname *Na Casúraigh* ('of the hammer blows') 'as an indication of their prowess as faction fighters'.[18] They appear to have flourished during the 1820s and 1830s (and the incident at St Finnan's Well may have been their work).

> There was a family in Iochtar Cua by the name of Na Casúraigh and at that time it contained four well-built, strong brothers who were "cliste" with their "bataí draighin" [skilful with their blackthorn sticks]. It was considered a sign of manliness to be athletic and agile with the blackthorn stick at the time. There was a long running feud between the Casúraigh and a family from the parish of Prior who were known as 'Clann Gleanncach na Priaireachta', even though both families were quite closely related. It was a regular occurrence for a skirmish to break out between them on fair days, pattern days, at funerals and at weddings. They were considerate though in a way, as they would never strike the first blow without giving a warning. The usual phrase was 'Cosain tu féin' or in English 'Guard yourself'. Fighting would be ferocious with little mercy shown by either side.

> Eventually, it was decided to have one 'decent' battle where both sides would gather together as many as they could and finally settle the matter once and for all.

The parties determined to fight one Sunday after Mass at Mastergeehy church. The congregation became swelled by their numbers, and the Casúraigh brothers 'made sure they were at the back wall of the church with their "bataí" gripped firmly behind their backs':

> After the gospel, the priest turned and faced the people in full regalia and started off 'I notice we have a large gathering here today from outlying parishes and they're not here for any good reason but fighting and disorder and quarrelling. If that is what they want, why don't they stay in their own parishes instead of fighting amongst us here and so close to this church?' This chat got the better of the Casúrs and one of them piped up and said 'Éist do bhéal, a bhodaigh agus tabhair aire dod' chúram féin ar eagla gur duit ba mheasa' which roughly translates 'Shut your trap you pompous old [fool] or it'll be the worse for you.'

The cleric appealed to his flock to have nothing to do with the coming fight and declared that the Casúrs would come to a bad end. 'The priest continued in this vein for some time and finally mass ended and the people dispersed quietly and calmly without a blow being struck. By all accounts, each of the four brothers died within a year "gan ola gan aithrí" [without the last sacraments and without repentance].'[19]

Another Irish-language account noted a fight between *Na Casúraigh* and the O'Sheas, held on a hillock in Mastergeehy one Sunday before Mass, around the year 1825. A priest found out who was responsible and 'took hold of a stick and struck Ó Súilleabháin for starting the fight ... Father Mac Cárthaigh was nicknamed "the priest of the stick" after that'. Afterwards, the young O'Sullivan man left the parish and called into a shebeen, where he drank down a jug of whiskey and collapsed and died (presumably of alcohol poisoning). 'A while after that the brother of the man who died was at the races in Prior and some kind of incident happened there and he died.'[20]

A party of O'Sullivans were subsequently involved in a fight with the Currans (or O'Currans) and the O'Sheas (although it is not quite clear whether these O'Sullivans were of the *Casúraigh* or not):

> An argument arose between them in a drinking house the previous Sunday about which of them was the best man among them. They met each other on the hill above the chapel that Sunday morning before Mass, and every one of them carrying a blackthorn stick ... each man with a strap on the stick in case the stick would be snapped away from them in battle. The O'Sullivans were winning and they drove the other crowd back west to Cúinne Máighréide and eastwards down towards the southern side of the chapel and then a crowd of the O'Sheas came down from the top of Barr na hAoine to help the O'Currans and they drove the O'Sullivans back again.[21]

A priest came along and put a stop to the fight, but, fearing that passions were still inflamed among the parties and not wishing to see blood spilled in the church, he held Mass at a rock on a nearby farm that day.

Another man recalled a story related to him by his grandfather about two parties who met at Mastergeehy one Sunday. The Pilibees were a local party of O'Sullivans, while their opponents, known as the Drins, or Doirins, were Sheehans, from around Bantry, West Cork, whose 'noses were crooked from fighting':

> This fight was at Mastergehy bridge because of a boast from the Drins that they would cross the bridge that day, and a counter by the faction that if they tried to cross it they would be ducked in the river. One conscience-stricken Pilibee said they would all be damned together if they drowned the others.
>
> They had at it, and the strength of the Drins was already broken when the priest came and ruined the finish of the fight. But it looked as though none of them had the stomach to finish it, seeing as how few words by the priest were enough to put an end to it.[22]

It is unknown whether or not many altercations took place around Derrynane, the home of Daniel O'Connell. Earlier factions may have been put down successfully by Maurice 'Hunting Cap' O'Connell (1728–1825), Daniel's uncle. On one occasion, it was much later claimed, when Hunting Cap heard that a fight was to take place at Derrynane strand, 'he loaded a brace of pistols, jumped on his horse, rode down at top speed to the scene of the action. Swore that he'd shoot the first man dead … who struck a blow. Then putting spurs to his horse he rode rough-shod through both factions, lashing out right and left with his hunting crop and put both parties to flight.'[23]

There was some fighting at Sneem fairs. On the evening of 15 December 1844, 'two parties who had been kept in order during the day' through the presence of the police, began to fight, and a man named Sullivan, who had initiated the combat, was killed by another named Dwyer.[24] The latter was arrested by the Sneem police that night, and it seems that this was a fortunate occurrence, as immediately afterwards 'an infuriated party of the friends of the deceased arrived at his house and would have, in all probability, taken summary vengeance, were they not anticipated by the vigilance of the police'.[25] The newspaper report described the dead man pointedly as 'a pledge-breaker' – a man who had taken, and abandoned, the oath against drinking alcohol administered by Fr Mathew's temperance movement.

Another incident in the village, in September 1850, was described as one of the fiercest faction fights to have occurred in Kerry:

> Unfortunately the parties were after purchasing reaping hooks for cutting their corn on the day following; but they turned them to a very different purpose, for they cut and mangled each other in a shocking manner with the instruments, which they freely used. Several of the mad and foolish [combatants] are not expected to recover. There were women, too, engaged in the *melée*, busily employed in gathering stones for those who were not possessed of sticks or reaping hooks. The magistrates have committed several of the rioters. There were but two policemen in the village; and all they could do was to take down the names of the principal rioters.[26]

The paucity of newspaper accounts may not reflect the true number of fights in the village. Recalling the fairs held there, a folklore interviewee later commented: 'When the people of their respective districts went to the fairs they stayed together in companies for fear of faction fights which took place frequently.'[27]

KENMARE AND THE BEARA PENINSULA

The town of Kenmare was visited by German traveller Fürst Hermann von Pückler-Muskau in September 1828:

> It was fair-time when I arrived in Kenmare, and I could hardly penetrate through the bustling crowd with my one-horse vehicle, especially from the number of drunken men who would not – perhaps could not – get out of the way. One of them fell in consequence of an attempt to do so, and knocked his head so violently on the pavement that he was carried away senseless – a thing of such common occurrence that it attracted no attention.[28]

Afterwards, the visitor dined with a window view of the street and saw several stick fights:

> First a knot of people collect, shouting and screaming; this rapidly thickens; and all at once, in the twinkling of an eye, a hundred shillelahs whirl in the air, and the thumps – which are generally applied to the head – bang and snap like the distant report of fire-arms, till one party has gained the victory … through the mediation of mine host I bought one of the finest specimens of this weapon, yet warm from the fight. It is as hard as iron, and that it may be sure to do execution, it is also weighted at the end with lead.[29]

In 1831 two local factions known as the Dennehys and the Mores fought in Kenmare, and nearby, at 'the fair of the Cross-roads', near Roughty bridge. The former group was led by Deree O'Sullivan, condemned in court as 'a person prone to turbulence and rioting'.[30] They fought at the crossroads on 10 September, and afterwards, in town, Deree was assaulted by Jeremiah O'Sullivan More and his party.

In what may have been a reappearance of these groups, at a July fair in Kenmare in 1836, 'a tremendous riot took place … between two factions in that part of the country'.[31] Sixteen men were arrested, including an individual described as one of the principal leaders of his party, who had been held to bail the previous March, when an earlier fight had been expected.

By 1858 the town was a significantly quieter place, with a newspaper correspondent writing:

> although I have been acquainted with the police of many towns in Munster I never saw a place where the constabulary had so little to do. Fair day and week day are all the same in this place. There is never any attempt at faction fighting and very seldom a drunken man is heard in the streets, so that the police force of this place have as easy a life as they could wish for.[32]

Further along the Beara peninsula, the pattern day at Bonane on 10 November 1846 was the occasion for a stick fight between Sullivans and McCarthys, following which one of the latter died. At the pattern field the whole congregation was assembled, some dancing and others playing hurling. After both parties exchanged some hostile words, John McCarthy admonished his son, 'you are not a son of mine or you would break his skull'. In a public house afterwards, he declared that if he had three others with him 'they would beat half the field full of the Bunane fellows'. A Sullivan man told him he was full of 'blundering and wind', whereupon McCarthy asked him if he wished 'to have a trial'.[33] A general fight followed outside, during which some of the Sullivans struck McCarthy with a hurley, a stick and a candlestick, leaving him fatally cut on the head and face, and coughing up blood.

Events at another pattern day in the district, at Lough Quinlan (or Lough Mackeenlaun), Kilmackillogue, were detailed in a disapproving letter from Protestant clergyman Edward Cowen to *The Kerry Evening Post* in 1851:

> there is a bog-hole about the size of a horse-pond called Quinlan's Lake;– and on the Sunday previous to each returning 8th of July, on every road, cars laden with tents, barrels of porter and whiskey … are seen going towards this bog-hole; and thither too in crowds resort Romanists of every grade, the respectable and decent along with trick o' the loop men, prostitutes, fiddlers … and cripples with the diseased and disabled.[34] Up to some twenty years ago mass was celebrated at a little mound, the remains of some rude cell or altar close to the hole; confessions heard; prayers prayed to Quinlan; penances undergone – some afoot, some on their bare knees on the well-worn paths round the mound, and each person plucking a hair at each round, placed it on a skull set on the mound for this purpose, to deepen superstition by the awe it inspired; and then they dipped in the dirty bog-hole, the men and girls strictly naked, the women with only their shifts on and dipped by the naked men; and factions too, from time immemorial, met here to slake their murderous thirst for bloodshed and violence, and this 8th had its usual assaults and battery, and finally, in and about the tents, night closed on orgies the most brutal and abominable. The next sun saw them disperse through the parishes with all the marks of their brutality and ferocity. But one Shea from Clunee was murdered at one [of] these fights, and then, the mass ceased; and now, save the mass, confessions and the skull, – all else continue.[35]

Factions there included the O'Sullivans and the Dorans. The former were 'led by the O'Sullivans of Cloonee, lineal descendants of a branch of the family of O'Sullivan Beare formerly seated at Ardea castle', while the latter faction were, unusually, a middle-class Protestant family from Sneem. On one occasion, a young man of the Dorans (a medical student noted for his long hair) got into an argument with one of the O'Sullivans:

> An altercation ensued and Doran left the pattern in fury. That night the Dorans sent horsemen out among the people of the other side of the bay … round Sneem, and even as far afield as Cahirciveen and Killorglin, summoning up their faction. Next morning, accompanied by their followers in forty or fifty small boats (which would presumably have accommodated some two hundred men), they landed at Canfey adjacent to Kilmakillogue. They led their faction across the shoulder of mountain called Béicín, where they were met by the O'Sullivans with forces summoned from the pattern. The ensuing battle lasted eight or nine hours. Eventually the Dorans were forced back over Béicín and retreated to their boats.[36]

Faction fighting at Kilmackillogue pattern may have been carried on over a significant length of time. At the event in 1898, a visitor heard that 'there had been some fun the first day and a little fighting', and he observed 'one lad who was being taken to Kenmare on a cart with a very badly smashed face and head'.[37] The latter account remains the last report of fighting at the pattern.

8

'BIG MICK' AND THE FOLEY FACTION

'For many years they fought full fierce
With the blackthorn stick
Till one day out from Anglont House
Dashed forth the great Big Mick
His legions came from east and west
In front himself was seen
He crushed the rival factions
And put down the Botha Dreen.'

Poem about Puck Fair by James J. Coffey, 1935[1]

Of all the towns or villages of Iveragh, Killorglin was the most associated with faction fighting. There, the Foley party held sway. Their leader, Michael James Foley (1783–1867), was reputed to have been six feet four inches in height, and derived his nickname, Big Mick, 'from his great strength and size'.[2] He was a larger-than-life figure in more ways than one, memories of whom lived on in story and song around Killorglin through the late 1800s and even into the next century.

The Foleys were strong farmers of Anglont, a townland near Killorglin, overlooking the Laune river which flows through the town. They became prominent in the locality during the last quarter of the eighteenth century, ceasing to be tenant farmers and buying out their land from the MacCarthy of Dungeel. The latter was a Catholic landowner who had avoided the land confiscations that had reduced many of his peers in earlier centuries, only to fall into financial difficulties by the 1770s.[3]

The Foleys benefited from associations with local Protestant landlords too. In 1798 Richard Blennerhassett granted James Foley (probably Michael's father) a lease of certain lands for 999 years at a yearly rent of £113.[4] The Foleys thereafter became allies of the Blennerhassetts and supported them and their interests in general elections – and in the fights and riots that sometimes went with them.

Around the year 1800 the Mullins family bought out some of the Blennerhassett lands as well as various property rights, and they sold their right to the ownership of the August fair – subsequently made famous as Puck Fair – to the Foleys. Michael himself became the Baron of the Fair, the man to whom tolls on sales of animals had to be paid by visiting farmers.[5]

Michael appears to have been involved in faction fighting mostly during the first two decades of the 1800s. 'Mick had made his mark in many a row … even as a stripling,' commented an elderly letter writer to the *Kerry Sentinel*, who described himself in 1896 as an octogenarian.[6] Some bouts took place at Killorglin, others at Kilgobnet, a hamlet a few miles from the town that held an important fair on St Gobnait's pattern day, 11 February. According to one account, the Kilgobnet fair ran for three days, and featured up to 200 tents where whiskey was sold to the fair-goers. There was horse racing over ditches and 'nothing but singing and dancing carried on'.[7] It seems that faction fighting was another component to this pattern, however. A folklore source later explained that if there was any quarrel or enmity between families, 'it was usual for the families concerned to collect a faction for the Pattern Day and a great fight took place. The weapons used were sticks.'[8] Another folklore interviewee remembered: 'in the evening when the day's work was done and a lot of drink taken, tis often they would be fighting and as a result many broken heads would be evident going home after the day.'[9] Among those who fought were the Coffeys from Coill and the Cronins of Meallis.

The letter writer recalled the story of a stick fight on a certain fair day there that featured Big Mick, when a 'collision of the mob with the Milltown "yeomanry" took place'.[10] The time span in which this incident occurred may be roughly inferred from the information provided by another correspondent, who said it played out in the presence of 'the newly-established police', probably a reference to the Peace Preservation Force ('the Peelers') who were legislated for in July 1814, but whose first appearance at the fair would have been in February 1815. The writer also said that Michael was afterwards charged before Judge Robert Day, who retired from the bench in 1819.[11] Another article about this incident records:

> I had a talk many years ago with Denis Casey[12] … He witnessed the fray, and took part in many a fray in Killorglin. Casey was a left-hander, and could whirl two sticks on occasion. When the yeomanry were routed, Casey saw one of them, a relative and a friend, in sore distress and peril of his life pressed by too many foes. Casey flew to his assistance, whirling his two cudgels to make room, but too late … the beaten man was past friendly aid. Denis Casey said it was the wild Iveragh devils and their neighbours of

> Glenbeigh that turned what was merely a 'scrimmage as usual at fairs' into the life-and-death conflict of this unhappy event. He said that Mick Foley – then only a stripling – did wonders in saving life that day. Casey himself had a finger cut off by a sword slash, in the act of shielding his friend Huggard.
>
> Mick Foley saw two [yeomen] thrown into the river – then in full flood – he seized a pony, jumped on his back, and plunged into the surging stream, just in time to collar the two men and drag them (only half alive) to the opposite shore.[13]

The man named Huggard was a member of a family of strong farmers and freeholders who lived at Anglont and Dungeel, who were both neighbours and peers of the Foleys. Another correspondent shared a different recollection of the event:

> [T]he version of the fight where 'Big Mick' Foley saved the Orangemen's lives from the Laune, or the stream flowing into it, which I heard, puts it that Mick was a grown man at the time, and the row originated in a challenge which Huggard, on behalf of himself and friends, sent to Mick and Mick's friends to meet them on the top of the old fort at Kilgobnet on the occasion of the fair.[14]
>
> Mick met Huggard personally and had rather the worst of the row when his adherents broke in.
>
> The yeomen were being disbanded at this time, but came to the aid of the newly-established police, while the Tipperary pig and cattle buyers went for the yeos [yeomanry] and drove them into the river.[15]

After the fight, Michael was charged before Judge Day, 'but had reasons of his own to feel confidence in the judge,' the writer commented.[16] The Foleys were aligned with Day and his family politically, as both families supported the Blennerhassetts and the Tory political interest in Kerry, and Michael may have felt himself protected by this connection. In 1817 a Kerry gentleman certainly felt that Day, 'being connected with the political opponents of the Petitioner in that county, behaved with partiality' in the case of a man who had killed his son in a duel but was acquitted.[17] It is unclear whether or not Michael received a prison sentence for any of the battles in which he and his party were involved; while there are no press reports to suggest so, a lawyer at a court case in 1841 stated that he had been 'tried and convicted for riots'.[18]

The fight involving the yeomen was afterwards recorded in a local song, related one of the correspondents, who wrote out a phonetic snippet and translation as:

> *Le hash clee broom the bruick an Orangemen*
> *Thamsa er colo, agus na dousíg me.*
>
> Beside the broom-clad hedge we battered the Orangemen
> I am asleep, do not waken me.[19]

The story of a previous fight at Kilgobnet was also related:

> In that fair the Protestants of Kerry came riding on horses with their swords hanging by their sides to behead Big Mick Foley of Anglont. … The Protestants came in a big army of horsemen. They broke into the fair field and surrounded him. At that time he had a black thorn stick in each hand. The captain of the Protestant army who was called Sugerson he drew his sword on big Mick Foley and made two halves of his black thorn stick. The Protestants thought

> they were too strong for the Catholics. The fair was in full swing with people from all parts of Kerry. They turned at the Protestants with sticks and stones ... The Protestants had to clear away. That is the day that broke down the Protestants of Kerry.[20]

This Kilgobnet conflict must have occurred some time before September 1812, when Magistrate John Segerson was shot dead near Killorglin while trying to execute a warrant.[21] It is possible that the above story actually stems from a famous fight that took place in 1807, when Michael would have been about twenty-four years old. That conflict had been significant enough to have been reported to national newspaper *The Freeman's Journal*: 'a desperate affray took place between two parties at the fair of Kilgobnet, County Kerry, in which several persons received severe wounds, and different lives are despaired of'.[22] But as one of the writers of the above recollections noted of these fights: 'The rows and the ructions at Kilgobnet were, no doubt, so many and so great that ... it's no wonder present versions got mixed up.'[23]

Fights also took place in Killorglin, and while names were not recorded, Michael and the Foley faction would seem to be the most likely participants. At the August fair of 1813, a serious riot took place 'as usual, between two well known factions', during which members of a military recruiting party were injured. 'This induced the military, who were ordered there from Milltown to keep the peace, to interfere, when some shots were fired; the consequence was, that a man of the name of Connor, was killed, and many others wounded.'[24] Of the August fair of 1819, an eyewitness later reported that the custom of raising and displaying a puck goat could not be carried out due to the outbreak of a faction fight.[25] On a Sunday in January 1820, a major fight was prevented by the combined forces of local priest Fr Luony (or Looney), a local magistrate and the military. Fighters – to the number of hundreds – poured into the village to decide a battle between two factions, and the conflict was only averted after magistrate and militia surrounded a house where 'some of the chiefs of one of the parties were', and made them prisoners; then Fr Luony made them swear to keep the peace.[26] Afterwards one of the leaders was reported to have said to one of his opponents: 'Surely ... it is well known if we were allowed to meet this day we would not have left one of you alive in the town.'[27]

As well as being remembered as a fighting man, Michael, who was described as 'of athletic frame', was well regarded as a sportsman.[28] It was recalled in 1894 that during the 1820s football was played with a heavy ball made of a donkey's bladder tied around with cord and 'that only big Mick Foley, of Killorglin, and Bryan Connor, of Boherbee, Tralee, could raise with a kick.'[29] (This game may have been 'Caid', a forerunner of Gaelic football, which was played in Kerry at the time.) Similarly, at a hurling match in Killorglin in 1824, 'four parishes, two against two, were pitted at a place called "Knockane-ard-anig", where there is a huge mound, over which Big Mick drove the ten-pound ball in a *puck-in-airde* that finished the game'.[30]

We do not sense a lot of Michael's own personality in reports or recollections of his activities. A photograph of him can be found in Kieran Foley's *History of Killorglin*, showing a smiling, avuncular man.[31] In 1829 he may have been portrayed in fictionalised form as Jack Foulue, 'a strong farmer that lives over Laun', in Crofton Croker's *Legends of the Lakes* (the Foleys were also known as the Foulues (or Foulowes, Foulowos) from the pronunciation of their surname in Irish, Ó Foghlú):

> He rode a tight cut of a horse, and led another by the bridle … 'Come here,' says he, 'I want to *spake* to you'. So I went into the next field, and Jack, dismounting, pulls a big bottle of the right stuff out of his pocket, and sets down by the side of the ditch. 'Sit down, Paddy,' says he, 'till we take a drop of the *crater* this *could* morning'.[32]

RIC officer George Garrow Green, who was posted to Killorglin around 1869,[33] was told a story of Michael at Puck Fair in former days, when:

> [He] was quite disappointed at the unusual harmony that prevailed. 'What's this for,' he cried, as the day waned apace, 'Six o'clock and no battle! Faith, yez ought to be ashamed of yeeselves.' Saying which he hurled his coat in an opponent's face, and was soon with some hundreds of 'the boys', retrieving the honours of the day.[34]

Whether these depictions represent his real character or speech is impossible to say.

The faction continued to fight during the 1830s. One Sunday in February 1835, the Foleys, the Macks, the Doyles and others were due to engage after Mass, 'to decide their differences by a grand general battle' but were put off by heavy rain and the appearance of the police, reinforced by the military. *The Kerry Evening Post* understood that the cause of the proposed battle was 'nothing more than that the leader of one of the factions lent another a cudgel, which he bestowed on a third person, and this affront could not be forgiven until expiated by torrents of human blood'.[35]

PARTY-POLITICAL FIGHTS

Younger men of the family, and their associates, were engaged with later bouts, which often had a political element. John Michael Foley and Philip Michael Foley (most likely Michael's sons) were active in a fight in Killorglin on 12 August 1837. The fight was one in a sequence of conflicts that took place in August, which had their origin in that year's county election. The Foleys supported Arthur Blennerhassett, the Conservative candidate.

There was a riot in the village on Sunday 6 August, the day before the poll; a day of fighting on Saturday 12 August, the day after Puck Fair; followed by further fights, or plans to fight, for days afterwards. The first skirmish of the Saturday morning commenced between the Foleys and the Dodds of Killorglin:

> as some freeholders in the interest of Mr Blennerhassett were returning from Tralee, passing through the village of Killorglin, some stones were thrown at them; this act of violence brought up some friends of Mr Michael James Foley, to their aid and protection, when they were attacked by the hostile faction, and a riot ensued, which ended in the defeat of the assailing party.[36]

A policeman later described in court how the Rev. John Day (a nephew of Judge Robert Day) passed through Killorglin:

> accompanied by several voters from Valentia … they voted for Mr Blennerhassett; there was violence offered to them by the people

> of Killorglan, it was done through party spirit … they were hooted at and booed by the people; stones were thrown at them, and [he] heard the people cry out, 'pelt the devils' … two of the freeholders were struck; the prisoners [John Michael Foley and Philip Michael Foley] interfered to prevent it; Parson Day was then in danger; it was the Dodd party that attacked them first.[37]

A more serious fight between the two factions began around four o'clock on the same day, and according to one report lasted for two hours. Philip Foley and a man named Hurly, the latter backed by other men, engaged in a 'scolding match' (in which two men insulted each other so as to raise their tempers). This was afterwards followed by a general fight. The two Foleys and one John Sullivan 'had sticks flourishing them, and crying out, "here are the Foleys for them"'. Hurly and another man named Gearan were subsequently surrounded by 'a great mob', struck and left bleeding. The Foley faction then left the scene, only to have stones thrown at them:

> from the opposite side by a parcel of small boys, women, and some men; they threw at them both from the street and houses; a general row then commenced, and several groups commenced fighting in different parts of the street … The Foley party then beat them up the street, and stones were thrown; the Dodd party made a rush down the lane.[38]

The latter appear to have been led by Henry Dodd, who was described in court as 'the Captain-General of his party'.[39] (Like Michael James Foley, Dodd may have been an imposing figure, as he was portrayed by a witness at a court case as 'very nearly as big as … himself'.)[40] As the fight went on, John Michael Foley and Philip Michael Foley struck a man named Thomas Daly with their sticks, after which Sullivan took a pair of iron tongs that Daly had been using as a weapon and hit him with them, leaving him stretched out on the ground. This event brought the fight to a close and Daly was carried into a nearby house. (The Sullivans were allies of the Foleys: in 1828 John, Michael and Cornelius Sullivan had helped Mick to take items of salvage from a shipwreck, on the latter's argument that he 'thought he had as good a right to them as any body else'.)[41]

On Sunday the two factions battled again: 'both parties assembled in vast multitudes, and a dreadful conflict took place with sticks, stones, and all manner of murderous weapons, during which a man had his leg smashed in a most dreadful manner by a stroke of a stone … All the windows in the village were broken to atoms.'[42] John Michael Foley was afterwards charged with breaking the leg of a man named Keliher.[43] On Monday 'the fight was renewed with increased numbers, and redoubled ferocity'.[44] Both parties intended to extend their conflict into Tuesday but were put off when they learned that magistrates meeting in the village that day to take evidence about the earlier fights were accompanied by a strong force of police.

Following these events almost 200 people were summoned to appear in court.[45] Daly died three weeks after being assaulted and John Sullivan was charged with his murder, agreeing at his trial to plead guilty to manslaughter. Philip Michael Foley was also charged with murder, but the offence was downgraded to that of aiding and abetting; the judge in the Sullivan trial grumbled that Foley's murder charge 'was sent up to the Grand Jury and it was ignored; I had a communication with them on the subject'.[46] Clearly the Grand Jury, which would have been made up of men from a similar class and background to Foley, did not wish to see one of their own charged with the more serious crime of murder. Similarly, when John Michael Foley had appeared in court over breaking Keliher's leg, the high sheriff, John O'Connell of Grena, reportedly declared that the case represented a conspiracy against the Foleys.[47] A degree of partisan legal protection may indeed have been in place for the Foleys among the Kerry establishment, if we tally these two elements alongside Michael supposedly benefiting from a rapport with Judge Day.

It is possible to detect a shift in Big Mick's role during the 1830s – less the leader of a faction as a group of field and street brawlers and more the leader of a faction as a group of partisan political supporters. By 1835 he was characterised in a police report as 'formerly a notorious rioter and leader of a faction'.[48] As an ally of local landlords and as a strong farmer, his political tendencies leant towards the established social and political order: 'he took an earnest and most active part in the desperate election contests that were held in this country, both before and after the Reform Bill [1832], as an ally to the landlord and Conservative party,' recalled *The Kerry Evening Post*.[49]

In advance of the 1835 election, Foley wrote to Tory MP Maurice Fitzgerald, the Knight of Kerry, giving him information he had gleaned about the voting intentions of landlords and tenants, and warning that if Maurice O'Connell was returned for the Tralee constituency, 'that would be a great blow against you'.[50] *The Kerry Evening Post* also observed: 'So heartily did he work' for the successful election of Arthur Blennerhassett of Ballyseedy in 1837, that he was presented after the election by the Carlton Club, a London gentlemen's club established for MPs and supporters of the Conservative party, 'with a valuable silver snuff box, which he treasured with pride to his dying day'.[51]

A public meeting held in Killorglin in 1837 in support of the local magistrates, chaired by John Michael Foley, and at which Mick spoke, finished with calls for 'three cheers for McGillycuddy of the Reeks, a kind and considerate landlord … three cheers for David Peter Thompson, who, as an agent, is kind and forbearing … three cheers for Judge Day, and the landlords of Kerry'.[52] The Conservative-supporting *Kerry Evening Post*, encouraging Kerry tenants to be loyal to their landlords in the way they voted, advised them to look to strong farmers 'like the Foleys of Killorglin … who will tell them plain and wholesome truths conducive to their interests, and cementing the ties between them and their natural protectors'.[53]

This was no longer the political inclination of most of the local and national population, however, who, following the victory represented by Catholic Emancipation in 1829, sided with Daniel O'Connell and their priests against the Anglo-Irish Protestant establishment represented by the majority of landlords, magistrates and political figures. Accordingly, Michael James Foley and the Foley faction were heroes to some but not to all.

Still, the Foleys remained loyal, despite the often difficult circumstances. At the general election held in July 1841, Michael was asked by Mr Herbert, the chairman of Mr Blennerhassett's election committee, to marshal men to ride alongside and shield a large party of his Killarney freeholders as they passed through

Killorglin, Milltown and Castlemaine on their way to vote in Tralee. At this time Michael was in his late fifties. As the party of seventy or eighty freeholders went through Killorglin in a convoy of carts and carriages, a hostile crowd of 500–600 people showered them fiercely with stones.[54] One man, named Spillane, was struck on the head and died later as a result. The crowd followed the convoy some way out of Killorglin, and a witness explained that were it not for another party of 'young Foulowes' and others on the outskirts of the town, who assisted in keeping the mob at bay, others would have been killed.[55]

Some men pursuing the convoy stripped to the waist and broke away to race along a bridle road to get to Milltown before them, where they helped to round up others against them. When the voters and their protectors passed through Milltown, they were then harassed by a screeching mob who threw stones, dirt and dung at them. Some of the gentlemen had to ride hard and fast, and flourish their pistols and swords, to discourage further violence, and Michael, with prominent Tory William Denny, 'rode furiously through the mob … to escape danger'.[56] Denny was later challenged by a lawyer in court about the wisdom of calling on Foley and his party to chaperone the convoy, rather than recruiting soldiers or policemen. It seemed that Foley's reputation as a faction fighter was still remembered by some:

> *Have you heard that he was a man at whose command in former times, and at present, a great many men of violent feelings could be collected for any purpose he choose?*
>
> He has a great deal of influence among the respectable class of farmers of the county.

I do not mean to annoy Michael James Foley by the question, but did you hear he was the leader of a faction?

Yes.

Did you hear it said how many men he brought?

I did not.

I expect another candid answer from you: if you were to have made the arrangements, would you have selected a man who was the leader of a faction, and what do you think it would be likely to lead to?

If I was going to bring in freeholders from Killorglan I would ask him to help me.

Though you knew him to be the leader of a faction?[57]

At a different court case that followed from the Milltown riot, another lawyer repeated the contention that Foley was an inflammatory figure and put it to Denny that 'Foley is a great faction fighter'. Denny denied it, instead describing him as 'an honest, respectable, decent man'. The advocate instead asserted to the court that 'Mr Denny had no right to go with Foley that day, a man so unpopular, so much disliked, as he is. Foley's presence was, of itself, calculated to cause confusion. Of course he gets a good character from Mr Denny, but that would not make him still popular.'[58]

Foley faction activity continued a little during the 1840s. After the Kilgobnet fair of February 1844, Michael Foley (probably a son) was challenged by several men who cried out 'Dodds against Foleys', to which he responded, 'Here's a Foley.'[59] He was struck with a stick, and a fist fight took place, after which he was held down and one of his assailants bit off part of his lip. In 1846, at Puck Fair, the Foleys and the Cliffords, 'both most powerful factions, fell out and continued fighting for two hours, notwithstanding the exertions of a large body of police,' reported *The Kerry Evening Post*. 'We have heard that this was one of the most severe faction fights known for years in this county. Neither of those factions have for some time past mingled in the feuds about them.'[60]

In contrast, Michael James Foley appears to have settled into the role of community patriarch. In 1840 he supported a celebration of Killorglin's temperance society.[61] By 1846 he was described by a correspondent of *The Cork Examiner* as a man who was 'considered a sort of Kaiser' by the local peasantry.[62] A year later he backed a public meeting held in the town to encourage local employment following the entrenchment of famine conditions.[63]

After the Famine, faction fighting did not continue strongly in Killorglin. At Puck Fair 1863 there was 'an attempt to revive an old faction fight' by the Foleys and the Breens, but the leaders of both parties were quickly arrested by the police, while at Killorglin's May fair 'there was a great deal of rioting, though not in large bodies'.[64] In reality, the days of the Foleys' fights had passed.

Michael died in 1867. At Anglont, the residence of his son, 'died this remarkable patriarch, at the advanced age of eighty-four years', *The Kerry Evening Post* noted on the occasion of Michael's death.

> Mr M J Foley – so well known in this county as 'Big Mick', from his great strength and size – occupied for nearly three parts of a century

> a very prominent position in the Killorglin district. Leader of a very strong sept, and of athletic frame, he was always prepared some fifty years ago, after the manner of the Munstermen of the time, to maintain the pre-eminence of his party, either single-handed, or at the head of his friends. … His remains were attended to the grave by one of the largest funerals ever seen in Killorglin, including the clergy and gentry of the surrounding district.[65]

He continued to be remembered afterwards. In the 1890s he was numbered 'in the list of heroes' in a local song.[66] His role in the Kilgobnet fight of the early 1800s remained part of local lore into the 1920s, when another song, about a well-regarded storyteller, listed the many tales the latter could recite:

> *He'll tell you of the 'patron' of the ructions and the battering,*
> *At Kilgobnet when the faction fights began;*
> *How they always kept on fighting and slashing took delight in*
> *Until big Mick Foley cleared them with his clan.*[67]

9

'PLENTY WHISKEY'

> 'It was deeply to be regretted that such a fine body of young men should be shut up from their families for so long a period through their own folly in being engaged in this deplorable vice.'
>
> Christopher Copinger, QC, June 1861[1]

Judge Copinger's remarks were made after a particularly intense fight at the great fair of Molahiffe, a hamlet that lay just outside the present-day village of Firies. Despite its small size, Molahiffe hosted a long-established May fair which was considered to be 'one of the most remarkable' in the county, 'owing to the critical season on which it falls and its central position'.[2] In 1840 it was also described as 'for years remarkable for riots'.[3] In 1867 *The Kerry Evening Post* commented that 'we have long been hearing of Molahiffe fair and Firies cross as scenes of more faction fighting than any other similar localities in this county'.[4] In 1873 a local correspondent of the same newspaper could reminisce: 'Molahiffe was famous in the "good old times" for those premeditated and preconcerted faction fights which were the pride of every "true Irishman", and thousands on thousands were in the habit of flocking thither, either to take part or to see the fun.'[5]

A detailed and vivid portrait was presented by former RIC man George Garrow Green, which is worth quoting at length. One day (around 1870, it would appear) he was dispatched to the fair with forty-five men to marshal crowds that he was told would reach over 3,000 people. 'They're rale divils to fight over there,' another officer warned him. 'The last time, Constable Cox lost an eye from a blow of a stone, and another had his leg mostly cut off with a scythe.'[6] He turned up with his men, consulted with a magistrate, and spent the day enjoying the business and the diversions, until he was tipped that trouble might be imminent:

> It appeared that one of the O'Connors, who had a powerful faction at his back, had been informed by an O'Sullivan, equally well provided, that his (O'Connor's) wife's sister's son was a poor-spirited creature, having paid every penny of rent due on the previous gale day.[7] This was a dreadful insult, but mutual friends interfered and a quart or two of whisky smoothed matters for a time, especially as business was not over, but the spark thus kindled steadily smouldered and dark looks began to be exchanged as the story circulated. Molahiffe was getting on the boil …
>
> As six o'clock drew near I sent out a party to warn the vendors of drink to strike their tents, their occasional licenses expiring at that hour, and then, for the first time, I noticed a change. The cattle, &c., had almost disappeared, and men were collecting in groups, apparently absorbed by some exciting theme, judging from their vehement gestures and talk, which, being in Irish, I could not comprehend … The tents now taken down, disgorged their crowds in various stages of inebriety … There happened to be one little licensed public [house] in Molahiffe a few yards from our quarters, and therein many of the dislodged ones whose thirst was unslaked took refuge … Suddenly, out staggered two tall fellows who capered round each other in a sort of war-dance for a few seconds, flourishing their blackthorns and uttering fearful yells. Then, one of them shrieking, 'Here's an O'Sullivan, aboo-Ah-h-h!' dealt the

other a dreadful blow on the head. As the blood spouted out a savage cry arose. It was taken up in the distance and swelled, rising and falling in dismal cadence until it culminated in one hoarse roar which seemed to rend the very air. I saw the old sergeant's horrified face and heard him mutter, 'Begor, we're in for it now,' and then I tried to collect my senses. For an instant I looked around. I saw a sea of struggling forms, of sticks descending, and heard the sickening thud as they struck home … In a moment we were upon them, and, like a wedge, forced our way into the seething mass; and what a meleé it was. Stripped to their shirts and trousers, the former in shreds, they were fighting more like wild beasts than men. Frothing from the mouth, streaming with blood and uttering horrid cries, they struck at and bit each other, writhing in insensate fury …

'Take that, ye black divils!' screamed a shrill voice, and, whiz, down came a shower of young rocks on us. Some of the men were hit, one having his cheek laid open, and another getting a nasty gash on the forehead; but the volley, though well intended, made more havoc among the belligerents, several of whom were put *hors de combat*.[8] Seeing this, the women stopped throwing, for to a detachment of old hags standing on the road bank were we indebted for this striking tribute of affection. But the men's blood was now up, and our position sufficiently critical. Whack, whack, whack went the batons, and down they went on all sides, despite their attempts to retaliate with their shillelaghs … Seeing that the conflict near us had ceased, though going on as briskly as ever in front, I ordered a retreat to the barracks with some prisoners we had made, and then, charging through the mob which had followed us, we once more plunged into the thick of the fray; but the cry of 'The peelers are coming!' had gone before us, and spread demoralisation, while loss of blood helped to weaken the combatants, who now began to give way on all sides. In a few minutes more the baton had decided the day, and we were able to introduce some more prisoners to their

> companions in custody. A nice looking lot they were truly. Half naked, their shock-heads dripping with blood, bruised, mutilated and half senseless, they sulkily submitted to their fate. And then ensued a strange scene. Women, with streaming eyes and heaving bosoms, implored me in the wildest excitement to restore to them their warriors. They embraced my knees and besought me with all their native eloquence to have mercy …
>
> 'Will you promise me, if I let them go, to keep them quiet, and take them home at once – no more fighting?' said I.
>
> 'Fighting, is it?' they cried. 'Oyeh, sure they were killed enough already. *Thau an diaol huha neerev snawha gudthee na groun* (Devil's luck to them, they haven't a rag left to their back).'
>
> Here the local sergeant handed me in a list of the names and addresses of the delinquents, who, I may here say, were all fined at the next Petty Sessions. I thereupon restored them to freedom and the arms of their fair intercessors, who, between cajolery and abuse soon led them from the field.[9]

After the crowds had finally cleared away, the officer and his men 'were marching for home by the light of a young May moon … some pools of coagulated blood, torn fragments of coats and broken sticks alone testifying that it had been so recently the theatre of a battle'.[10]

If scenes like this were common at Molahiffe fairs much earlier in the century, it is not until 1822 that a man was reported to have been killed at the fair.[11] Ten years later a man died as a result of 'a very severe beating' there.[12] In 1837 'a most desperate riot took place … between two hostile factions … the riot act was at length read by the Magistrate, and the riot was suppressed, but not before many of the unfortunate wretches were brutally mangled, and lay bleeding in their glory!'[13] The following year, after the police and military had left the fair, there were a number of fights 'between barbarous hostile factions, in which numbers of people were severely injured'.[14] In the latter case the parties were the Moynihans, stated to be from the parish of Currans, who were opposed by the Costelloes of Molahiffe; the former 'were at first defeated, but … they afterwards rallied, repulsed, and soundly drubbed the Costelloe faction'.[15] At nightfall after the fair of 1843, two factions began to fight, and when some arrests were made, reported a police officer, the crowd turned on the police, 'stones flew like hail' and several policemen were struck; the officer then ordered the men to prime and load their rifles, 'and told the people "on their own heads would the blood that would be spilled rest". The people then ran as quick as they could.'[16] Both gangs planned to renew the battle on a Sunday a couple of days afterwards, but police prevented it from taking place by arresting two of the principal fighters.[17]

Although several unnamed parties were found guilty of fighting at the fair of 1845, faction fighting disappeared from Molahiffe in the succeeding years of famine and did not re-emerge until the 1850s.[18] In 1855 the Brosnahans and the Leynes (possibly the factions from Castleisland) held a fight, and in 1857 the Tangneys and the Learys, 'from near Listry' (about seven miles away), went 'rioting and fighting with each other'.[19]

The story of a particular fight, which seems to have taken place around 1857, between the Larkins and the Connors, was later recalled. When Jack Larkin, 'a robber', died, the Connors tried to prevent his burial in Aglish churchyard, which both families had long shared. The Larkins 'hunted them out of the graveyard and buried the corpse', but the Connors attacked them afterwards as they made their way home. Con 'Bacach' Meara finished that fight for the Connors by striking Dave Larkin (who was also known as Daithín Na bhFoithre) on the head, leaving him badly wounded. Both parties swore to fight again at the fair of Molahiffe. There, the Larkins were aided by the Brosnans, Allens and Corcorans, while the Connors had the MacGillycuddys, Mearas, Burkes, Dalys and Sullivans. 'Seán "Liath" Connor, from Rath, Firies was the leader of the Connor faction. On the fair morning he had a barrel of whiskey on top of the "Rock" at Molahiffe.[20] All his supporters got plenty whiskey. He walked through the fair shouting, "five pounds for a Larkin's head".'[21]

The Larkins gathered their supporters and the fight began, going on for about two hours, but leaving them 'tired and wounded'. A man named Big Bill Fitzgerald, 'a powerful fighter', who had been watching as a spectator, joined in and by his efforts won the fight for the Larkins.

> During the fight Dáithín Na bhFoithre found Con Bacach Meara stretched between the shafts of a car. Dáithín stood over Meara and beat him on the head with a hurley. Meara was nearly dead and had to be taken home on a door. Since the fight the Larkins never allowed a member of the Connor Liath family to be buried in the graves at Aglish.[22]

A singular battle at the fair of 1861 was described as 'one of the most determined and brutal engagements' to have taken place in Kerry for many years.[23] It started as a fight between two parties, the Quinlans and the Callaghans, which was taken up and carried on by the Learys and the Crowleys, who were 'two more powerful factions'.[24] (The Learys may have been the group from Listry that had fought in 1857.) Fighting began after six o'clock in the evening, when the business of the fair was over. 'It being one of the largest fairs of the county and characteristic for its faction fights', a large force of police had attended, but the men from Tralee and Castleisland stations then departed for their own barracks at the end of the day's business, leaving behind a smaller cohort from local stations.[25]

The Callaghans appear to have begun the fight, shouting out 'Callaghans against Quinlans'.[26] Jeremiah Quinlan was standing by himself when he heard a Callaghan cry out, '£5 for a Quinlan's head', upon which 'Quinlan said he was a Quinlan; Callaghan then struck him'.[27] At one point there were forty or fifty men fighting with sticks, and Sub-Inspector Lynch had to ride in among the crowd in an effort to get them to disperse; he claimed that one among them, Cornelius Crowley, 'seized my horse by the mouth-piece, and attempted to strike me with a huge stick'.[28] Lynch could make no progress in stopping the fighting and instead got Constable Cowming of Milltown Station to stand by and identify the participants for later arrest. Cowming later recounted: 'I heard the shouts of "Quinlans" and "Callaghans"; I heard the shouts frequently, and they came from the parties engaged in the fight; I saw John Riordan beating others with a stick; I saw him knocked down and six or seven others beating him when down.'[29]

Jeremiah Leary, 'a powerful looking man not long since arrived in this town [Killarney] from Wales'[30] then proclaimed his own identity and was 'immediately followed by a crowd', and another fight took place.[31] He was 'rushing up and down the fair, wheeling a stick and saying he was "a Leary and a Molahiffe boy"'.[32] A

Darby Gearen was also involved, flourishing a stick which was later shown in court (a 'long deal stick about two inches square, with sharp corners, and covered with blood').[33]

Afterwards, five men were given prison terms of twelve months with hard labour, and one man six months with hard labour, upon which their relatives 'raised a loud cry which they kept up for some time'.[34] Judge Copinger commented:

> This was one of the worst cases of this description that he had met with in his experience of thirty years in the Crown Court … For the time they would have to remain in prison, he turned and hoped they would recollect that it would be but folly to carry out that bad spleen which seemed to have descended from their grandfathers, and which had already caused so much affliction and misery in this country.[35]

The cases of other men involved were deferred. When they came to trial, a policeman stated that 'some of the jurors were tampered with', and allegations circulated of 'strange and unconstitutional efforts made by some parties in the rank of gentlemen to tamper even with magistrates on the bench, on behalf of the persons whose trial has been postponed'.[36] No more of that came to light, but Cornelius Crowley's trial for assault on the police officer was postponed 'on the grounds that an impartial trial could not now be had' because 'the matter was so much canvassed among the jurors'.[37]

At the May fair of 1862, some men who had been involved in the Quinlan-Callaghan-Leary affray made an attempt to start another fight, 'but receiving no encouragement from those with whom they were anxious to come into collision, they were forced to leave the fair disappointed'.[38]

There were later incidents by others. In 1865 'there was a good deal of desultory rioting and fighting'.[39] Around 1870 there occurred the scenes described by George Garrow Green. In 1872 'things went on smoothly for the greater part of the day' until 'some rowdies … considered that it would be no Molahiffe fair unless they had a tip at each other with the "kippeen", which was the cause of sore heads to some of the combatants'.[40] In 1876 a serious disturbance appeared to have arisen 'out of an old faction feud', reported *The Tralee Chronicle*, without mentioning the parties involved. The newspaper explained:

> Many years ago Molahiffe fair was celebrated for faction fighting, but latterly the practice had almost disappeared. For the past few weeks, however, symptoms of its revival were manifested, and large numbers of police … were present at the fair during the day … About nine o'clock … two hostile factions assembled near Firies, when blows were freely given at both sides and some of the leading parties had to attend in Killarney to get their wounds dressed.[41]

A final outbreak at Molahiffe occurred in 1887: 'The mob were fighting and striking each other with sticks and stones. Stones came from all directions and hit the police.'[42] After that, however, the fair became a more peaceful event.

CASTLEMAINE, KEEL AND KILTALLAGH

'Local prejudice still exists between the two divisions of the Castlemaine parish namely Keel and Kiltallagh', a folklore collector noted during the 1930s.[43] In such feelings they were not unique. Another collector noted, for example, that in Co.

Roscommon 'the people south of the Clocher bridge never liked the people of Cootehill, Knockvicar, Crossna or Keadue and this prejudice exists to the present day'.[44] In Co. Mayo, too, 'Long ago, the people of many towns and villages hated each other. Caherlistrane and Shrule were very much against each other. When the Caherlistranes used to come to a football [match] in Shrule, the Shrules used to beat them with sticks.'[45]

The animosity between the factions from Keel and Kiltallagh was particularly intense, however. A hundred years earlier, factions from Keel and Kiltallagh engaged each other at Castlemaine village. 'Several faction fights took place in the past between the people of these two places, and they met at Castlemaine fairs and fought with sticks of all kinds', it was recalled. 'At the last fight … the roof was torn off a house to provide sticks for the fight … A man named Whelan, who was a weaver at the time, owned the thatched house when the contending parties attacked it.'[46] The Teahans and McCarthys of Keel regularly fought against the Flynns, Fitzgeralds and Broders of Kiltallagh.

An early fight between the districts was much later described by a folklore interviewee. Although he does not say so, it appears to have been the notable fight that took place on 23 November 1812.[47] The fighters were described at the time as farmers and farm labourers, with a party of Doolings stated to be the ringleaders, on this occasion.[48]

> The reason for the fight was because the most of the Kiltallagh people were Protestants and soupers and they always disliked the people of Keel.[49]
>
> When ever a fight was to take place the people of Dingle and

[Abbeydorney] would come to help Keel and from Castlemaine to Killorglin would help Kiltallagh.

When the fight began the people of Kiltallagh started to advance towards the Keel people and to drive them back.

After a great struggle four of the Keel people had to take cover. It was in a small little house they took shelter and locked themselves in.

When the Kiltallagh people got to the house they tried to burst in but it was in vain. A Kiltallagh man named Barry rushed at the door but as he was about to strike it a Keel man fired at him from Anagh height and killed him. It was the leg of a spoon he fired at him so he killed him all of a sudden.[50]

When they found it in vain to break in they jumped in top of the house and began to tear the thatch and break in.

When the Keel people saw this they sent word to Edward Rae to come and help them.[51]

Edward Rae refused to go and help them. After this the Keel people got broken hearted but again the Keel people sent word to him.

Edward Rae refused to go at first when the messenger went to him. There was a stranger and one of Lankford Rae's sisters there and when she heard Edward refuse to go she said 'If my father were here he would go and help the Keel people'.

At these words Edward went into the room for his gun and his armour suit and told the stranger do the same.

They rode to Castlemaine as fast as they could on two horses and when they landed over, the Kiltallagh people['s] house [was] nearly torn down.

When they reached Anagh height they came off of their horses and Edward put his gun to his shoulder and told the stranger do the same.

They started to fire at the Kiltallagh people until all the people that were up in the house fell off dead.[52]

(The man who was killed first was 'David Barry, farmer, of Fieries, killed on the spot, having received a ball in the breast', a newspaper reported at the time.)[53]

The Kiltallagh party 'raised a cry ... to stop firing or they would kill them all'.[54] They approached their opponents and instead challenged them to a fight, 'without any guns but sticks and hurleys', to be held in Tralee.[55] On the day, Rae turned up with a sword and led the Keel men, who outnumbered their rivals. The Keel faction were keen to fight, but 'all the priests around the place' turned up and forced the parties into a reluctant peace.[56]

Fights may also have taken place in Keel village itself, although only a dramatic reference to one event exists. 'About seventy-five years ago [the 1860s] a faction of men from Kiltallagh raided Keel ... to take some cattle. The Keel men met them with clubs and stones ... and slaughtered every one of them.'[57]

The principal faction in Castlemaine itself was a group known as the Sullivans Keonagh (or Conuahts),[58] who fought between the 1830s and 1850s, both at the fairs in the village and at locations beyond. They and their first rivals, the Riordans, were reported to be near neighbours.[59] It was said that these gangs were 'headed by the richest farmers on the banks of the Main, who supply their men plentifully with whiskey'.[60] The first part of that observation may account for the Sullivans' nickname (*conách*, wealthy). While the conflict was portrayed as a 'bitter feud', it was at the same time claimed to be 'carried on in a spirit of unusual fairness, and, if I may use the word, chivalry'.[61]

In November 1845 the Sullivans and the Riordans interrupted the business of the day at four or five o'clock, to fight until about eight. One account said that there was 'a fair stand up fight with cudgels', while another characterised it as having been 'fought desperately with sticks and stones'.[62] The battle had been arranged well in advance, as 'picked men were brought all the way from Glanflesk and other equally remote districts to assist in the fight'.[63] Word of their intentions had circulated in the locality, and Fr Carmody and his curate, Fr O'Flaherty, attempted to thwart the fight for a number of days beforehand. Nevertheless, so determined were the combatants on the day that they started fighting in their presence and 'in the very presence of a large force of police and five magistrates'.[64] On this occasion the Riordans forced the Sullivans to retreat. Several people were injured, among them 'a poor woman, who had her skull fractured with a stroke of a stone while carrying a pail of milk on her head'.[65]

Both groups met again at the village of Currans in December, although the fight was forestalled by police after the exchange of a few blows.[66] It appears that these factions had a long geographical reach, travelling to several towns and villages both near and far to fight each other or different factions. 'The fairs, and Sunday and holyday meetings along the Main from Castlemain to Castleisland are disturbed by the combats of the rival factions of Sullivans (Kieonaghs) and Riordans,' observed *The Kerry Evening Post*.[67] In Tralee, in January 1846, 'some persons belonging to the Kieonagh party, who had been shouting for the Riordans' were arrested.[68] The Riordans in turn travelled to Currans in May 1846 to engage the Flynns (the party from Kiltallagh) where they 'arranged themselves in hostile attitude' at about five o'clock, but thirty policemen were present and succeeded 'in arresting one of the ringleaders and dispersing the rest'.[69]

The Sullivans of Castlemaine appear to have been the 'farmers, named Sullivan', described as strangers to Tralee, who fought another group there in 1856 in the incident that so annoyed Bishop Moriarty.[70] It is likely that the Sullivans and Riordans also fought at nearby Molahiffe, and that a man named Sullivan, killed there in 1822, and the John Riordan who fought there at the great fight of 1861 may be indicative of a more extensive involvement by both gangs there than newspaper records suggest.[71]

Sentences for the November 1845 affray, of nine months with hard labour, followed in January 1846, with the bench threatening to condemn every man who repeated his offence to transportation to Australia: 'It is disgraceful to the County that such things should be allowed to go on, and they hope that the example now set by the present sentence will have the effect of putting an end to them.'[72] That did not deter them, however, for in August the Sullivans and the Riordans renewed their feud at Firies chapel, on a Sunday, and, further, it was understood that it was 'the avowed intention of those parties to have a pitched battle at Castlemain fair' on 3 September.[73]

One evening in Castlemaine in early November 1849, after what was described as a remarkable consumption of whiskey in the public houses, 'there was the greatest disposition shown to revive the old practice of faction fighting – indeed at a late hour there was, we understand, a very serious riot'.[74] Perhaps this was the Sullivans and Riordans renewing their feud once more – though there were other contenders.

By 1858 the Sullivans were fighting the Flynns, both parties characterised as 'the old factions'.[75] It may have also been these two groups who had planned to fight in November 1857: Fr Carmody strongly addressed the people in church on two previous Sundays, 'on the folly and wickedness of their conduct', but in the event the parties were prevented from battle by the arrest of their leaders and their being bound over to keep the peace (paying a cash bond which they risked losing if sentenced again).[76]

The two groups succeeded in meeting in May 1858, when what threatened to develop into 'a bitter and bloody' fight was stopped chiefly by Fr Sheehan, 'who threw himself in amongst the raging combatants'.[77] Despite showers of stones he 'went into the thick of them and took their sticks from many'.[78] (Both parties agreed among themselves to fight instead at Molahiffe fair, although this becoming known to the police, they were again bound over.)

When members of both factions afterwards appeared in court they declared that 'they had become friends again', and did not wish to proceed with the cases they had initiated against each other. The judge did not agree, and in his assessment he recalled the fight that had been held in Castlemaine between the Keel and Kiltallagh fighters in 1812, in which Barry had been shot:

> If the farmers of the country were full of money, and if they could make no better use of it than getting drunk, they should teach them to behave themselves, and to find some other amusement than breaking each other's heads at fairs and markets, for no reason on earth but that one party happened to be called Sullivan, and to be from one parish, and another party were named Flynn, and were from another district … The riots at that fair in former times used to be attended even with loss of life, as on one occasion especially shots were fired and one man killed and others were severely

> wounded. They should take measures to prevent such scenes from being renewed again.[79]

One man pleaded that they would be 'friends for ever again, and they never again will have a fight', but the defendants, who included five members of the Flynn family and one of the Sullivans, were sentenced to a month in jail with hard labour. This was evidently too much for them:

> Some of the offenders (who were all of a very respectable appearance, being for the most part sons of comfortable farmers) said they could never live in the jail, and applied to have the sentences changed to fines; but the court refused to change the sentences, observing that some of the parties would not care what they had to pay for it, [as long as] they could wheel a stick and engage in the row at a fair, but they … would punish them severely, and in a manner which would have far more effect on them.[80]

Afterwards, the Sullivans no longer appear in press accounts of fighting in Castlemaine, although two Flynn men assaulted a Sullivan man in Milltown in 1863 in what a policeman believed was 'an attempt to renew an old faction fight'.[81]

The Flynns continued against the Teahan (or Tehan) faction from Keel. When both groups engaged in a fight at a fair in Castlemaine in 1860, a newspaper hinted that they had often done so previously.[82] Whatever faction was to blame, it is clear that faction fighting did continue for several more years in the area. On Sunday 21 April 1861 a very serious fight occurred which a police constable characterised as the renewal of a feud between two factions, although he did not name the parties; afterwards *The Tralee Chronicle* rebuked 'the patronisers of those "rural sports" and Sunday evening pastimes'.[83] At the fair of Castlemaine in November 1866, a man named Coakley 'passed through the town in a riotous manner, shouting out faction cries, and wheeling a cudgel over his head, and calling on some warrior of a rival faction to fight him'.[84] In May 1869 another serious riot took place: 'From some motives, two factions met. Sticks were freely used at both sides. Blood ran copiously from the combatants.'[85] Jer Tehan and two other men 'fought and struck each other with sticks' but escaped custodial sentences because all three of them were 'jobbers' – cattle dealers – 'and it would ruin them to send them to jail'.[86]

So ended the Sullivan, Riordan and Flynn factions. What is perhaps most notable about them is that they illustrate the observation often made during the nineteenth century that rural factions were not run by the lowest orders of society. Fighting gangs were not formed by labourers, beggars or criminals, but by comparatively well-off farmers who possessed a respectable status. The question then arises whether their rough games were a method, however unusual and violent, by which they asserted that status among their peers and their communities at large.

MILLTOWN

Faction fighting also took place in the nearby village of Milltown. Although the names of the parties involved were not recorded, it must be suspected that the gangs of Castlemaine and its environs may have been involved. 'Two parties of *whiskified heroes*, high in blood – who *drink for love – quarrel for nothing, and fight for fun*, thought proper to *amuse* themselves, by cannonading each other in the street with showers of stones', one evening in September 1825, after sunset, during which a publican standing at the door of his premises had his skull fractured by a blow from a stone and died afterwards.[87] There was some rioting in the evening after the May fair of 1829.[88] The June fair of 1834 also hosted a fight, which lasted for four hours and led to eighteen arrests.[89] Similarly, the May fair of 1836 was 'a constant scene of riot, and many fractures were exchanged by the combatants', while at the fair the following month four or five factions 'from different parts of the surrounding country' fought with cudgels before showering each other with stones.[90]

A report of the August fair of 1846 finished with the comment that – contrary to expectation – there was no faction fighting during the day.[91] At the fair of December 1847, however, there was a good deal of fighting and sixteen people were arrested. That affray may have been well fuelled by alcohol, as the correspondent observed: 'A friend informs us that the quantity of whiskey drank during the day exceeded all belief.'[92]

It was reported in *The Kerry Evening Post* in September 1863 that there had been 'a general free faction fight' late one night (probably at the August fair). During the resulting court case several witnesses claimed they could remember nothing of the event and they were afterwards generally regarded as having committed perjury. In a sermon in Milltown on a following Sunday, Fr O'Connor 'dwelt strongly on the sin they were guilty of, and pointed how they were disgracing their religion by swearing falsely, in so barefaced and shameless a manner before Protestant magistrates'. On the same day, Fr O'Sullivan, in nearby Killorglin, also denounced the perjury 'for which his parish has become infamous'. The newspaper added: 'We hope that the exhortations of these clergymen … will have a good effect on the morality of the country with regard to the sanctity of an oath, of which, particularly when swearing to get a friend out of a scrape, our peasants appear to have a very faint idea.'[93]

At the Milltown fair of June 1872, 'a serious fight took place between some faction fighting parties; sticks were used, and blood was spilled':

> Constable James Coyle, Sub-constables Keane and Fennel … separated the combatants. Just at the moment when things were getting cooled down, a farmer named Brien rushed into the crowd and began to shout and lay about fiercely. He was at once arrested by Keane, and was going to the barrack when a shout was raised from the crowd, 'Don't let him go with the devils'; and the three constables were immediately hemmed in. Three or four half-drunken fellows caught Sub-constable Fennel, and began to drag him, while others took hold of Constable Coyle. The crowd, or at least the part of it which did not belong to the place, kept shouting 'Oh, the devils. – Don't let Brien go with the peelers' …
>
> Just then some young men from this town and neighbourhood, seeing the exhausted appearance of the police, at once identified themselves in showing these 'mountain chaps' that they would not be allowed to assault the police in Milltown.[94]

A stick fight reputedly took place between the landlord of Milltown, Mr Godfrey, and one Tadhg Ruadh, from Portmagee, a strongman who was 'the champion of the hurling fields and faction fights of those days'.[95] According to one account, as Tadhg was returning from Co. Limerick, where he had been working as a farm labourer, he passed Godfrey's property and:

> went in to a plantation and cut three blackthorn sticks. The owner of the wood came on him and he asked him what did he want the sticks for and Tadhg said he wanted one for himself and one for each of his two brothers. The owner of the wood asked him would he fight him and Tadhg said he would. The man told Tadhg to come to his own house in order that his wife would see the fight. When they got to the house they started the fight and after a while Tadhg hit him across the head and made him unconscious.[96]

A more colourful account of the incident carries the quality of a folk tale rather than a report. It related that Tadhg had 'daringly leaped over the wall ... The keeper alarmed at his great size and apparent strength fled in terror to his master to inform him of the occurrence.'[97] Godfrey followed Tadhg on horseback and 'overtaking him at a crossroad presented a pair of pistols and asked him where he found those sticks'.[98] Tadhg, 'who was as fearless as he was bulky answered "In Mr [Godfrey's] orchard sir"'. Asking Tadhg if he was 'a good hand at the stick', the latter replied, 'I can defend myself', and Godfrey, 'who was a good swordsman there challenged him for a bout'.[99]

> As the offence he had committed was punishable [with] death by hanging at that time he gladly accepted the challenge and the gentleman being an old soldier of the class who admired courage and bravery in others was more likely to shield him from the law than endeavor to secure his conviction. They both returned to the house and

> Mr [Godfrey] procured two sticks and handed Tadg one. He then asked his wife to come out and see him drub a west Kerry spalpeen. The fight then began, [Godfrey] attacking in military fashion.
>
> Tadg gallantly warded off his blow, trusts [thrusts] and parries till at length exhausted from the combat he invited his opponent into his parlour and ordered a dinner followed by a couple of stiff bumpers of whiskey.[100]

The gangs of Mid Kerry most clearly demonstrate that alcohol was a fundamental element in faction fighting. Tadhg Ruadh may have had some civilised drinks over dinner, but excess was generally the order of the day. The fight witnessed by George Garrow Green at Molahiffe was first avoided by some friendly drinks and then exploded into life after the parties emerged from a public house. The Castlemaine factions supplied their men 'plentifully with whiskey', and on one occasion a newspaper reporter noted that it was 'several years since we saw so much whiskey sold' there, after which a serious fight followed.[101] In Milltown a Cork newspaper condemned two parties of '*whiskified heroes*'.[102] Around 1841 Samuel Carter Hall and his wife Anna Maria had a conversation about faction fighting with a country man, who commented:

> We ask each other how we were ever drawn into them, what brought them about; and the one answer to that, is – Whisky! – No gun will go off until it is *primed*, and sure whisky was the priming. That made more orphans and widows than the fever or starvation. Thanks be to God, if death come upon us now, it is by the Lord's will, and not our own act.[103]

10

'WHO'S AFRAID?'

> 'It was common at that time for people to be in contention with each other at all hours, trying to be the best man over each other. A man was no use without a party of hard men to back him up. A man whom a faction followed would be sooner received than great wealth with a man who had nobody behind him.'
>
> Peig Sayers, *An Old Woman's Reflections*[1]

Although faction fighting was not as often reported on the Dingle peninsula as it was for other districts in Kerry, stick fighting flourished there from the eighteenth century, when it was evidently popular. 'Around the year 1780 there was a fencing master in the parish,' wrote Tomás Mac Síthigh, of Ballyferriter, who had the information through the recollections of his father, Pádraig, 'and all of the young men of the parish would come to him to be taught.'[2] The instructor was one Gearóid Ó Maonaigh, from Rathkeale, Co. Limerick.

> The fencing masters used to have them very well trained at the sticks. The master had two sticks, and the learner had two sticks, when he used to teach the craft, the skill and the brandishing of the sticks. The men were very keen and eager at the art of stick fighting. It was rare that anyone was badly hurt in the feuds, as they were extremely adept and knowledgeable in how to defend themselves and in how to avoid the blows.[3]

A folklore interviewee from Annascaul also commented that there once were 'fencing Masters going about the district, a school was held for practicing the art of fencing. The pupils paid a small fee … per week. In these schools they learned all the tricks of the game, and became efficient in wealding a stick.'[4]

Early fights appear to have taken place on local holy days, such as St Gobnait's Day, Ferritersquarter, Dunquin, held on 11 February, and another at Minard, Lispole, held on 25 August. Along with dancing and drinking, Mac Síthigh noted, 'stick battles also used to take place at the patterns. Two evenly balanced groups would vie with one another.'[5] St Gobnait's Day was much later described as having been 'a riotous occasion with fun and games, drunkenness, and fighting, until a man was killed'.[6] The local priest who put an end to the tradition there died in 1803, which may date some of these activities to the late eighteenth century.

Fights continued during the first decades of the following century. During the battles held in Castlemaine between factions from Keel and Kiltallagh, 'the people of Dingle … would come to help Keel', such as at the engagement that went off in November 1812.[7] Around 1817 there was a big fight between the Kennedys from Annascaul and the Mannings (or Mannions) from Ballyferriter and their respective followers from the west, which was arranged to take place in Dingle town. 'There were 120 men on each side,' Mac Síthigh related.[8] Another account details the fight:

> The men from the West were picked from three parishes, and all were big, strong fellows.

> The Annascaul forces marched to the Little Bridge, every man with a stout cudgel in hand. The men from the West gathered at Tigh-na-mBocht, on the height.
>
> The Annascaul men saw that if they advanced up the road their opponents would have them at a disadvantage; so they swung round the Mall and out to the Green.
>
> At that time, the Green was common land, hoked over by the pigs of the town.
>
> Hither came the men of the West, and the two parties hurled themselves upon each other with their cudgels.
>
> The West-men were obliged to retire before those of Annascaul. They retreated about a mile, to Cill-Fhionntain; and here, in a big space of land, the conflict was fought out.
>
> Nobody was killed. The worst injury was a broken nose, suffered by a Mainíneach from the West. The Annascaul [men] were dexterous with the cudgel, but the others were stronger in close fighting.[9]

The main stage for faction fighting on the peninsula was Ballinclare fair, near Annascaul, which had been established since 1758, and which was held every May Day and 4 October. (Dingle, despite being the only major town of the barony of Corkaguiney – which consisted of most of the peninsula – and holding several market days, lacked any fairs until the second half of the century, and it appears to have been comparatively quieter as a consequence.) A folklore source described the scene of the Ballinclare fair. Publicans from Annascaul, Castlemaine and Dingle erected their tents, '[a] counter made of ladders ran the whole length of one side of the tent', and stout, whiskey, rum, wine and lemonade were made available.[10] Plenty of meat pies in soup were presented there, as the favourite food of every fair-goer:

> A fire was made a little way outside the tent and a three legged pot was placed on it. This was attended by a capable woman throughout the day. Several waitresses dressed in neat white aprons served the pies. Very often a fight would start when the fire pot and all disappeared half way across the fair field, and too the delph, tables etc. were often upturned by a call from a Faction Fighter to join in the fray.[11]

Faction activity at the fair appears to have been strongest before the Famine. In January 1829 Maurice Kennedy and a number of men named Bowler were imprisoned for an assault on a man named Canny (probably carried out in 1828).[12] At the fair of May 1835, 'there was more savage rioting than ever was known at that fair before', during which Thomas John Kennedy of Aunalack struck 'an inoffensive man' named Namock with 'a deadly blow of a cudgel with an iron ferule, which it is feared fractured his skull'.[13] In May 1837 a reporter noted that the farmers of the Dingle peninsula had suffered a hard winter, so that '[t]he distress in that part of the country is supposed to have dampened the ardour of the rival factions, as there was no appearance of riot at the fair'.[14] At the October fair of 1844 a 'great faction fight' was due to take place, although it did not go ahead following the appearance of a phalanx of fifty policemen to keep the peace.[15]

There were some later incidents, however. On the night of the October fair of 1863, a man named Connor was arrested for assault 'and calling out party names'.[16] In 1866 the May fair was recollected as having featured a 'riotous and disgraceful display', when over 200 people engaged in a fight, in which 'party cries' were made.[17] A newspaper correspondent hoped that this event did not signify a renewal of the faction fighting that was 'at one period very prevalent in that district'.[18]

'WHO'S AFRAID?'

A select number of established gangs fought at Ballinclare and along the Dingle peninsula. Among the most pre-eminent were the Kennedys. The family's grandparents on their father's side had come to Kerry from Nenagh, Co. Tipperary. A relative, Tadhg Kennedy, a prominent member of the IRA in Kerry during the War of Independence, later stated that they had been transplanted to Kerry around 1656 by the Earl of Cork and Orrery, along with a number of other families from the county, including the Curranes, the Coughlans and the Cournanes. He also related:

> I heard from old people that the Kennedys were very troublesome to the landlords and at one time a cavalry barracks had to be maintained at Ballinacourty to deal with a grand-uncle of mine named Jack Tadhg Kennedy of Coolnacuppogue. He was imprisoned for some time in Galway's Gaol in Dingle, and I remember a ballad in Irish 'Coppul Jack Thaidhg' being sung at Kennedy weddings recounting his escape from there on a black mare.[19]

The Kennedys flourished in Kerry: in 1831 a Timothy Kennedy was described as 'an opulent farmer residing in the barony of Corkaguiney'.[20] Given that the name Timothy was sometimes equated with that of Tadhg, this man may have been the celebrated fighter Tadhg Kennedy. A folklore source recalled that:

> Thig Kennedy was the Aunascaul leader. He lived at Anagap. He was known locally as 'whose afraid' [i.e. who's afraid?]. It is said he always started the row. He used take off his coat and drag it about the field shouting 'whose afraid' in a defying manner. Anyone who stepped on the coat would start the faction fight. Needless to say there always was someone of the rival clansmen more than anxious to get the opportunity of doing so.[21]

He was also famous for wielding a favourite stick which he had nicknamed '*Bás gan Saggart*' ('Death without a Priest').[22]

The Kennedys' foremost rivals were the Curranes. Their faction members were drawn from Garrynadur as well as from Lispole, Minard, Aglish and Dingle. Michael Currane was their leader. 'This man was very tall and strong. On May morning all his faction gathered together in Garrynadur crossroad. Each man armed with a stick. There he gave instructions to them for the coming fight. He mounted a big grey sire [shire] horse and rode in front of his clan till they came to Ballinclare Fair.'[23]

Months before the fair was held 'the faction fighters used cut sticks and put them away seasoning. They were put up in the chimney so as they would be dry and tough' for the fair day.[24] 'Many the bloody fights that were fought between rival factions in Ballinclare. The feud between the Currans and Kennedys went on for years 'till finally the Kennedys beat them. The Kennedys remained victors for a great number of years, always beating any small clan that would try to fight them.'[25] The feud appears to have been most active during the 1820s and 1830s: in June 1825 John Kennedy was arrested for the murder of Patrick Currane, 'a respectable farmer of good character', who had been attacked with a blunt instrument.[26] In another incident, in March 1833, when both parties were returning home from Dingle one night, Thomas Kennedy beat Michael Currane (possibly the faction leader) with a stick.[27]

One May Day, long afterwards, another of the former Tipperary families, the Coughlans, 'a strong faction from Dingle', appeared at the fair. They 'meant to give battle to the Kennedys and beat them'; their arrival 'was a great surprise to the Kennedy faction, and they sent word around to muster full strength for the fight'.[28]

> The Coughlans been [being] a much stronger faction succeeded after a long time in driving the Kennedys out on the road, and was beating towards Aunascaul village. Reinforcements being coming the Kennedys fought fiercely and every foot of road was fiercely contested.
>
> Tidg Kennedy been a very old man at this time and was unable to come to the Ballinclare Fair. However he happened to be out in his farm looking at sheep and from where he was he saw the great battle raging in the distance.
>
> When he saw his clan being [beaten] back, his old fury returned once again. He came down to his own house and much to his surprise he saw his own [son] sitting near the fire. This added more to his timpir and he said to his son 'Is it there you are sitting down near the fire and our clan [beaten] and killed along the road to Aunascaul you should be ashamed of yourself a young man like you[.]'
>
> When the young man heard that, he jumped up and got his stick and was about to start off to join his clan[.] 'Don[']t go yet[,'] says old Tidg[. ']Tidg will be with you[.'] He took down his 'Bás gan Saggart' and with his son[']s assistance he reached the scene of the fight.

> When the Kennedys seen him it gave them new courage. He started shouthing words of encouragement to them, and giving orders in general. The fight became very fierce and buckets of blood was spilled.
>
> The Kennedys being reinforced succeeded in driving the Coughlans back a small bit but after another while it became evident that the Kennedys were getting the best of the fight and the Coughlans started to retreat. However they fought (still retreating) a half a mile of the road back and at last they were forced to run through the fields.[29]

There was a postscript to the battle. Some of the Coughlans went to Annascaul and remained in the village. 'That night a row started in a public house between some of them and the Kennedys['] supporters. One of the Coughlans struck one Hamilton man with a stick in the head and he died as a result of the blow.'[30]

It is possible that the above fight was the battle involving 200 people that was reported in 1866.[31] By 1870, however, the Kennedy faction appears to have been considered defunct. A man who identified himself as one of the Kennedys' followers was jeered by a group of men after leaving a public house in Boolteens: 'when they came up to us Clifford cried out and said was there a Kennedy alive – that there was none of them now from Dingle to Keel but a little, and that the devil would soon take the rest of them'.[32]

THE FITZGERALDS AND THE MORIARTYS

The other great faction of the Dingle peninsula was the Fitzgeralds (also known as Na Gearaltaigh or the Mac Gearailts). 'The Gearaltaigh had a great name for agility and prowess with sticks, especially the Gearaltaigh Dhubha from Leataithe,' noted Tomás Mac Síthigh, who provides much of what we know about the factions of the barony.[33] They often fought against the Moriartys, and appeared at Ballinclare, and apparently as well in Dingle town and at the Ventry races.[34] Most of the Fitzgeralds and Moriartys were said to be from west of Dingle.[35]

'The way these fights usually started was a hero follower of the Fitzgeralds, primed with drink, would prance through the fair, waving his blackthorn cudgel and at the same time shouting for a Moriarty,' wrote Patrick Foley, who published two somewhat obscure books about the folklore and history of Corkaguiney and who was seemingly a native of the barony, in 1916.

> Then a fight was started in which whole parishes became involved. They fought each other without any individual ill-will, using stumps of furze, sticks of hawthorn or oak as their weapons. Sometimes big fights were started by a man holding out a stick and having one member of a faction spit on it and asking a man of the opponent's faction then to let him spit on. If he did, this was a challenge and the fight started. Tents were upset and the people scattered leaving the fair grounds to the combatants.[36]

Only a single newspaper report of the parties appears to exist, following their being charged for riotous assembly at Ballinclare in May 1840, to the number of 300, where they stoned the police, and one man who 'was wheeling his stick and shouting' was arrested.[37] An account of a significant fight between the parties was later noted down from a folklore interviewee. He explained that 'a judge named Barrister Freeman who was in

Aunascaull Court jailed and put heavy fines on anyone who was caught fighting at Ballinclare Fair afterwards'; this battle would thus appear to have taken place between 1829 and 1835, when William Deane Freeman served on the Kerry bench.[38]

> The leader of the Fitzgeralt faction was armed with an oar of a boat. One woman of the clan fought with a stone inside a stocking. She had nine brothers in the fight.
>
> The Moriartys [sent] for help to Killarney and Cahirciveene, they came from Cahirciveene in boats, and landed near Minard Castle about 2 miles from Ballinclare.
>
> The fight started in the field and there was'ent a sweet stall or pie tent that was'ent knocked. The Moriartys were beaten and all their backers were also hunted. They were chaced out of the field and those who came from Cahirciveene were followed down to Minard Strand where their boats were. The[y] just managed to escape before the Fitzgeralds got down there.
>
> There were three [canoes] belong[ing] to local fishermen in the strand. The Fitzgeralds gathered stones and put out the canoes and followed them half way out Dingle Bay but they could not catch up to the Cahirciveene men as they had too much of a start on them.[39]

The parties' enmity was believed to have had a remarkable origin. Patrick Foley stated that '[t]he origin of these factional fights in those parts was the betrayal of the Earl of Desmond – a Fitzgerald – by a Moriarty' – an event which had taken place in 1583.[40] According to Limerick journalist Michael MacDonagh, a barrister friend of his was told the same story in Abbeyfeale around 1883.[41] (Of course whether the feud had continued from the 1580s onwards or was a later eruption that merely utilised a historical incident as a handy taunt is another matter.)

There also used to be fights between the Fitzgeralds and the Mannings, another strong party. Some of the men involved were portrayed in a song, *Hup-saí-rá na nGearaltach*, later collected by local folklorist Seán Ó Dubhda in 1933:

Gluaisigheann an Gearaltach muar,
Ó Bhaile 'n tSléibhe anuar go ceannasach,
Níl aon Mhainníneach thoir ná thuaidh
Ná go mbainfeadh sé an chluas le maide dhe
Is ar phairc Éamoinn Dáith bhí an greadadh 'ca.

Gluaisigheann Éamonn an Ghárda,
Is helm an bháid mar bhata 'ge,
Nuair a bhaineann sé crothadh as a láimh
Critheann an tsraid le heagla.

Gluaisigheann Seán Éamoinn Taidhg,
Is a mhaide breágh meidhrach ó Shasana,
Buaileann sé flíp ar Chlár Gheáits
A thógann naoi bhfeádh ó thalamh é.

Gluaisigheann Muiris is Gearróid,
Is faobhar ar a n-órd chun marbhuithe,
Nuair a chíd siad an gasra rómpa,
Tuitid ar a dtóin le heagla.

Maireann na Gearaltaigh fós,

Is céad fear óg a leanas iad,
Beidh aca rinnce 's ceol,
Ag an Holy Shtone Dé Sathairn.

This translates as:

Big Fitzgerald travels boldly from
Baile an tSléibhe in the west,
There is no Mainíneach east or west
That he wouldn't remove his ear from him with a stick
They had their thrashing on Éamonn Dáithí's field.

Éamonn an Ghárda travels along,
Holding the helm of a boat as a stick,
When he shakes his hand
The street shakes with fear.

Seán Éamoinn Taidhg moves along,
With his fine, sporty stick from England,
He hits Clár Gheáits a heavy blow
Which lifts him nine feet off the ground.

Muiris and Gearóid travel along,
With their hammers sharpened to kill,
When they see the band of young warriors ahead of them,
They fall on their backsides with fear.

The Gearaltaigh still live on,
With the hundred young men that follow them,

> They will have dancing and music,
> At the Holy Shtone on Saturday.[42]

Fainter traces of other factions and fighters along the Dingle peninsula exist. Ó Dubhda wrote that 'stick fights ... were always held at the Gleann Fair day', not far from Dingle town, 'where there were "half on either side" as the old saying goes'.[43] At Lateeve, Ballyferriter, in August 1833, a man named McDonnell was followed from his home:

> by some men of the name of Collins, and a man named Moriarty, who belonged to an opposite faction, between whom and the McDonnell clan, a savage feud subsisted; and in accordance with the system of warfare adopted by *the finest people on the face of the earth*, poor McDonnell being found alone and unprotected, was so cruelly beaten, that he died in consequence.[44]

Some men engaged in episodes of single combat: Paid Eoghain Ó Súilleabháin from Baile Eaglaise, Ballyferriter, and Conchubhar Ó Curráin from Ceathrúin an Phúca, near Ventry, had a stick fight, wrote Tomás Mac Síthigh: 'Ó Curráin was a warrior of a man but Paid Eoghain got the better of him or got the upper hand on him. Paid Eoghain was a great man with the stick. He used to work as a farm labourer.'[45] He was also told of a woman who declared that she was from sweet Ventry, where men could achieve success not with arms, swords or fire, 'but with the green branches of the wood, and from the strength of their veins'.[46]

Blasket Island storyteller Peig Sayers (1873–1958) also had a story in her repertoire – 'Red Tommy and Margaret O'Brien'

– about a young man from Ventry who comes to the aid of his father-in-law's faction: 'It happened that another farmer had a notice put up that he and his men would be in the town of Tralee on a certain day and that he expected O'Brien leading his men to be there'; the young man appears at a crucial moment when defeat seems complete and goes on to win the older man's respect by demonstrating his strength and courage in the contest.[47] Fellow islander Tomás O'Crohan (1856–1937) mentioned a man from Ballyferriter: 'When the country people used to brawl and fight at the markets and fairs, Big James was captain of one of the factions.'[48] Finally, in her survey of activities connected with the August festival of Lughnasa, Máire Mac Neill characterised the pattern day of Cloghane, on the northern side of the peninsula, as 'the great assembly of the year' in the barony, 'a day of games, athletics, vaulting over horses, dancing, singing and courtship, of faction-fighting and feasting'.[49]

Ultimately, as elsewhere in the county, the practice of faction fighting in Corkaguiney came to an end, though perhaps it declined earlier there than in other districts. 'Feuding with sticks was very commonplace right up until the Famine. There was very little of this type of combat then after the Famine,' observed Tomás Mac Síthigh.[50] Seán Ó Dubhda also concluded: 'Bad times and the Famine put an end to that kind of fury.'[51]

AFTERWORD

'FACTION AND FEUD ARE PASSING AWAY'

After this survey of stick fights, beatings, injuries, deaths, court cases and imprisonments, it remains to be asked how faction fighting ended. Throughout its course, the practice was condemned and opposed by most local gentlemen and magistrates (although perhaps not by all), as well as by local priests and their bishops. To these forces were added during the first half of the nineteenth century the police, the Catholic Association, the Repeal Association and Fr Mathew's temperance movement. The national decline and death of faction fighting has been attributed by contemporary commentators and later analysts to these elements, and to the Famine, although the case of Co. Kerry does not appear to conform easily to such views.

RECONCILIATION AND 'PACIFICATION'

Among the middle-class leaders of the campaign for Catholic Emancipation, faction violence represented an embarrassment because it threatened to foster an impression among British politicians and the British newspaper-reading public that Irishmen might not be deserving of their rights. At a dinner for Daniel O'Connell, held in Cork city in 1828, William Crawford declared of the factions that he 'could not help indulging in ludicrous emotions upon hearing the names of *Black Hens* and *Magpies* given to them. What thought I, will honest John Bull say to us when he finds us engaged in contests and quarrels about such absurd names?'[1]

O'Connell regularly expressed his frustration with the faction fighters. In 1827, for example, he called upon Irishmen 'to leave off those disgraceful quarrels which were so frequent at fairs, where the Twohys are against the Duggans, and the Mahonys beat down the Scanlans':

> [H]ad [they] not enemies enough amongst themselves, without wasting their strength and exhausting themselves, quarrelling with each other, and degrading themselves below the rank of men? He had seen five men sentenced to be transported during the Assizes which had just concluded, for being engaged in a riot at a fair, which ended in the death of a man. They were to be transported to an ungenial climate – to another hemisphere; removed for ever from mothers, and wives, and children, and all who were dear to them on earth. Such were the consequences of those fateful broils, originating in folly and absurdity, ending in crime, and calling down punishment in this world and the vengeance of the God of Charity in the next.[2]

In the summer of 1828 the Catholic Association began trying to reconcile some of the major factions around the country, in partnership with the clergy. In one meeting, a ceremony was arranged in August between the parties of the Rieskavallas and the Coffees at a chapel in Newport, Co. Tipperary. After speeches by prominent members of the Association, twenty faction leaders agreed to put aside their animosities for what they were told was the greater good of their country. 'The Clergyman then took down the crucifix from the Altar, on which they swore ... They, in conclusion, went on the Altar – embraced each other, and exchanged medals, in token of future friendship.' There was then an emotional scene:

> A grey-headed old man, who, though advanced in age, was strong in mind and feelings, had lost his favourite nephew. He was brought reluctantly to the altar by his friends, and, when solicited to make an offering of his feelings, 'I will not', he said, 'they brutally murdered my nephew. If they killed him by a blow in fair fight – but they fired several shots through his body, and not satisfied with that, they broke his legs and thighs – I must have justice of them'. Being remonstrated with, and told that his present vow was one promotive of future peace, that a recurrence might be prevented of such a melancholy casualty as he himself was afflicted with, he did kneel to make the pledge, but when the crucifix was tendered to him, he became very much agitated, and rising from his knees, said he would not go against his conscience, he would not injure his soul, he should have justice of them ... but being reasoned with, after a long struggle, he again knelt down, and vowed future peace and friendship with the slayers of his nephew.[3]

In July 1828 two factions of Co. Limerick met under the auspices of a priest, formed one procession, 'preceded by a garland, in the centre of which was placed one of O'Connell's handkerchiefs' and attended a ceremony in which the priest asked them to raise their eyes to Heaven and repeat, 'I swear solemnly to that God, in whose presence I must one day appear for judgement, that from this hour to the last I shall live in this world, the hands that are now lifted towards His Eternal Throne, shall never more be raised against my fellow-man.'[4]

In Kerry, analogous scenes were played out. German visitor Fürst Hermann von Pückler-Muskau noted that the O'Donoghues and the Moynihans who fought around Killarney performed a marching penance, 'and ever since the war is at an end'.[5] Similarly, in December 1828, in order to pacify two unnamed factions (probably the Cooleens and the Lawlors), a large crowd of people from the parishes of Ballylongford, Lisselton, Tarbert and the area of the Galey had to assemble at Tarbert and walk to Tralee, then a distance of about thirty miles. This was 'by way of penance on this poor deluded people for having violated the commands of the Catholic Association, by rioting among themselves', reported an unimpressed eyewitness to the scene:

> Every individual concerned in the affray, men and women, combatants and lookers-on, prize-fighters and battle-holders, were condemned by their spiritual guide and ruler to perform this pilgrimage, and submit to whatever further chastisement the Parish Priest of Tralee may feel disposed to inflict on them, and from whom they were to receive tickets to that effect, before they should be reconciled to the Church. These tickets, which are nothing more than ab[b]reviations of two or three Latin words, are considered indispensable by the people, and are a prime article of profit with the Priests. Away went the multitudes on this worse than Quixotic expedition – Some few of them, tis true, very reluctantly, but none daring to refuse ... A few sturdy farmers, who grumbled, not a little ... determined to make the grievous punishment of so long a jaunt

> in this inclement season as easy as possible, and bestrided their gallant greys, and, in the plenitude of good nature, helped a less affluent neighbour to a lift.[6]

When the priest found out afterwards that some men had ridden rather than walked the journey, they were commanded to repeat it again on foot. Locally, this particular procedure did not have any lasting effect, as the killing of a man at Lisselton on Christmas Day (of all days) and a faction fight at Ballylongford on another holy day in June the following year both suggest.[7]

More generally, too, the years 1828 and 1829 (the latter the year Emancipation was achieved) went on to represent the two most active periods of faction fighting in Kerry during the decade of the 1820s. According to Mathew Barrington, crown solicitor for the Munster Circuit, faction fights went into decline after Catholic Emancipation was achieved.[8] If that was true nationally, however, it was not the case in Kerry, where the decade of the 1830s represented the busiest period of the violence in the county, with at least forty-three incidents during the decade.

The apparent futility of pacification was satirised in a comic verse, published in a Waterford newspaper, about a faction fighter who 'laid by his cudgel … no more to be seen'.

> *Thady Flyn was a mighty good warrant to lend*
> *A fist to his faction and fight for his friend;*
> *They call'd him 'Black Hen', but a pout of his size*
> *Would strike the beholders with fear and surprise.*
> *There was not in Clare a more frolicsome stripling,*
> *Nor one more addicted to fighting and tipling,*

Till O'Connell came down, saited on his barouche,
And praiched paice between Dublin, and Dingle-i-couch.

Thady goes on to demonstrate his desire for peace by beating two Caravats who will not give up fighting: 'And therefore shake hands and put down your Alpeens,/Or I'll lick yeez agin, ye two lousy spalpeens'.[9]

O'Connell had to address the vexed issue once again during the campaign for the repeal of the Act of Union. At a public meeting in 1836 he again complained:

> There was one foul blot on their history ... he alluded to what is called clanship, and the disgrace and enormities of which it is so prolific a source. This evil of Ireland is not even understood in England. The people there cannot comprehend how it is that 'Three-year-olds' and 'Four-year-olds', 'Caravats' and 'Shanavests', 'Black-hens' and 'Magpies' should meet and knock each others['] brains out.[10]

He then produced an address he had written to the people of Ireland, pleading with them 'to abstain altogether, and for ever, from fighting at fairs or other meetings, from waylaying or beating one another'.[11]

Another process of control was adopted by the Repeal movement. On this occasion it marshalled local 'pacificators', whose role was to report on and discourage factions in their districts. Messrs O'Sullivan and Murphy had the unenviable task of preventing faction fights at that great centre of riot, Molahiffe fair. 'In this, our first report, we are happy to record the tranquillity of these parishes,' they stated to the Association in August 1837 concerning Molahiffe and Keelanean. 'There had been some symptoms of faction fights, but the exertions of our peace-preserving and patriotic clergy, aided by our humble exertions, have put a final stop to such attempts; neither are there any illegal societies, clubs, &c, in the parish.'[12]

That may have been true in August, but May was when the fairs took place (and at the event of that year a fierce fight between two parties had gone off, after which 'many of the unfortunate wretches were brutally mangled, and lay bleeding in their glory!')[13] At the following fair of 1838 there were several brutal fights 'between barbarous hostile factions, in which numbers of people were severely injured', for which the appointment of the pacificators, in that case, does not seem to have mattered.[14]

Nevertheless, the great period of fights in Kerry represented by the 1830s began to decline from 1837 and continued to do so until 1843. This did cover much of the period of the Repeal campaign, which effectively ended in the latter year. In most of those years only a single faction fight was reported in the county annually. While it is possible that the Repeal movement, popular as it was, may have encouraged a climate of self-discipline or diverted men's interests in a political direction, there was another element that came into play during that period, and may have also been responsible for the effect: the introduction of a reformed and more effective police force.

POLICE INTERVENTION

Policing had been introduced to Ireland by an act of the Irish parliament in 1789. But the force was 'corrupt and useless', and the baronial constables or 'barneys' were 'almost all elderly men and would be of no help in controlling a faction fight,' wrote historian of Irish fairs Patrick Logan.[15] A new model was introduced in 1814 by Chief Secretary Sir Robert Peel as the Peace Preservation Force, known commonly as 'the Peelers' (a nickname that continued to be applied to later versions of the police). Yet in 1821 Chief Secretary Charles Grant still bemoaned the state of the country, with its robberies, burglaries in search of arms, murders and 'fightings at fairs'.[16] As a result, in 1822 a County Constabulary was formed, but neither it nor the earlier force was particularly useful in suppressing or controlling faction fights, as their policy was often to avoid getting involved. Under-Secretary Thomas Drummond later explained that 'it was a Practice at one Time not uncommon to draw the Police from the Fairs ... and leave the People to fight among themselves unrestrained, rather than risk the Loss of Life by Collision with the Constabulary'.[17]

The number of incidents of both political violence and faction fights was intolerable to Drummond, who set about establishing a more efficient force in 1836, the Irish Constabulary (from 1867 termed the Royal Irish Constabulary). From its very inception it was intended that faction fighting would be a particular target of the new police. A general order was issued in 1836 stating that:

> It is the Determination of the Lord Lieutenant that every Exertion shall be made to suppress Party and Faction Fights at Fairs, Markets, or on any other Occasion ... Such Scenes cause a Disregard for the Law ... nothing can be more calculated to keep up Habits of Ferocity and Ill-will ... The Inspector General promulgates those views in order that every Officer and Constable of the Force may be aware that the Orders upon this important Point proceed from a

> fixed Determination on the part of his Excellency to call upon the Constabulary Force … to put down Fights arising from whatever Cause.[18]

By 1839 it certainly seemed that faction fights had almost disappeared in Kerry. In that year a single incident was reported for the county and such continued to be the pattern for each year up to and including 1843. It appeared to be the same elsewhere, too. 'Have Faction Fights diminished in the County of Kilkenny?' a witness was asked at a parliamentary inquiry in June 1839. 'Very much; I scarcely know of a Faction Fight.' 'To what do you attribute their Cessation?'; 'I attribute it principally to the constant Attendance of a strong Police Force and a Government Magistrate at Fairs, which had not been heretofore the Case.'[19] Thomas Drummond agreed with the same committee that the mere appearance of the police and the prospect of likely arrest were enough to prevent fighting.[20]

Yet if these effects had been produced following the introduction of the constabulary, it was temporary, as Co. Kerry afterwards experienced a resurgence of faction fighting between 1844 and 1846, when nineteen episodes were reported by the press, across a wide geographical range, and police intervention seemed unavailing.

CLERICAL CENSURE

Clerical opposition to faction fighting was repeated and ubiquitous. Parish priests waded into fights in efforts to stop them, condemned perpetrators from the pulpit and urged the participants to obey the law of the land. At a higher level, too, censure was made. David Moriarty, bishop of Kerry, turned to the subject in a Lenten Pastoral of 1858. He warned that if any members of the diocese were found guilty of the activity, and did not repent and make reparations, he would have a sentence of excommunication passed against them:

> We thought that a quarter of a century of civilizing education had effaced for ever the last vestiges of this savage practice, and had afforded sufficient guarantee against its recurrence but, where drunkenness prevails, neither education nor the teachings of religion can avail, our happiest hopes are frustrated, and we are doomed in sorrow to see our country and our people disgraced by feuds more barbarous than those of the wild children of the forest. This evil is yet confined to certain localities, it has not acquired considerable extent; but, unless it is vigorously suppressed, we fear the worst consequences, for we know that it is the revival of what once stained the country with blood and we know, too, that one faction fight – such are the clannish habits of the people, may sow so deep and spread so wide the seeds of hatred and revenge, that years may not suffice to extirpate them.[21]

The role of alcohol in faction fights, particularly noted by contemporaries in the cases of the Castleisland area and the fair of Molahiffe, was well accepted nationally. The Irish MP who pointed out in 1786 that people could seldom meet at fairs without a fight ensuing, attributed it to the consumption of whiskey and remarked, unflatteringly, 'Take an hogshead of whiskey, place it on the top of a hill, knock out the bung, and the country people will be attracted by the scent of it, as rats are by oil of rhodium.'[22]

A much-heralded clerical intervention, performed by the work of Fr Theobald Mathew and his temperance movement, sought to change these circumstances. Beginning in 1838, Fr Mathew created a mass movement dedicated to eliminating drunkenness from Irish life, as well as the various criminal activities, including faction fighting, which he and others felt were the result of it. He traversed the country speaking to huge crowds, appearing several times in Kerry between 1840 and 1845, and encouraging his audience to take 'The Pledge'. ('I promise, with the Divine assistance, to abstain from all intoxicating liquors, and to prevent, as much as possible, by advice and example, intemperance in others.')[23] In March 1841 he addressed an open-air meeting on the Knight of Kerry's lawn at Glanleam, Valentia, where he stated:

> Most of the crimes of Ireland had been engendered in whiskey houses, or perpetrated under the influence of whiskey. Such crimes have nearly ceased; the gaols are, comparatively, empty, and the criminal business of assizes materially diminished. Faction fights are unknown, and breaches of the peace are rare, such were the general effects of a change from whiskey to total abstinence.[24]

In the same year *The Kerry Examiner* published a poem on the local effects of the movement; formerly, 'each manly heart was ardent glowing/For the faction fight or the measured sod':

But now from Erin's verdant green
Have duelling dire and faction fled,
No more is heard the avenging keen,
Nor wildly wave the ribbons red.

The sun of Temp'rance bright is shedding
It's peaceful rays o'er vale and hill.[25]

Only five faction fights were reported in Kerry between 1839 and 1843, which appears to contrast very favourably with the twenty-three that had been waged in the five-year period previously. Generally, it was felt that temperance had curbed faction fights significantly.

A question nonetheless remains about whether the temperance movement had a long-term effect on faction fighting in Kerry. The nineteen reported fights between 1844 and 1846 suggest that the practice was soon taken up again after the brief hiatus. Indeed, a man who was killed in a fight at Sneem in December 1844 was himself 'a pledge-breaker'.[26] In 1845 *The Kerry Evening Post* felt that:

> The temperance movement ... has dwindled, – at least in Kerry, and, we believe, all over Ireland – from a mighty river to an unimportant stream. Of this lamentable fact, we have increasing evidences presented to our eyes every day. Numerous applications for spirit licenses come before the Court at every Quarter Sessions; the fairs and markets abound with drunken men, and in consequence, faction fights again disgrace the country.[27]

In 1846 a speaker at a temperance meeting in Killarney admitted that 'the people who were kept back from intoxicating liquor by the first flush of temperance, have fallen into their old ways'.[28] In a modern assessment of the effectiveness of Fr Mathew's campaign between the years 1839 and 1845, in relation to reducing crime as a whole, the writer concluded that Kerry showed 'almost no decrease' in *per capita* convictions.[29]

THE AFTERMATH OF FAMINE AND THE LAND WAR

The Great Famine (1845–49) appears to have diminished faction fighting in some areas but not in others. Fights at the great fairs of Molahiffe, for example, ceased until the mid-1850s, but others continued elsewhere in the county. While there had been fights in Kerry earlier in 1845, after the potato blight struck, in late summer, there were five more incidents in the county during the remainder of the year. Following a fight in Castlemaine in November 1845 between the Sullivans and the Riordans, strong farmers of Castlemaine, magistrates stated that they 'regretted to find that a system which had been for many years given up in this county should be now revived'.[30] In January 1846 a policeman 'called the attention of the Court to the fact that since he had come to this county in September last, his force had been met at every fair and meeting by faction fighting. In O'Dorney a police constable's jaw was broken; the other night his men were attacked in Castleisland.'[31] Even in the year of 'Black '47', when famine conditions intensified, there was a big, whiskey-fuelled battle at Milltown in December, after which a writer in *The Kerry Evening Post* concluded: 'This, taken in connection with the riotous disposition of the young farmers, shows that among that class at least there is not much distress – no hungry bellies, nor empty pockets.'[32] In 1848, when three episodes were reported in the county, the same newspaper commented: 'We always look upon faction fighting as a sign that the farmers are not in distress.'[33]

It was in the aftermath of the Famine that the first break in the tradition of fighting appeared in the county. For the first time, there was a two-year absence of fights between 1851 and 1852, and when a fight took place at Castleisland in 1853, it was characterised as representing a disposition among the farmers 'to renew the faction fighting practices of their fathers'.[34] Thereafter faction fights in the county carried on at a rate of only one or two per year.

From the 1860s onwards, the activity in other counties also began to be described as a phenomenon of the past. 'Faction fights have, thank Heaven, nearly ceased. There is no rioting, worthy of the name, at fairs and markets,' the *Southern Reporter and Cork Commercial Chronicle* felt in August 1862.[35] In Co. Clare, in July 1864, a newspaper noted that 'large fairs are held in this county, which in former years were the source of much disturbances, and would now, if the people were not better disposed, generate faction-fights, riotous assemblies, and other acts of lawlessness'.[36]

During the 1870s occasional gaps of a year or two began to appear in which no incidents were reported in Kerry. In the 1880s faction fights for the first time began to disappear from the county for longer periods of time and never reappeared in large numbers. *The Freeman's Journal* noted a national trend in February 1881: 'There are two denominations of crime after which we are particularly glad to see blanks in the returns. One is the denomination of "Faction Fights", and the other that of illegal "Party Demonstrations". May it be an omen that faction and feud are passing away!'[37] The farmers may have been absorbed instead by the collective campaign of the Land War, a movement that particularly concerned their self-interest; in Kerry, folklore collector Díarmuid Ó Múimhneacháin observed of the Gearaltaigh and Daithínigh factions that their fights, which had been running since the 1820s, 'died down when the Land war became hot'.[38]

THE INTRODUCTION OF SPORT AND THE GAA

Another factor in the decline of faction fighting may have been the promotion of sport, although the evidence is contradictory. Recalling the pattern day of Knockanure, one of the battle-grounds of the Cooleens and the Lawlors, a folklore source commented: 'The young men of the different parishes when "The Pattern Day" came round organised sports', which:

> turned the minds of the youth into other channels and faction fighting was completely forgotten. The only people who tried to keep it alive were the old seasoned veterans and at fire side and crossroad they recalled the 'brave deeds' of the men of their day and rebuked the youths taunting them with cowardice, but their encouragement was in vain.[39]

In this regard the formation of the GAA in 1884 (in the chief county for faction fighting, Tipperary) may have had a role in discouraging faction fights, instead diverting men's energies in the direction of competitive sport. A guide to the history of Ballinamere GAA club in Co. Offaly stated that it was following the death of a young man in a faction fight that a local priest 'grasped the opportunity to actively promote hurling as an alternative'.[40] A folklore interviewee commented of the Three

Year Olds and Four Year Olds of Co. Limerick that the GAA, cleverly, established a football team with members drawn from both sides, which 'united the parties and silenced the "party cries"'.[41]

Nevertheless, fighting inspired by loyalty and identity, such as had been expressed through the factions, also continued within the new context of sport. In November 1887, 'A Gaelic athletic faction fight took place on Sunday near Limerick. The hurleys were vigorously used by the athletes, not upon the ball, but upon each other's heads, only one of which, owing to the strength of the material of which heads are composed in that part of the world, was "opened."'[42] At the Wicklow championships in the same year, a newspaper reported that stewards and spectators were 'freely using ash saplings on one another's heads in a manner worthy of the halcyon days of faction fighting'.[43]

In Kerry, in 1890, a newspaper complained that meetings of the GAA 'are fast becoming a public nuisance. Scarcely a football or hurling match takes place, in this county at all events, that a dispute, followed by a free fight, does not arise', and it described a match between the Tralee Mitchels and the Killorglin Rangers in which sticks were flourished. 'According to the account given by an on-looker the famous faction fights at "Puck" fair in days of yore were "nowhere" in comparison to the wild cheers and charges of the Rangers.' The secretary of the Mitchels club stated that the Killorglin fans attended in very large numbers, and 'almost every man was armed with a blackthorn'. After dominating the early part of the game, two Killorglin players then struck a Tralee man 'and the Killorglin outsiders then rushed in with sticks and belaboured everybody from Tralee. Some clergymen who happened to be on the field, and other impartial gentlemen interfered, and the savage instincts of the Killorglin men were quelled.'[44] Nevertheless, despite these evident setbacks, thirty years after its formation, a priest at a meeting in Castlegregory was enthusiastic in his feeling that the GAA had turned young men away from faction violence:

> With all his virtues, the Irishman – and especially the poor and illiterate Irishman – has some vices and defects of character. He has a proclivity to drunken brawls and faction fighting, to many of those unseemly practical jokes [which] emanate from the spirit of mischief. His strong point is not respect for law and order … on the whole the Gaelic sports have had the effect of bringing a good deal of sunshine, happiness and joy into Irish life. They have a most refining and educating effect on the minds of the rising generation, and as a proof of that I can point to this one fact that those streets and squares of villages, those cross-roads, and … glens which in the days of the faction fights used to rebound so often with the murderous blows, the savage shouts and the groans of the wounded men – these very places are to-day the scenes of music and song and dance, of innocent merriment and of joyous laughter.[45]

THE END

At length, the fighting sticks were generally laid aside, and became relegated to the status of souvenirs of Irishness that were sold to tourists as harmless relics of a bygone time. In October 1889 the wife of a Home Rule MP 'obtained a true specimen of the Irish "shillelagh"', although a writer in the *Kerry Sentinel* noted that its 'spick-and-span newness' suggested it had never been used in a faction fight.[46] Shops for foreign visitors continued to sport poor imitations of the weapons long into the twentieth century, so that the writer Padraic Colum complained that the 'varnished blackthorn with green ribbons round it that the tourist brings back from "The Emerald Isle" was merely a simulacrum of a shillelagh'.[47]

However, a scattering of late incidents did take place before stick fighting finished for good. In Kerry there was a fight following Knocknagoshel pattern in 1900, and another the following year in which young men from Kilflynn and Stacks Mountain attacked each other fiercely with sticks and stones.[48] Thereafter, almost ten years of uninterrupted peace followed. Two politically motivated conflicts then went off in the election campaign of 1910, which were reminiscent of the battles that had taken place so often in Tralee. One of these was the incident that set the former East Kerry factions of the Gearaltaigh and Daithínigh against each other again, just over the county bounds in Knocknagree.[49] The other involved the rival supporters of two candidates, O'Sullivan and Murphy, who fought along High Street, Killarney.[50] In a related incident, some of O'Sullivan's supporters carried sticks and tried to drive off their opponents at a crowded polling station in Firies, after which a judge in a resulting court case recalled how that district had once been so noted for faction fights, seemingly with the famous days of Molahiffe fair in mind.[51] There was a further altercation after the case had been heard, which was witnessed by Jeremiah Murphy as a young child: 'There was a large crowd around Killarney courthouse and a big fight broke out. The police quelled the riot and order was restored. I saw a woman using her stocking as an offensive weapon ... it was reinforced in the toe by a good-sized stone. She was flattening men left and right and I was scared.'[52] After these very final flourishes, however, Kerry faction fighting could be declared dead.

A handful of old heroes lingered as living spectres of the practice. 'In my early youth I often saw some of the prime actors in those foolish and disreputable scenes,' revealed a man in 1917. 'In life's wane they appeared to be God-fearing and respectable men who belonged to the sturdy class of farmers who inhabited North Kerry more than sixty years ago.'[53] In Castleisland, a noted faction fighter, 'Black Maurice Fitzgerald ... in the poverty of old age, lived in Pound lane, when we were boys', recalled another man in 1927. 'We had great respect then for Black Maurice, because our fathers told us that he was a "terrible man with a stick" at faction fights.'[54]

For some, however, the passing of the old days was a matter of regret. Church of Ireland clergyman and writer George Birmingham, who was familiar with the West of Ireland, commented in 1912:

> Those reprobate ancestors of ours drank hard, fought frequently, and outraged every canon of economic science. But after all they lived vigorously, and that is something to their credit ... The faction fights are over, but have we gained greatly? ... We are better men and women now, no doubt, but, no doubt also, we have lost something which all our earnestness will not give back to us.[55]

ENDNOTES

PREFACE

1 McMahon, Richard, *Homicide in pre-Famine and Famine Ireland* (Liverpool University Press, Liverpool, 2013), p. 53.

2 Lewis, George Cornewall, *On Local Disturbances in Ireland* (B. Fellowes, London, 1836), pp. 279–95.

3 Donnelly, James S. Jr., 'Factions in Prefamine Ireland', in Eyler, Audrey S. and Garratt, Robert F. (eds), *The Uses of the Past: Essays on Irish Culture* (University of Delaware Press, Washington, 1988), p. 113.

INTRODUCTION

1 Larkin, Emmet (ed.), *Alexis de Tocqueville's Journey in Ireland: July–August, 1835* (Wolfhound Press, Dublin, 1990), p. 53.

2 Barlow, Stephen, *The History of Ireland, from the Earliest Period to the Present Time*, Vol. I (Sherwood, Neely and Jones, London, 1814), p. 261.

3 'Limerick Assizes', *Limerick Chronicle*, 9 March 1836.

4 Lewis (1836), p. 285.

5 Conley, Carolyn, 'The Agreeable Recreation of Fighting', *Journal of Social History*, Vol. 33, No. 1 (1999), p. 60.

6 'Faction Fight', *The Kerry Evening Post*, 26 November 1845.

7 Bary, Valerie, *Houses of Kerry* (Ballinakella Press, Whitegate, 1994), pp. 7, 177.

8 'Summer in Ballybunnion. Sketches by J. A. O'C. The Faction Fight at Ballyeagh', *The Tralee Chronicle*, 25 September 1868.

9 *The Tipperary Vindicator*, 18 January 1845.

10 Reid, Thomas, *Travels in Ireland in the Year 1822* (Longman, Hurst, Rees, Orme and Brown, London, 1823), pp. 280–1.

11 Barrington, Sir Jonah, *Personal Sketches of His Own Times*, Vol. III (Henry Colburn and Richard Bentley, London, 1832), p. 253.

12 *Ibid.*, pp. 254–6. 'If the drop was in': if they had drink taken. Emphases in original.

13 Anon., 'Notes of a Journey in the Kingdom of Kerry', *Blackwood's Edinburgh Magazine*, January 1828, p. 50. Note: some punctuation in the original account has been modernised in this excerpt.

14 von Pückler-Muskau, Fürst Hermann, *Tour in England, Ireland, and*

France, in the years 1828 & 1829, Vol. I (Effingham Wilson, London, 1832), pp. 227–8.

15 O'Toole, Terence, 'National Emblems', *Dublin Penny Journal*, 7 July 1832, p. 10.

16 Hurley, John W., *Shillelagh: The Irish Fighting Stick* (Caravat Press, Pipersville, 2007), pp. 118–21.

17 'Summer in Ballybunnion. Sketches by J. A. O'C.', *The Tralee Chronicle*, 11 September 1868.

18 Edgeworth, Richard Lovell, and Edgeworth, Maria, *Essay on Irish Bulls* (J. Johnson, London, 1802), p. 107.

19 For these and other terms see Hurley (2007), pp. 126–49.

20 Hall, Mr, and Hall, Mrs S. C., *Ireland: its Scenery, Character*, Vol. I (How and Parsons, London, 1841), p. 426.

21 Hurley (2007), p. 181. Frieze coats were heavy winter coats made of coarse woollen cloth.

22 Evidence of Major Richard Willcocks, Inspector of Police, to a House of Commons committee in 1824, cited in Lewis (1836), p. 284.

23 'Killarney Quarter Sessions. The Faction Fight at Molahiffe Fair', *The Kerry Evening Post*, 22 June 1861.

24 Ó Danachair, Caoimhín, 'Faction Fighting in County Limerick', *North Munster Antiquarian Journal*, Vol. 10 (1966), p. 49.

25 'Old Kerry. Octogenarian writes again', *Kerry Sentinel*, 19 February 1896.

26 Wagner, Paul and Rector, Mark (eds), *Highland Broadsword: Five Manuals of Scottish Regimental Swordsmanship* (Chivalry Bookshelf, Highland Village, Texas), p. 134.

27 Ó Danachair (1966), p. 52.

28 'The Faction Fights at Ballinclare Fair', National Folklore Collection (hereafter NFC) 782: 277. '*Bás gan Saggart*': 'Death without a Priest'.

29 O'Donnell, Patrick, *The Irish Faction Fighters of the 19th Century* (Anvil Books, Dublin, 1975), p. 17.

30 Logan, Patrick, *Fair Day: The Story of Irish Fairs and Markets* (Appletree Press, Belfast, 1986), p. 103.

31 Anon., 'The Darling Ould Stick', *Songs of Ireland and Other Lands* (D. & J. Sadlier, New York, 1847), p. 268. The song was also printed in England; see Broadside Ballads Online, http://ballads.bodleian.ox.ac.uk/search/?query=the+darling+ould+stick.

32 Hall and Hall (1841), p. 427.

33 Cronin, Dan, 'An Ancient Characteristic of Ireland: Faction Fights', *Sliabh Luachra, Journal of Cumann Luachra*, Vol. 1 No. 14 (2010), p. 61.

34 'A Description of the County of Kerry', in O'Conner, Morgan, *Poems, Pastorals and Dialogues* (J. Thompson, Dublin, 1726), p. 20. In other editions and publications the writer was always styled Murroghoh O'Connor, and that form has been adopted here.

35 *The Kerry Evening Post*, 15 October 1864.

36 'The Humours of a Munster Village', *The Kerry Weekly Reporter and Commercial Advertiser*, 12 August 1933.

37 'Old Kerry Records – Over One Hundred Years Ago. Summer Assizes 1762 – Sept 3', *The Kerry Evening Post*, 16 November 1864.

38 'The Convicts – A Sketch', *Mayo Constitution*, 16 August 1832.

39 'Faction Fighting', National Folklore Schools Manuscript Collection (hereafter NFCS) 0451: 408; NFCS 0358: 510.

40 Lewis (1836), p. 289.

41 In other words, she had a cataract on her eye like a boiled cockle.

42 Anon., 'Notes of a Journey in the Kingdom of Kerry', p. 50. 'Fortin': fortune, dowry.

43 'O'Dorney Petty Sessions – Friday', *The Kerry Evening Post*, 11 May 1892.

44 Townsend, Horace, *Statistical Survey of the County of Cork* (Graisberry and Campbell, Dublin, 1810), p. 71.

45 Larkin (1990), p. 53.

46 Carleton, William, 'The Battle of the Factions', in *Traits and Stories of the Irish Peasantry*, Vol. I (William Frederick Wakeman, Dublin, 1834), pp. 309, 316.

47 Conley, 'The Agreeable Recreation of Fighting', pp. 59–60.

48 Evidence of Major Thomas Powell, 'Minutes of Evidence taken before the Select Committee of the House of Lords, appointed to examine into the Nature and Extent of the Disturbances which have prevailed in those Districts of Ireland which are now subject to [...] the Insurrection Act [...] 18 May–23 June, 1824', in *Selection of Reports and Papers of the House of Commons* (House of Commons, 1836), p. 108.

49 Evidence of Rev. Costello to a House of Commons committee, 1825 cited in Lewis (1836), p. 287.

50 Hall, Rev. James, *Tour through Ireland; Particularly the Interior and Least Known Parts*, Vol. I (R. P. Moore, London, 1813), p. 310.

51 Letter from magistrates of County Tipperary, 14 May 1825, Chief Secretary's Office Registered Papers, National Archives of Ireland (hereafter NAI), CSO/RP/SC/1825/436; Captain Brady to Major W. Miller, Constabulary Inspector-General for Munster, 25 June 1834, quoted in O'Donnell (1975), p. 152.

52 Evidence of Major Richard Willcocks to a House of Commons committee in 1824. Willcocks had been chief magistrate of police in counties Tipperary and Limerick. Cited in Lewis (1836), p. 283.

53 'Sean Burns', NFCS 0407: 513; 'Listowel Petty Sessions – Saturday. Constable Arthur v Peter Hurley', *The Kerry Evening Post*, 3 May 1871.

54 Garnham, Neal, 'Accounting for the Early Success of the Gaelic Athletic Association', *Irish Historical Studies*, Vol. 34, No. 133 (2004), p. 76.

55 Le Fanu, W. R., *Seventy Years of Irish Life* (Edward Arnold, London, 1893), p. 32.

56 *The Kerry Evening Post*, 13 May 1829. Emphasis in original.

57 Anon., *Leaves from my Note-Book ... by an Ex-Officer of the Royal Irish Constabulary* (Dean and Son, London, 1879), p. 68.

58 'Killorglin Fair of Puck', *The Kerry Evening Post*, 13 August 1870. 'Faction Fighting', NFCS 0357: 337–8.

59 O'Neill Daunt, William J., *Personal Recollections of the late Daniel O'Connell, MP*, Vol. I (Chapman and Hall, London, 1848), p. 47.

60 Bossy, John, 'The Counter-Reformation and the People of Catholic Ireland, 1596–1641', in Williams, T. D. (ed.), *Historical Studies VIII: Papers read before the Irish Conference of Historians 27–30 May 1969* (Gill and Macmillan, Dublin, 1971), p. 158.

61 O'Conner (1726), p. 19.

62 *Ibid.*, p. 14. 'A Pastoral in Imitation of the first Eclogue of Virgil, inscrib'd to the Provost and Fellows of T. C.'

63 Anon., 'O'Donoghue of the Glenns', *Tait's Edinburgh Magazine*, No. VI (1832), pp. 665–6; Mac Neill, Máire, *The Festival of Lughnasa* (Oxford University Press, London, 1962), p. 268.

64 Evidence of Robert Day, 'Minutes of Evidence taken before the Select Committee of the House of Lords, appointed to inquire into the State of Ireland ... 24 March–22 June, 1825', in *Selection of Reports and Papers of the House of Commons* (House of Commons, 1836), p. 532.

65 *Tralee Mercury*, 31 December 1831.

66 'The Emigrant's Return. A Legend of the South', *The Kerry Evening Post*, 6 July 1842. At the Battle of Callann in 1261, near the present-day village of Kilgarvan, the MacCarthys and their allies inflicted a famous defeat upon the Hiberno-Norman Fitzgeralds.

67 O'Conner (1726), p. 18.

68 Examination of Elizabeth O'Gormelly, TCD MS 838, Fols 214r–214v, and Examination of Ellizabeth Gormally, TCD MS 838, Fols 235r–235v, TCD, 1641. Depositions Project, online transcript, www.1641.tcd.ie.

69 Williams, N. J. A., *Pairlement Chloinne Tomáis* (Dublin Institute for Advanced Studies, Dublin, 1981), p. 45.
70 'An Act for the better Observation of the Lord's-Day, commonly called Sunday', 7 William III c.17.
71 MacLysaght, Edward, *Irish Life in the Seventeenth Century* (Cork University Press, Cork, 1950), p. 164.
72 Thomas Dineley, quoted in Cullen, L. M., 'Economic Development', in Moody, T. W. and Vaughan, W. E. (eds), *A New History of Ireland, Vol. IV: Eighteenth-Century Ireland 1691–1800* (Clarendon Press, Oxford, 1986), p. 176.
73 'Cáth Bearna Chroise Brighde' ('The Battle of the Gap of St Bridget's Cross'), trans. Mrs Nessa Doran, in McKay, Robert (ed.), *An Anthology of the Potato* (A. Figgis, Dublin, 1961), pp. 38–9.
74 O'Conner (1726), p. 19.
75 *Dublin Intelligence*, 10 June 1729, cited in Kelly, James, *The Liberty and Ormond Boys: Factional Riot in Eighteenth-Century Dublin* (Four Courts Press, Dublin, 2005), p. 21.
76 *The Freeman's Journal*, 24 September 1765.
77 *Ibid.*
78 Kelly (2005), p. 10.
79 Andrews, J. H., 'The French School of Dublin Land Surveyors', *Irish Geography*, Vol. 5, Issue 2 (1965), p. 282. The map is 'A Survey of Corballis being part of the Manor of Kilkea ... by John Rocque, 1760', plan 32.
80 'Country News', *Finn's Leinster Journal*, 31 August 1782.
81 Corish, Patrick J., *The Catholic Community in the Seventeenth and Eighteenth Centuries* (Helicon, Dublin, 1981), p. 112.
82 'Police Bill', (Belfast) *News Letter*, 24 March 1786.
83 Jupp, Peter and Magennis, Eoin, *Crowds in Ireland c. 1780–1920* (Macmillan Press, London, 2000), p. 6.

1 EARLY FACTION FIGHTING IN KERRY

1 'Old Kerry Records – Over One Hundred Years Ago. Summer Assizes 1762 – Sept 3', *The Kerry Evening Post*, 16 November 1864.
2 Corish (1981), p. 31.
3 Richard Hedges writing to Secretary Dawson in 1714, cited in Froude, James Anthony, *The English in Ireland in the Eighteenth Century*, Vol. I (Longmans, Green and Co., London, 1872), pp. 469–70.
4 O'Neill Daunt (1848), p. 194.
5 O'Conner (1726), p. 20.

6 Froude (1872), p. 470.
7 *The Nation* (Dublin), 10 January 1846.
8 'Old Kerry Records – Over One Hundred Years Ago. Summer Assizes 1762 – Sept 3', *The Kerry Evening Post*, 16 November 1864; 'Country News', *Saunders's News-Letter*, 13 September 1782.
9 'The Raid on Fuller's Cattle by Daniel Maurice O'Connell', *Kerry News*, 14 June 1935; 'Tadhg na (Stiall) Striall', NFCS 0474: 134.
10 Denis Casey (1766–1867). 'Longevity in Kerry', *The Freeman's Journal*, 20 March 1867.
11 Anon., 'O'Donoghue of the Glenns', pp. 665–6. 'Pattern': a patron day, held in celebration of a local saint, usually at the site of a holy well.
12 'Dreadful Affray and Wholesale Slaughter in Kerry', *The Standard* (London), 30 June 1834.
13 Ní Chinnéide, Síle, 'A New View of Eighteenth-Century Life in Kerry', *Journal of the Kerry Archaeological and Historical Society*, Vol. 6 (1973), p. 99.
14 'Old Kerry Records. (From *Anthologia Hibernica*, for October 1794). Extract of a letter from Tralee, September 24th', *The Kerry Evening Post*, 11 May 1870.
15 *The Times*, 31 August 1798.
16 'Faction Fights', NFCS 0444: 461.
17 Ferris, Fr William, *Fr. Ferris's Parish Histories: BallymacElligott, Ballyseedy, O'Brennan and Nohoval* (Cló Staire Chiarraí, Tralee, 2018), p. 161. 'Can': a pail of milk.
18 *The Times*, 18 August 1803.
19 *Carlisle Journal*, 9 March 1805.
20 Carr, John, *The Stranger in Ireland: or, a Tour in the Southern and Western Parts of that Country in the Year 1805* (Samuel F. Bradford, Philadelphia, 1806), p. 247. Emphasis in original.
21 *The Belfast Commercial Chronicle*, 28 June 1806.
22 *The Freeman's Journal*, 27 August 1806.
23 *The Freeman's Journal*, 21 February 1807. The fair was on 11 February (Saint Gobnait's Day).
24 *Saunders's News-Letter*, 1 July 1808.
25 'Village Factions', *The Freeman's Journal*, 16 June 1808. Emphasis in original. 'Career': a fast, meandering movement.
26 *Saunders's News-Letter*, 4 January 1810.
27 Stewart, Alexander and Revington, George (eds), *Memoir of the Life and Labours of the Rev Adam Averell* (Methodist Book Room, Dublin, 1848), pp. 322–3.

28 *The Freeman's Journal*, 25 June 1810. Emphasis in original.

29 *Saunders's News-Letter*, 20 October 1810.

30 Day to Maurice Fitzgerald, Knight of Kerry, Listowel, 15 April 1811, Public Record Office of Northern Ireland (hereafter PRONI) MIC639/5.

31 Letter from John Raymond, 20 May 1811, State of the Country Papers, NAI (hereafter SOC), 1384/11.

32 *The Belfast Commercial Chronicle*, 5 June 1811.

33 *The Freeman's Journal*, 26 June 1811.

34 'Swan shot': large-gauge ammunition used for shooting wildfowl.

35 *Chute's Western Herald*, 26 November 1812.

36 'Copies of Informations', made before John Day, 1813, SOC 1532/2.

37 *The Freeman's Journal*, 19 August 1813. The report was drawn from *The Kerry Evening Post*.

38 Foley, Kieran, *History of Killorglin* (Killorglin History and Folklore Society, Killorglin, 1988), p. 41.

39 Lawlor to Gregory, 26 July 1814, SOC 1553/30.

40 *The York Herald and General Advertiser*, 21 May 1814.

41 'Tralee, Jan 16', (Belfast) *News Letter*, 25 January 1814.

42 Culhane, Thomas F., 'Traditions of Glin and its Neighbourhood', *Journal of the Kerry Historical and Archaeological Society*, Vol. 2, 1969, p. 89.

43 *Ibid.* 'Seven guards' may have been defensive movements of the stick to protect the left or right side of the head, the left or right leg, the left or right ribs, and the top of the head – see Hurley, John W., *Fighting Irish: The Art of Irish Stick-Fighting* (Caravat Press, Philadelphia, 2018), pp. 53, 60–1.

44 Mac Síthigh, Tomás, *Paróiste an Fheirtéaraigh; Stairsheanchas an Cheantair i dtréimhse an Ghorta Mhóir* (Coiscéim, Baile Átha Cliath, 1984), p. 107.

45 *Chute's Western Herald*, 20 January 1820. Quoted in O'Donnell (1975), p. 184.

46 'Munster Circuit', *London Courier and Evening Gazette*, 30 March 1826.

2 THE COOLEENS AND THE LAWLORS

1 *Saunders's News-Letter*, 21 July 1829; 'Tarbert Petty Sessions', *The Kerry Evening Post*, 9 July 1859.

2 Letter from M. Fitzgerald, 2 July 1814, SOC 1553/29; Statement from Captain Chambre, 11th regiment, stationed at Listowel, 16 November 1825, SOC 2727/1.

3 NFCS 0415: 259–60; *Southern Reporter and Cork Commercial Courier*, 13 September 1825; 'Limerick, Nov 30', *The Dublin Evening Post*, 3

December 1825; *The Kerry Evening Post*, 21 October 1846; *The Belfast Commercial Chronicle*, 5 June 1811; 'Tralee Assizes', *Tralee Mercury*, 24 March 1830.

4 'Tralee Quarter Sessions', *The Kerry Evening Post*, 9 July 1834.

5 'Dublin, June 27. Dreadful Affray and Wholesale Slaughter in Kerry', *The Standard* (London), 30 June 1834.

6 'Riot at Ballyeagh. Investigation at Listowel', *Tralee Mercury*, 27 August 1834; 'Savage and Fatal Affray', *Limerick Chronicle*, 28 June 1834.

7 According to John Francis Hewson, magistrate and deputy lieutenant of the county. Hewson lived at Ennismore, near Listowel, and indicated that he knew both the area and its factions well. 'Riot at Ballyeagh. Investigation at Listowel', *Tralee Mercury*, 27 August 1834.

8 Herbert, E., 'The Cooleens and the Lawlors – The Story of a Faction Feud', in *The Irishman's Annual 1955* (Tralee, 1955), p. 28; NFCS 0416: 138.

9 'Summer in Ballybunnion. Sketches by J. A. O'C. The Faction Fight at Ballyeagh', *The Tralee Chronicle*, 25 September 1868. A 'curtain lecture' was a reprimand delivered by a wife to a husband in the privacy of their bedroom.

10 Ó Danachair (1966), p. 50.

11 Herbert (1955), p. 28.

12 'Gunsboro Petty Sessions', *The Tralee Chronicle*, 13 January 1865. Emphasis in original.

13 'The Ballyeagh Riot and Murders', *The Kerry Evening Post*, 3 September 1834.

14 Herbert (1955), p. 28.

15 'The Ballyeagh Fight', *The Kerryman*, 26 July 1924.

16 Herbert (1955), p. 28.

17 'Faction Fights. Culeens and Lawlors', NFCS 0415: 045.

18 'Notes on Ardfert, and Anecdotes of the Last Earl of Glandore', *The Tralee Chronicle*, 16 November 1869.

19 'Faction Fights', NFCS 0412: 027.

20 Culhane (1969), p. 90.

21 Gaughan, J. Anthony, *Listowel and its Vicinity* (Mercier Press, Cork, 1973), p. 191.

22 'The Ballyeagh Fight', *The Kerryman*, 26 July 1924.

23 *Ibid.*; 'Tralee Assizes', *The Kerry Evening Post*, 21 March 1835; 'Gunsboro Petty Sessions', *The Tralee Chronicle*, 13 January 1865.

24 'Summer in Ballybunnion. Sketches by J. A. O'C. The Faction Fight at Ballyeagh', *The Tralee Chronicle*, 25 September 1868.

25 'Tralee Assizes', *The Kerry Evening Post*, 21 March 1835. He was involved in a fight at Lixnaw in December 1828 – see *The Kerry Evening Post*, 13 May 1829.
26 'Old Kerry Records. Coroner's Inquest', *The Tralee Chronicle*, 29 May 1877, drawn from *The Kerry Weekly Reporter and Commercial Advertiser*, 1 July 1826.
27 *The Kerry Evening Post*, 13 May 1829. Emphasis in original.
28 'Quarter Sessions', *The Kerry Evening Post*, 9 May 1829.
29 'Tralee Assizes – Monday, Oct 15', *The Kerry Evening Post*, 17 October 1832.
30 (Belfast) *News Letter*, 16 December 1831, reprinted from *Limerick Chronicle*.
31 'Wilful Murder', *The Kerry Evening Post*, 10 December 1831.
32 *Chute's Western Herald*, 10 December 1831.
33 *The Kerry Evening Post*, 17 March 1832 and 'Tralee Assizes – Monday, Oct 15', 17 October 1832.
34 'The Ballyeagh Murders', *Cork Constitution*, 2 September 1834.
35 'Investigation at Listowel', *The Kerry Evening Post*, 23 November 1836.
36 *The Kerry Evening Post*, 19 February 1848.
37 'Listowel Quarter Sessions', *The Kerry Evening Post*, 27 October 1858.
38 'Notes on Ardfert, and Anecdotes of the Last Earl of Glandore', *The Tralee Chronicle*, 16 November 1869.
39 'A Tardy Tribute', *The Kerryman*, 6 July 1929.
40 *Chute's Western Herald*, 14 June 1832.
41 *The Kerry Evening Post*, 14 July 1832.
42 'Desperate Riot – Attack on the Police', *The Cork Examiner*, 5 June 1846.
43 'Distribution of the Constabulary', *The Kerry Evening Post*, 12 September 1857.
44 NFCS 0404: 351.
45 *Chute's Western Herald*, 8 January 1829. Emphasis in original.
46 'Tralee Assizes', *The Kerry Evening Post*, 25 March 1829.
47 'Tralee Quarter Sessions', *Tralee Mercury*, 13 April 1839.
48 'Faction Fighting', NFCS 0406: 395.
49 'Notes from Asdee and District. Aonach an Bheil', *The Kerryman*, 15 September 1928.
50 NFCS 0405: 288.
51 *The Belfast Commercial Chronicle*, 28 June 1806; *The York Herald and General Advertiser*, 21 May 1814.
52 NFCS 0404: 351–2.
53 'Letter to the editor, by "Faucon"', *The Kerry Evening Post*, 17 December 1828.

54 *Tralee Mercury*, 28 July 1832.
55 'Strong man', NFCS 0405: 163.
56 'Historical Sketches of Abbeyfeale', *The Kerryman*, 1 April 1916.
57 'Local Heroes', NFCS 0405: 617.
58 'Sean Burns', NFCS 0407: 514.
59 '"Shown" Burns' Prowess', *The Kerryman*, 15 April 1916.
60 'Shóne (Byrnes) Burns', NFCS 0494: 234.
61 *Ibid.*
62 'Seón Burns', NFCS 0410: 203.
63 'Seán Burns the Strong Man', NFCS 0491: 227–8.
64 '"Shown" Burns' Prowess', *The Kerryman*, 15 April 1916.
65 'Tralee Assizes – Monday, Oct 15', *The Kerry Evening Post*, 17 October 1832.
66 *The Kerry Weekly Reporter and Commercial Advertiser*, 28 March 1908: 'Shawn Burns, who died about 35 years ago'.
67 'Weight-throwing and Wrestling', NFCS 0406: 413–14.
68 Ó Danachair (1966), pp. 51–2.
69 Culhane (1969), pp. 91–2.
70 'Keane of Lybes', NFCS 0406: 392.
71 'Great Wrestlers', NFCS 0406: 415–16.
72 'Faction Fighting', NFCS 0406: 395–6.
73 'The Ballyeagh Fight', *The Kerryman*, 26 July 1924.
74 'Listowel Petty Sessions – Saturday. Constable Arthur v Peter Hurley', *The Kerry Evening Post*, 3 May 1871. A comforter was a scarf, usually made of wool.
75 Verses in Irish from Culhane (1969), p. 91. English translation by Jim O'Malley.

3 THE BATTLE OF BALLYEAGH, 1834

1 'Summer in Ballybunnion. Sketches by J. A. O'C. The Faction Fight at Ballyeagh', *The Tralee Chronicle*, 25 September 1868. The writer stated in a previous article: 'I think it necessary to say, that I have gleaned the facts relating to the fight from various sources and from prominent members of both parties', *The Tralee Chronicle*, 8 September 1868.
2 'Riot at Ballyeagh. Investigation at Listowel', *Tralee Mercury*, 27 August 1834.
3 'The Ballyeagh Riot and Murders', *The Kerry Evening Post*, 27 August 1834. Account reprinted from the *Limerick Herald*.
4 *The Kerry Evening Post*, 27 June 1832.

5 'The Ballyeagh Riot and Murders', *The Kerry Evening Post*, 3 September 1834.
6 'Riot at Ballyeagh. Investigation at Listowel', *Tralee Mercury*, 27 August 1834.
7 'Summer in Ballybunnion. Sketches by J. A. O'C.', *The Tralee Chronicle*, 11 September 1868. Emphasis in original.
8 *The Kerry Evening Post*, 17 October 1832. Emphasis in original.
9 'Summer in Ballybunnion. Sketches by J. A. O'C. The Faction Fight at Ballyeagh', *The Tralee Chronicle*, 25 September 1868. Hewson too noted that 'upon the occasion of "great fights", they are reinforced by bodies from the counties of Limerick and Clare' – see 'Riot at Ballyeagh. Investigation at Listowel', *The Tralee Chronicle*, 27 August 1834.
10 'The Ballyeagh Riot and Murders', *Tralee Mercury*, 3 September 1834.
11 'The Ballyeagh Riot and Murders', *The Kerry Evening Post*, 3 September 1834. Emphasis in original.
12 *Ibid.*
13 'Riot at Ballyeagh. Investigation at Listowel', *Tralee Mercury*, 27 August 1834.
14 *Ibid.*
15 *Ibid.*
16 NFCS 0416: 140.
17 'Kerry Assizes', *Tralee Mercury*, 28 March 1835.
18 'Riot at Ballyeagh. Investigation at Listowel', *Tralee Mercury*, 27 August 1834.
19 'The Ballyeagh Murders', *Cork Constitution*, 2 September 1834: 'In the early part of the day the Lawlors, it seems, tried to help their superior numbers by generalship, and concealed a part of their force in ambuscade behind a bank.'
20 'Riot at Ballyeagh. Investigation at Listowel', *Tralee Mercury*, 27 August 1834.
21 *Ibid.*
22 'The Ballyeagh Riot and Murders', *The Kerry Evening Post*, 27 August 1834.
23 'The Ballyeagh Riot and Murders', *Tralee Mercury*, 3 September 1834.
24 'The Ballyeagh Riot and Murders', *The Kerry Evening Post*, 27 August 1834.
25 O'Donnell (1975), p. 143.
26 'Riot at Ballyeagh. Investigation at Listowel', *Tralee Mercury*, 27 August 1834.

27 'The Ballyeagh Riot and Murders', *The Kerry Evening Post*, 3 September 1834.

28 'Riot at Ballyeagh. Investigation at Listowel', *Tralee Mercury*, 27 August 1834.

29 'Summer in Ballybunnion. Sketches by J. A. O'C. The Faction Fight at Ballyeagh', *The Tralee Chronicle*, 25 September 1868. 'Lighter': a type of flat-bottomed boat.

30 *Ibid.*

31 'County Election', *The Kerry Evening Post*, 14 July 1841.

32 O'Conner (1726), p. 20.

33 Mc Coluim, Fionán, 'An Old Man's Memories', *Béaloideas*, Iml. 4, Uimh 2 (1933), p. 180. The remark was made in relation to Co. Roscommon.

34 'Tralee Assizes', *The Kerry Evening Post*, 21 March 1835.

35 'Dreadful Faction-Fight and Loss of Life. Thirty-Five Men Killed', *The Waterford Mail*, 2 July 1834, reprinted from the *Limerick Herald*.

36 'Summer in Ballybunnion. Sketches by J. A. O'C. The Faction Fight at Ballyeagh', *The Tralee Chronicle*, 25 September 1868.

37 'The Fight of Ballyeagh 1834', NFCS 0400: 180. Paddy Hackett was portrayed afterwards as a leader of the Cooleens ('Summer in Ballybunnion. Sketches by J. A. O'C. The Faction Fight at Ballyeagh', *The Tralee Chronicle*, 25 September 1868) and according to a much later account by a folklore interviewee, his grandfather, a Cooleen, accompanied Hackett to the fight (NFCS 0416: 140). Another folklore source related that one of the men who died as a result of the fight, Sylvester Ahern, was one of the leaders of the Cooleens ('The Fight of Ballyeagh 1834', NFCS 0400: 181).

38 O'Donnell (1975), p. 145; 'Kerry Assizes – Convictions', *Tralee Mercury*, 16 March 1836.

39 O'Donnell (1975), p. 146.

40 *Ibid.*, pp. 144–5.

41 'Riot at Ballyeagh. Investigation at Listowel', *Tralee Mercury*, 27 August 1834.

42 'Summer in Ballybunnion. Sketches by J. A. O'C. The Faction Fight at Ballyeagh', *The Tralee Chronicle*, 25 September 1868.

43 'Riot at Ballyeagh. Investigation at Listowel', *Tralee Mercury*, 27 August 1834.

44 *Ibid.*

45 'The Ballyeagh Riot and Murders', *The Kerry Evening Post*, 27 August 1834.

46 Captain Brady to Major W. Miller, Constabulary Inspector-General for Munster, 25 June 1834, cited in O'Donnell (1975), p. 152.

47 'Riot at Ballyeagh. Investigation at Listowel', *Tralee Mercury*, 27 August 1834.

48 'The Fight of Ballyeagh 1834', NFCS 0400: 181.

49 'The Ballyeagh Riot and Murders', *The Kerry Evening Post*, 3 September 1834.

50 'Riot at Ballyeagh. Investigation at Listowel', *Tralee Mercury*, 27 August 1834.

51 'Barbarous and Disgraceful Riot, and Loss of Lives', *The Kerry Evening Post*, 28 June 1834.

52 'Riot at Ballyeagh. Investigation at Listowel', *Tralee Mercury*, 27 August 1834.

53 'Summer in Ballybunnion. Sketches by J. A. O'C. The Faction Fight at Ballyeagh', *The Tralee Chronicle*, 25 September 1868.

54 'Riot at Ballyeagh. Investigation at Listowel', *Tralee Mercury*, 27 August 1834.

55 'Savage and Fatal Affray', *Limerick Chronicle*, 28 June 1834; 'Riot at Ballyeagh. Investigation at Listowel', *Tralee Mercury*, 27 August 1834.

56 'The Ballyeagh Riot and Murders', *The Kerry Evening Post*, 3 September 1834.

57 'Barbarous and Disgraceful Riot and Loss of Lives', *The Kerry Evening Post*, 28 June 1834.

58 'Riot at Ballyeagh. Investigation at Listowel', *Tralee Mercury*, 27 August 1834.

59 'Summer in Ballybunnion. Sketches by J. A. O'C. The Faction Fight at Ballyeagh', *The Tralee Chronicle*, 25 September 1868.

60 Matheson, Steve, *Maurice Walsh, Storyteller* (Brandon Books, Dingle, 1985), p. 15.

61 'Summer in Ballybunnion. Sketches by J. A. O'C. The Faction Fight at Ballyeagh', *The Tralee Chronicle*, 25 September 1868.

62 Ó Danachair (1966), p. 51.

63 'Summer in Ballybunnion. Sketches by J. A. O'C. The Faction Fight at Ballyeagh', *The Tralee Chronicle*, 25 September 1868.

64 'Riot at Ballyeagh. Investigation at Listowel', *Tralee Mercury*, 27 August 1834.

65 'Summer in Ballybunnion. Sketches by J. A. O'C. The Faction Fight at Ballyeagh', *The Tralee Chronicle*, 25 September 1868.

66 'The Ballyeagh Riot and Murders', *The Kerry Evening Post*, 3 September 1834.

67 'Riot at Ballyeagh. Investigation at Listowel', *Tralee Mercury*, 27 August 1834.
68 'Tralee Assizes', *The Kerry Evening Post*, 21 March 1835.
69 Ó Danachair (1966), pp. 49–51.
70 'Late Dreadful Conflict. From the Kerry Evening Post', *Chute's Western Herald*, 7 July 1834.
71 'Tralee Assizes', *The Kerry Evening Post*, 21 March 1835.
72 *Ibid.* Emphasis in original.
73 *Ibid.*
74 *Ibid.*
75 O'Donnell (1975), p. 146.
76 'The Ballyeigh Fight', NFCS 0401: 112; 'The Ballyeagh Fight', *The Kerryman*, 26 July 1924.
77 'Seán Burns', NFCS 0407: 513.
78 'The Ballyeagh Fight', *The Kerryman*, 26 July 1924.
79 Captain Brady to Major W. Miller, Constabulary Inspector-General for Munster, 25 June 1834, cited in O'Donnell (1975), p. 152.
80 'The Ballyeagh Riot and Murders', *The Kerry Evening Post*, 3 September 1834.
81 'Riot at Ballyeagh. Investigation at Listowel', *Tralee Mercury,* 27 August 1834.
82 *Ibid.*
83 *Ibid.*
84 *Ibid.*
85 'The Ballyeagh Riot and Murders', *The Kerry Evening Post*, 3 September 1834.
86 NFCS 0416: 141–2.
87 'The Ballyeagh Riot and Murders', *The Kerry Evening Post*, 3 September 1834.
88 'Riot at Ballyeagh. Investigation at Listowel', *Tralee Mercury*, 27 August 1834.
89 'Dreadful Affray', *Tralee Mercury*, 25 June 1834.
90 'The Late Riot at Ballyhea', *Tralee Mercury*, 2 July 1834.
91 'Barbarous and Disgraceful Riot and Loss of Lives', *The Kerry Evening Post*, 28 June 1834.
92 'The Late Riot at Ballyhea', *Tralee Mercury*, 2 July 1834.
93 'The Fight of Ballyeagh 1834', NFCS 0400: 181; O'Donnell (1975), p. 148.
94 'The Ballyheagh Murders', *Reading Mercury, Oxford Gazette and Berkshire County Paper*, 14 July 1834.

95 'Barbarous and Disgraceful Riot and Loss of Lives', *The Kerry Evening Post*, 28 June 1834.
96 'Tralee Assizes', *The Kerry Evening Post*, 21 March 1835.
97 'The Fight of Ballyeagh 1834', NFCS 0400: 181.
98 'The Ballyeagh Riot and Murders', *The Kerry Evening Post*, 3 September 1834.
99 'Riot at Ballyeagh. Investigation at Listowel', *Tralee Mercury*, 27 August 1834; 'Ireland (From our own Correspondent). Government Inquiry into the Ballyheagh Murders', *The Times*, 28 August 1834.
100 'Riot at Ballyeagh. Investigation at Listowel', *Tralee Mercury*, 27 August 1834.
101 'Faction Fights. Culeens and Lawlors', NFCS 0415: 045, 046.
102 'Prisoners in Custody for Trial at the Next Assizes', *The Kerry Evening Post*, 28 February 1835.
103 *The Kerry Evening Post*, 6 September 1834 and 25 February 1835.
104 'Faction Fights. Culeens and Lawlors', NFCS 0415: 045; Smith, Babette, *The Luck of the Irish: How a Shipload of Convicts Survived the Wreck of the Hive to Make a New Life in Australia* (Allen & Unwin, Sydney, 2014), p. 17.
105 'Local Happenings', NFCS 0416: 160–1.
106 *Chute's Western Herald*, 23 March 1835. This newspaper named him as Thomas Leahy.
107 *The Kerry Evening Post*, 6 May 1835.
108 *Ibid.*, 13 May 1835.
109 *The Monitor* (Sydney), 19 December 1835.
110 'Tralee Assizes', *The Kerry Evening Post*, 21 March 1835.
111 *Cork Constitution*, 26 August 1834.
112 'Kerry Assizes', *The Kerry Evening Post*, 25 July 1835.
113 'Kerry Assizes. Crown Court – Monday, July 27', *The Kerry Evening Post*, 29 July 1835.
114 'Viceregal Clemency – The Ballyeagh Rioters', *The Freeman's Journal*, 22 April 1836.
115 'Sequel to Culeen-Lawlor Faction fight', NFCS 0415: 047.
116 'Conditional Pardons', *The Sydney Morning Herald*, 10 January 1849.
117 'Great Moral Revolution', *The Freeman's Journal*, 24 August 1840.
118 John Flaherty, 'The early, bloody years of racing in North Kerry', *The Kerryman*, 23 September 1977.
119 *The Wexford Conservative*, 3 December 1834.
120 *Limerick Chronicle*, 14 September 1836.

121 'O'Connell – Precursor Society in Listowel', *Tralee Mercury*, 23 January 1839.

122 Hall and Hall (1841), p. 44.

123 'Listowel Petty Sessions – Saturday. Faction Fighting', *The Tralee Chronicle*, 5 November 1867.

124 'Faction Fights. Culeens and Lawlors', NFCS 0415: 046. The 'night of the big wind' refers to a terrific storm that struck Ireland on 6 January 1839. The 'year the boat was drowned' recalls the massacre at the Ballyeagh shore.

4 ELECTION RIOTS AND FACTION FIGHTS

1 'Kerry Election. Great Meeting at Abbeydorney', *The Kerry Examiner*, 13 July 1841.

2 'County of Kerry. Number of Freeholders in the County of Kerry entitled to vote at the Election of Members of Parliament' in *Estimates, Accounts and Papers relating to Ireland, Session 3 February to 6 July 1825*, Vol. XXII (House of Commons, 1825), p. 6. (40s = 5,537. Other voters: £20 = 438, £50 and upwards = 741, total: 6,716.)

3 Palmer, Stanley H., *Police and Protest in England and Ireland 1780–1850* (Cambridge University Press, Cambridge, 1988), p. 272.

4 'Working of the Reform Act – Intimidation by Landlords', *The Spectator* (London), 5 December 1835.

5 *Ibid.*

6 *Ibid.*

7 Barrington, Sir Jonah, *Personal Sketches of His Own Times*, Vol. I (Henry Colburn and Richard Bentley, London, 1832), p. 5.

8 'Irish Elections', *Bell's Life in London and Sporting Chronicle*, 2 July 1826.

9 'The General Election. Election Anecdotes', *The Atlas* (London), 23 December 1832.

10 'Kerry Election. Dreadful Affray – Several Persons Killed and Wounded', *Southern Reporter and Cork Commercial Courier*, 27 June 1826; 'From a Kerry paper. Tralee, June 29', *The Freeman's Journal*, 5 July 1826.

11 'Old Kerry Records. Coroner's Inquest', *The Tralee Chronicle*, 29 May 1877, drawn from the *Kerry Advertiser*, 1 July 1826.

12 'From a Kerry paper. Tralee, June 29', *The Freeman's Journal*, 5 July 1826.

13 'Kerry Election. Dreadful Affray – Several Persons Killed and Wounded', *Southern Reporter and Cork Commercial Courier*, 27 June 1826.

14 'From a Kerry paper. Tralee, June 29', *The Freeman's Journal*, 5 July 1826.

15 *Ibid.* Corkaguiny is the area of the Dingle peninsula.

16 'Old Kerry Records. Coroner's Inquest', *The Tralee Chronicle*, 29 May 1877.
17 'Dreadful Affray in Kerry – The Coroner's Inquest', *Cork Constitution*, 4 July 1826.
18 *Ibid.*
19 *Ibid.*
20 'The Election – Dreadful Affray', *Cork Constitution*, 1 July 1826.
21 'Old Kerry Records. 1826', *The Tralee Chronicle*, 20 March 1877.
22 'Old Kerry Records. Coroner's Inquest', *The Tralee Chronicle*, 29 May 1877.
23 Cronin, Maura, 'Popular Politics, 1815–1845', in Kelly, James (ed.), *The Cambridge History of Ireland 1730–1880*, Vol. III (Cambridge University Press, Cambridge, 2018), p. 129.
24 McElroy, Martin, 'The Impact of the Parliamentary Elections (Ireland) Act (1829) on the Irish electorate *c.* 1829–1832', in Blackstick, Allan and Magennis, Eoin (eds), *Politics and Political Culture in Britain and Ireland 1750–1850* (Ulster Historical Foundation, Belfast, 2007), p. 35.
25 *The Kerry Evening Post*, 27 April 1831.
26 'A New Song in Praise of Our Favourite Candidates, of Tralee'. See Broadside Ballads Online, http://ballads.bodleian.ox.ac.uk/view/edition/22442.
27 Lyne, Gerard J., 'Daniel O'Connell, Intimidation and the Kerry Elections of 1835', *Journal of the Kerry Historical and Archaeological Society*, Vol. 4 (1971), p. 82.
28 'Kerry Election Petition', *Tralee Mercury*, 28 November 1835. Mr Brownrigg, a witness at a later inquiry, also said he had heard these words spoken – see 'The Late Kerry Election. Minutes of evidence taken before Select Committee on Bribery at Elections', *Tralee Mercury*, 9 December 1835.
29 'Kerry Election Petition', *Tralee Mercury*, 28 November 1835.
30 'The Late Kerry Election', *Tralee Mercury*, 16 December 1835.
31 Letters and papers of Maurice FitzGerald, Knight of Kerry, PRONI MIC639/8. Copy of 'The Patriot's Curse'.
32 'The Late Borough Election – Glorious Triumph', *Tralee Mercury*, 27 May 1835.
33 'County and Borough Elections', *The Kerry Evening Post*, 9 August 1837.
34 *The Kerry Evening Post*, 23 August 1837.
35 'County Election', *The Kerry Evening Post*, 14 July 1841.
36 'Kerry Election. Great Meeting at Abbeydorney', *The Kerry Examiner*, 13 July 1841.

37 'County Election', *The Kerry Evening Post*, 14 July 1841.
38 *Ibid.*
39 Ponsonby stood unsuccessfully for the Conservatives in the county election of 1835. 'Irish Elections. County Kerry', (Belfast) *News Letter*, 27 January 1835.
40 'Milltown Petit Sessions. Election Riots', *The Kerry Evening Post*, 28 August 1841.
41 'Limerick Assizes', *Limerick Chronicle*, 9 March 1836.
42 'Tralee. Riot Between the Followers of the Rival Candidates', *The Cork Examiner*, 24 March 1880.
43 O'Keefe, Jeremiah, 'A Shameful Day in History of Kerry', *The Liberator* (Tralee), 27 January 1917.
44 *The Kerry Evening Post*, 30 October 1833.
45 *The Belfast Commercial Chronicle*, 10 July 1809.
46 'Old Reminiscences of Tralee', *The Kerry Evening Post*, 30 May 1868.
47 'Johnston's Express and the Evening Mail', *The Kerry Evening Post*, 27 February 1836.
48 'Dreadful effects of Drunkenness and factious Riot', *Chute's Western Herald*, 9 November 1822.
49 *The Kerry Evening Post*, 21 January 1846.
50 *The Kerry Evening Post*, 12 January 1831. Emphases in original.
51 *The Kerry Evening Post*, 16 August 1856.
52 'The Bishop of Kerry and the Magistrates', *The Nation* (Dublin), 20 September 1856, reprinted from *The Tablet*, London.
53 'Tralee Petty Sessions', *The Tralee Chronicle*, 29 August 1856.
54 *The Tralee Chronicle*, 12 September 1856.
55 *The Kerry Evening Post*, 27 August 1856.
56 'Tralee Petty Sessions', *The Tralee Chronicle*, 29 August 1856.
57 *Ibid.*
58 *The Kerry Evening Post*, 27 August 1856.

5 THE GEARALTAIGH AND THE DAITHÍNIGH

1 Aodhagán O'Rahilly (*c.* 1675–1726). See 'Fiadnéid Aodagáin' ['Egan's Testimony'], in Dineen, Patrick S. (ed.), *Dánta Aodagáin Uí Rataille; the Poems of Egan O'Rahilly* (Irish Texts Society, London, 1911), p. 285.
2 *Saunders's News-Letter*, 17 October 1820.
3 'Faction Fighting', NFCS 0446: 419. Irish language material translated by Thomas O'Sullivan.
4 'Comhairle Uilig Uí Chéirín'. Audio recording made in 1928 by Dr

Wilhelm Doegen. See The Doegen Records Web Project of the Royal Irish Academy, www.doegen.ie.

5 'Limerick Assizes', *Limerick Chronicle*, 9 March 1836.

6 Culhane (1969), pp. 91–2; 'Death at Faction Fight', *Limerick Leader*, 30 November 1968.

7 'Limerick Assizes', *Limerick Chronicle*, 9 March 1836.

8 *Limerick Chronicle*, 29 June 1836.

9 *Limerick Chronicle*, 25 January 1840.

10 *The Kerry Evening Post*, 8 January 1845; *The Kerry Examiner*, 30 June 1848; 'Castleisland Fair', *The Tralee Chronicle*, 4 August 1854.

11 *The Kerry Evening Post*, 21 May 1853.

12 'Mat the Herder', NFCS 0410: 165.

13 'Buffer': a self-important individual. See Share, Bernard, *Slanguage* (Gill and Macmillan, Dublin, 2003), p. 44.

14 'Mat the Herder', NFCS 0410: 165.

15 'Mat the Herder', NFCS 0410: 166.

16 *Ibid.*

17 From the Irish *triail*: test.

18 'Mat the Herder', NFCS 0410: 167–9.

19 'Currens Fair', NFCS 0445: 132–3.

20 'Club Law', *Tralee Mercury*, 12 May 1830. Letter by 'Anti Club Law'.

21 'The Pleasures of Imagination', *The Kerry Evening Post*, 9 June 1838.

22 'Tralee Quarter Sessions', *The Kerry Evening Post*, 27 June 1860.

23 'Faction Fights', NFCS 0444: 461.

24 'The Faction Fight at Clogher', NFCS 0443: 101–3.

25 'Faction Fighting', NFCS 0494: 152.

26 'The Fair Field', NFCS 0494: 230.

27 'The Faction Fights', NFCS 0494: 231.

28 *Ibid.* Note: punctuation of the original has been corrected slightly here.

29 'Faction Fighting in Kerry. Desperate Conflict with the Police', *Lincolnshire Echo*, 10 October 1895.

30 'The Story of the Knocknagoshel Pattern', NFCS 0450: 077.

31 'Brosna Petty Sessions', *The Kerry Weekly Reporter and Commercial Advertiser*, 8 September 1900.

32 'Tralee Quarter Sessions', *The Kerry Evening Post*, 3 November 1832.

33 *Limerick Chronicle*, 12 January 1833.

34 'Convictions at the Quarter Sessions of the Peace for the Division of Tralee', *The Kerry Evening Post*, 12 January 1833.

35 *Máire Mór na Muinge*: Big Mary of the Marsh.

36 'Faction Fight', NFCS 0494: 151.

37 *Ibid.*

38 Anon., 'O'Donoghue of the Glenns', pp. 665–6.

39 'Longevity in Kerry', *The Freeman's Journal*, 20 March 1867; 'Old Kerry. Octogenarian writes again', *Kerry Sentinel*, 19 February 1896.

40 'Faction Fight', *The Kerry Evening Post*, 26 November 1845.

41 'Old Fighting Tinkers', NFCS 0451: 353–4.

42 *Ibid.*

43 *The Kerry Evening Post*, 29 August 1829.

44 'Faction Fighting at Castleisland', *The Kerry Evening Post*, 14 October 1893.

45 'Song of Cordal', NFCS 0449: 093.

46 'One of the O'Keefes was named David or Daithi and from him the Daithinigh got their name' – see 'Faction Fighting', NFCS 0357: 332. The Daithínigh may also have been called the Dhawheens – see 'Mallow Quarter Sessions – Tuesday', *The Cork Examiner*, 25 October 1858.

47 Mac Neill (1962), p. 269.

48 'Faction Fighting', NFCS 0452: 324.

49 'Na Daithinnigh agus na Gearaltaigh', NFCS 0451: 059.

50 NFCS 0358: 510.

51 'Faction Fighting', NFCS 0451: 408.

52 *Ibid.*

53 NFCS 0451: 059; 'Na Daithinnigh agus na Gearaltaigh', NFCS 0358: 510.

54 *Chute's Western Herald*, 25 August 1834.

55 *Ibid.*

56 '*Cláirín*': short stave. '*Cleath-ailpín*': knobstick.

57 NFCS 0358: 511.

58 'Faction Fighting', NFCS 0357: 332.

59 'Faction Fighting', NFCS 0357: 337–8.

60 Daniel MacDonald's 'The Fighter' can be seen in O'Sullivan, Niamh, *In the Lion's Den: Daniel MacDonald, Ireland and Empire* (Quinnipiac University Press, Hamden, Connecticut, 2016).

61 A differing account says that 'the Russian' was a man named Diarmaid Liam Sheehan. See 'Na Daithinnigh agus na Gearaltaigh', NFCS 0451: 059. It quoted a poem in Irish by Micheal Mór Moynihan praising Sheehan for his ability to put the fear of God into the opposition and comparing him rather grandly to Julius Caesar. (Information drawn from the poem by Thomas O'Sullivan.)

62 NFC 407: 281.

63 'Faction Fighting', NFCS 0357: 333.
64 'Local Songs' NFCS 0357: 324.
65 'Faction Fighting', NFCS 0357: 333.
66 'Faction Fighting', NFCS 0358: 511; 0357: 334.
67 NFC 266: 66.
68 'Faction Fighting', NFCS 0357: 336.
69 'Baffety': baft was a coarse cloth much used in men's clothing.
70 'Baitín': cudgel. '"A Botheen Boy" was and is applied to a rowdy whose cudgel and martial services could be hired.' – see 'Ashplant rowdies', NFCS 266: 14–15.
71 NFCS 0357: 334.
72 *Ibid.*
73 'Troda Móra', NFCS 0451: 417. Translated by Thomas O'Sullivan.
74 *Ibid.* 'Tawneys': the brown-skinned.
75 NFCS 0358: 510–1.
76 'A story about a tyrant', NFCS 0451: 402.
77 'Faction Fighting', NFCS 0357: 332.
78 'Faction Fighting', NFCS 0357: 332–3.
79 'Faction Fights', NFCS 0358: 509.
80 'Faction Fighting', NFCS 0357: 338.
81 'The Riot at Six-Mile Bridge,' *The Tralee Chronicle*, 27 September 1859. Some punctuation in this extract has been corrected.
82 'Killarney Petty Sessions – Wednesday', *The Tralee Chronicle*, 27 September 1859.
83 'Faction Fighting', NFCS 0357: 337. The folklore interviewee may be recalling the fight of September 1859, and the men's sentencing in October, as there does not appear to be any newspaper report which tallies with such events in 1860.
84 'Faction Fighting', NFCS 0357: 338.
85 'Kerry Intelligence', *The Cork Examiner*, 22 September 1869. The text as presented has been edited slightly.
86 'A Serious Faction Fight Suppressed', *The Cork Examiner*, 10 June 1873.
87 NFCS 0358: 482.
88 NFCS 0358: 509. The All for Ireland League was established by William O'Brien MP in 1909 to advance a moderate campaign for Irish Home Rule based upon a conciliatory approach towards Unionists, while the established Irish Parliamentary Party, led by John Redmond MP, was the popular standard-bearer of nationalist Ireland.
89 NFCS 0358: 482.

90 NFCS 0358: 483.

6 'THE SAVAGE CONFLICTS OF BARBAROUS MOBS'

1 Evidence of James Shaw Kennedy, 'Report from the Select Committee of the House of Lords, appointed to inquire into the State of Ireland in respect of crime ... Part I', in *Reports from Committees State of Ireland: Crime*, Vol. XI (House of Commons, 1839), p. 43.

2 Corish (1981), p. 31; Froude (1872), pp. 469–70.

3 O'Conner (1726), p. 20.

4 Explained by the writer as 'Larry of the Jaw or Cheek'. Copper mining was carried on at Ross Island from about 1750.

5 Anon., 'O'Donoghue of the Glenns', p. 665.

6 *Ibid.*, p. 666.

7 'Killarney Sessions. Important Trial', *The Kerry Evening Post*, 29 April 1829.

8 'Killarney Sessions', *The Kerry Evening Post*, 13 January 1830.

9 von Pückler-Muskau (1832), p. 295.

10 *The Mail* (Waterford), 10 January 1824.

11 *The Globe* (London), 30 October 1827, from a report in *Limerick Chronicle*; 'Tralee, October 27', *The Dublin Weekly* Register, 3 November 1827.

12 'Crubeens': salted pigs' feet.

13 'Squireen': a middleman, often a native Catholic Irishman, who rented large tracts of land from a landlord and sublet to tenant farmers at rents sufficient to allow him to live a life of some leisure and comfort. Traveller Caesar Otway met a poor man near Kenmare, who praised Lord Lansdowne who 'permits no middlemen to set and re-set over and over again, his estate – he allows no Jack of a Squireen to be riding in top-boots over the country, drinking and carousing on the profits of the ground, while the poor racked tenant is forced, with all his labour, often to go barefooted, and often to live and work on a meal of dry potatoes' – see Otway, Caesar, *Sketches in Ireland* (William Curry, Dublin, 1827), pp. 406–7. A 'Caroline hat' was a type of fur hat.

14 Croker, T. Crofton, *Legends of the Lakes*, Vol. II (John Ebers, London, 1829). Abstracted from pp. 24–8.

15 Anon., *Paddiana; or, Scraps and Sketches of Irish Life, Present and Past*, Vol. I (Richard Bentley, London, 1847), pp. 224–5. Emphasis in original.

16 von Pückler-Muskau (1832), pp. 295–6.

17 'The Championship', *Tralee Mercury*, 16 June 1830.

18 'Dreadful and Alarming Riot in Killarney', *The Kerry Evening Post*, 26 June 1833.

19 *Ibid.*
20 *Tralee Mercury*, 3 July 1833.
21 *Ibid.*
22 *The Kerry Evening Post*, 22 July 1829; *Tralee Mercury*, 31 December 1831; 'Tralee Quarter Sessions', *The Kerry Evening Post*, 3 November 1832.
23 'Killarney Sessions – March 29. Extraordinary & Interesting Case', *Tralee Mercury*, 3 April 1833. Emphasis in original.
24 'Convictions at Killarney January Sessions, 1829', *The Kerry Evening Post*, 14 January 1829.
25 *The Kerry Evening Post*, 25 July 1829.
26 Croker (1829), pp. 58–9.
27 *The Kerry Evening Post*, 3 April 1830.
28 *Chute's Western Herald*, 15 April 1830; *The Kerry Evening Post*, 31 December 1831.
29 *The Kerry Evening Post*, 29 December 1832.
30 *The Kerry Evening Post*, 1 January 1834.
31 'Riots at Killarney', *The Kerry Evening Post*, 25 January 1834. Some punctuation has been omitted or amended here, in line with modern usage. Emphasis in original.
32 'Killarney Sessions' Court', *Tralee Mercury*, 28 June 1834.
33 *The Kerry Evening Post*, 9 July 1834.
34 *Ibid.*
35 'Killarney Fair', *The Kerry Evening Post*, 8 July 1835.
36 *The Kerry Evening Post*, 13 June 1835.
37 *The Kerry Evening Post*, 28 October 1835.
38 'Killarney Sessions', *The Kerry Evening Post*, 17 October 1835.
39 'Killarney Fair. Dreadful Riot', *The Kerry Evening Post*, 15 August 1835.
40 *Ibid.*
41 *The Kerry Evening Post*, 28 October 1835.
42 'The Chairmanship of Kerry', *The Kerry Evening Post*, 30 December 1835.
43 'Killarney Fair', *The Kerry Evening Post*, 8 July 1835.
44 'A Sanguinary Faction Fight in Killarney', *The Kerry Evening Post*, 11 January 1888.
45 'Local Heroes', NFCS 0457: 228. Dan T. subsequently perished during the Famine 'and was buried without a coffin'.
46 Evidence of James Shaw Kennedy, 'Report from the Select Committee of the House of Lords, appointed to inquire into the State of Ireland in respect of crime ... Part I', in *Reports from Committees State of Ireland:*

Crime, Vol. XI (House of Commons, 1839), p. 43. (I take his comment to mean 3,000 in total.)

47 'Knut Jongbohm Clement (1839)', in Burke, Eoin (ed.), '*Poor Green Erin*': *German Travel Writers' Narratives on Ireland from Before the 1798 Rising to After the Great Famine* (Peter Lang, Frankfurt am Main, 2011), p. 300.

48 'Sketches of Scenery in the South of Ireland', *The Kerry Evening Post*, 20 January 1841, reproduced from the *Westmorland Gazette*. Fr Theobald Mathew led the popular mass temperance movement of the time; a 'drop of the creatur' represented an affectionate phrase for a glass of *poitín* or whiskey.

49 'Killarney Races', *The Kerry Evening Post*, 17 August 1844.

50 *The Kerry Evening Post*, 2 April 1845.

51 Possibly signifying Sullivans from Brackhill, Castlemaine.

52 *The Kerry Evening Post*, 31 December 1845. 'Caubeen': '*cáibín*', an old cap or hat.

53 *Ibid.*

54 *The Kerry Evening Post*, 4 July 1846.

55 *The Cork Examiner*, 13 July 1846.

56 Thackeray, William Makepeace, *The Irish Sketchbook, 1842* (Chapman and Hall, London, 1857), pp. 130–1.

57 *The Kerryman*, 2 July 1966.

58 *The Tralee Chronicle*, 28 December 1860.

59 *The Kerry Evening Post*, 17 January 1863.

60 'A Faction Fight in Killarney', *The Kerry Evening Post*, 4 June 1887.

61 'A Sanguinary Faction Fight in Killarney', *The Kerry Evening Post*, 11 January 1888.

62 'East Kerry election. Exciting scenes. People batoned. Several injured', *Kerry People*, 22 January 1910.

7 'THE WILD IVERAGH DEVILS' AND OTHERS

1 Trench, William Steuart, *Ierne: A Tale*, Vol. I (Longmans, Green and Co., London, 1871), p. 170. Trench was the land agent for the extensive Lansdowne estate in Kerry from 1849 until his death in 1872. He lived in Kenmare.

2 Corish (1981), p. 113.

3 *Ibid.*

4 Nicholson, Asenath, *Ireland's Welcome to the Stranger: or, Excursions through Ireland in 1844 & 1845* (Charles Gilpin, London, 1847), p. 318.

5 Fenton, Seamus, *It All Happened* (M. H. Gill, Dublin, 1949), p. 42.

6 O'Connell, Maurice R. (ed.), *The Correspondence of Daniel O'Connell, 1792–1814*, Vol. I (Irish University Press, Shannon, 1972), p. 344. Emphasis in original.

7 *Ibid.*, p. 382.

8 Lyne, Gerard J., 'The Pattern of Kilmakilloge', *Journal of the Kerry Archaeological and Historical Society*, No. 22 (1989), p. 26; 'The Faction Fights at Ballinclare Fair', NFCS 782: 282.

9 'Old Kerry. Octogenarian writes again', *Kerry Sentinel*, 19 February 1896.

10 'Bruíon', NFCS 0479: 103.

11 NFCS 0479: 104.

12 Kirby, Michael, *Skelligs Calling* (Lilliput Press, Dublin, 2003), pp. 96–8.

13 Mac an tSíthigh, Seán, 'St Michael's Well and Skellig Michael', in Crowley, John and Sheehan, John (eds), *The Iveragh Peninsula: A Cultural Atlas of the Ring of Kerry* (Cork University Press, Cork, 2009), p. 140; Ó Duilearga, Séamus, 'Cnuasach Andeas: Scéalta agus Seanchas Sheáin í Shé ó íbh Ráthach', *Béaloideas*, Iml. 29 (1961), p. 126.

14 Smith, Charles, *The Ancient and Present State of the County of Kerry: New Reader's Edition*, ed. Seán Moraghan (Bona Books, Killorglin, 2010), p. 40.

15 'County Kerry', *The Standard* (London), 16 October 1838.

16 Ó Duilearga (1961), p. 126; Ó Duilearga, Seamus (ed.), *Seán Ó Conaill's Book* (Comhairle Bhéaloideas Éireann, Dublin, 1981), p. 324.

17 *The Kerry Evening Post*, 22 March 1834.

18 'Friend and Piper of Liberator. Patrick O'Sullivan (Casure) of Eightercua', *The Kerryman*, 25 June 1938.

19 Ó Fiannachta, Donncha, 'Fraction [*sic*] Fight at Mastergeehy', *Barr na hAoine, Stories and Facts*, Vol. 1 (Dromid Heritage Group, Dromid, 2007), p. 45.

20 NFCS 0474: 221.

21 NFCS 0474: 220.

22 Quoted in O'Donnell (1975), pp. 180–1.

23 'Faction Fighting in Ireland Long Ago', *The Southern Star*, 19 May 1962. The writer does not cite the source of this information.

24 'Fair Fights', *The Kerry Examiner*, 24 December 1844.

25 'A Man Killed in a Faction Fight', *The Cork Examiner*, 3 January 1845.

26 'Faction Fights in the South', *The Northern Star and National Trades' Journal*, 21 September 1850, report drawn from the *Limerick Examiner*.

27 NFCS 0476: 297–8.

28 von Pückler-Muskau (1832), p. 306.

29 *Ibid.*, p. 307.

30 'Quarter Sessions, Killarney ... The Dennahys and the Mores', *Tralee Mercury,* 31 December 1831.

31 'Disgraceful Riot', *The Kerry Evening Post*, 6 July 1836.

32 'Kenmare – Saturday Night', *The Tralee Chronicle*, 7 December 1858.

33 'Manslaughter', *The Kerry Examiner*, 16 March 1847.

34 The trick o' the loop men were tricksters who offered a variety of gambling games that were rigged against the participants.

35 Letter to the editor by Rev. Edward Cowen, *The Kerry Evening Post*, 6 August 1851.

36 Lyne, 'The Pattern of Kilmakilloge', pp. 25–6. Story drawn from 'An Patrún – Troid – Dhá Pharóiste', NFCS 0463: 121–4.

37 Bigger, Francis Joseph, 'The Lake and Church of Kilmakillogue ...', *Journal of the Royal Society of Antiquaries of Ireland*, Vol. VIII (1898), p. 317.

8 'BIG MICK' AND THE FOLEY FACTION

1 'The Historic Fair of Puck', *Kerry Champion*, 10 August 1935. Poem by James J. Coffey of Carhoonahone, Beaufort. 'Botha Dreen': *bata draighin*, blackthorn stick.

2 NFCS 0471: 188; 'Death of Mr Michael James Foley, of Killorglin', *The Kerry Evening Post*, 16 January 1867.

3 Bary (1994), pp. 7, 177.

4 A James Foley Senior of Killorglin was still living in 1835 – see 'O'Connell Tribute, Killorglan', *Tralee Mercury*, 25 July 1835; named as the lessee of 1798, he was described as 'the late James Foley' in 1844 – see 'Meeting to Determine the Close Season', *The Kerry Evening Post*, 16 November 1844.

5 'Puck Fair', *The Tralee Chronicle*, 14 August 1857.

6 'Old Kerry', *Kerry Sentinel*, 7 March 1896.

7 'The Pattern Fair', NFCS 0471: 189.

8 'Kilgobnet. The Pattern Fair – Feb 11th', NFCS 0471: 216.

9 'Daoine Cáiliúla', NFCS 0471: 69–70. Translated by Thomas O'Sullivan.

10 'Old Kerry. Octogenarian writes again', *Kerry Sentinel*, 19 February 1896.

11 'Old Kerry', *Kerry Sentinel*, 7 March 1896.

12 Possibly Denis Casey (1766–1867) a famous faction fighter from Glenflesk. See 'Longevity in Kerry', *The Freeman's Journal*, 20 March 1867.

13 'Old Kerry. Octogenarian writes again', *Kerry Sentinel*, 19 February 1896.

14 The old fort may have been Lios Gobnait, which lay near the ruins of St Gobnait's church.

15 'Old Kerry', *Kerry Sentinel*, 7 March 1896. Letter by 'Padrig-na-Knock'.

16 *Ibid.*

17 'Imperial Parliament. House of Commons – Friday, July 11. Judge Day – Mr O'Connor – Mr O'Hanlon', *The Freeman's Journal*, 16 July 1817.
18 'Milltown Petit Sessions. Election Riots', *The Kerry Evening Post*, 28 August 1841.
19 'Old Kerry', *Kerry Sentinel*, 7 March 1896.
20 'The Pattern Fair', NFCS 0471: 188–9.
21 'Tralee, Sept. 21', *The Freeman's Journal*, 24 September 1812, original report from *The Kerry Evening Post* (early issues no longer extant).
22 *The Freeman's Journal*, 21 February 1807.
23 'Old Kerry', *Kerry Sentinel*, 7 March 1896. Letter by 'Padrig-na-Knock'.
24 (Belfast) *News Letter*, 20 August 1813.
25 'Gossip. Puck Fair'. (Letter by 'Octogenarian)', *Kerry Sentinel*, 8 October 1898.
26 *Chute's Western Herald*, 20 January 1820, quoted in O'Donnell (1975), p. 184.
27 SOC 2184/1.
28 'Death of Mr Michael James Foley, of Killorglin', *The Kerry Evening Post*, 16 January 1867.
29 *Kerry Sentinel*, 16 May 1894.
30 *Ibid.* '*Poc in airde*': a high stroke.
31 Foley (1988), p. 36.
32 Croker (1829), pp. 33–4. Emphases in original.
33 'To George Garrow Green, Esq, S.I.R.I.C.', *The Kerry Evening Post*, 20 February 1875.
34 Garrow Green, G., *In the Royal Irish Constabulary* (James Blackwood, London, 1905), p. 26.
35 *The Kerry Evening Post*, 28 February 1835.
36 *The Kerry Evening Post*, 16 August 1837.
37 'Criminal Court – Friday', *Tralee Mercury*, 17 March 1838.
38 *Ibid.*
39 *Ibid.*
40 'Milltown Petit Sessions – Monday. Election Riots', *The Kerry Examiner*, 3 September 1841.
41 'Kerry Assizes, August 20', *Tralee Mercury*, 22 August 1829.
42 *The Kerry Evening Post*, 16 August 1837.
43 'Criminal Court – Friday', *Tralee Mercury*, 17 March 1838.
44 *The Kerry Evening Post*, 16 August 1837.
45 'Investigation at Killorglin', *The Kerry Evening Post*, 26 August 1837.
46 'Criminal Court – Friday', *Tralee Mercury*, 17 March 1838.

47 *Ibid.* According to the evidence of a police sergeant.

48 Foley (1988), p. 41.

49 'Death of Mr Michael James Foley, of Killorglin', *The Kerry Evening Post*, 16 January 1867.

50 Michael James Foley, Anglont, to Maurice Fitzgerald, 29 December 1834, PRONI MIC639/7/160.

51 'Death of Mr Michael James Foley, of Killorglin', *The Kerry Evening Post*, 16 January 1867. Arthur Blennerhassett (1799–1843) was elected an MP for the borough of County Kerry in 1837 (the newspaper mistakenly cited the year as 1835).

52 'Important Meeting at Killorglan', *The Kerry Evening Post*, 1 February 1837.

53 'The County of Kerry Election', *The Kerry Evening Post*, 16 August 1837.

54 'Coroner's Inquest', *The Kerry Evening Post*, 17 July 1841.

55 'Milltown Petit Sessions. Election Riots', *The Kerry Evening Post*, 28 August 1841.

56 'Milltown Petit Sessions – Monday. Election Riots', *The Kerry Examiner*, 3 September 1841.

57 'Milltown Petit Sessions. Election Riots', *The Kerry Evening Post*, 28 August 1841.

58 'Kerry Assizes. Crown Court – Friday March 11', *The Kerry Evening Post*, 16 March 1842.

59 *The Tralee Chronicle*, 16 March 1844.

60 'Faction Fight', *The Kerry Evening Post*, 15 August 1846.

61 *The Kerry Evening Post*, 21 March 1840.

62 'Puck Fair', *The Cork Examiner*, 17 August 1846.

63 *The Kerry Evening Post*, 23 October 1847.

64 'Faction Fighting', *The Kerry Evening Post*, 12 September 1863; 'Faction Fighting in Kerry', *The Cork Examiner*, 29 May 1865.

65 'Death of Mr Michael James Foley, of Killorglin', *The Kerry Evening Post*, 16 January 1867.

66 'Old Kerry', *Kerry Sentinel*, 7 March 1896.

67 'Tuaith Tales', *The Kerry Weekly Reporter and Commercial Advertiser*, 19 December 1925.

9 'PLENTY WHISKEY'

1 'Killarney Quarter Sessions. The Faction Fight at Molahiffe Fair', *The Kerry Evening Post*, 22 June 1861.

2 'Fairs', *The Cork Examiner*, 3 June 1844. The fair was established in 1613.

3 The Morning Register (Dublin), 2 June 1840. From a report by the *Cork Constitution.*
4 *The Kerry Evening Post*, 9 January 1867.
5 'Molahiffe Fair', *The Kerry Evening Post*, 28 May 1873.
6 Garrow Green (1905), pp. 26–7.
7 The gale day was one of two occasions during the year on which a tenant farmer paid his rent.
8 '*Hors de combat*': put out of action through injury.
9 Garrow Green (1905), pp. 29–35.
10 *Ibid.*
11 *John Bull*, 17 June 1822.
12 *The Kerry Evening Post*, 13 June 1832.
13 *The Kerry Evening Post*, 27 May 1837.
14 'The Fine Pisantry', *The Kerry Evening Post*, 30 May 1838.
15 'The Pleasures of Imagination', *The Kerry Evening Post*, 9 June 1838.
16 'Killarney Petty Sessions – Tuesday', *The Tralee Chronicle*, 3 June 1843.
17 'The Riot at Molahiffe', *The Kerry Evening Post*, 3 June 1843.
18 'Killarney Quarter Sessions', *The Tralee Chronicle*, 28 June 1845.
19 *The Kerry Evening Post*, 9 June 1855 and 13 June 1857.
20 Perhaps the remains of an old castle described by antiquarian John O'Donovan as 'situated on a high rocky eminence'. O'Donovan, John, *Antiquities of the County of Kerry collected during the progress of the Ordnance Survey in 1841* (typescript of original manuscript, Killarney Library), p. 100.
21 'Faction Fights', NFCS 0460: 150.
22 *Ibid.*
23 'Faction Fighting in Kerry', *The Tralee Chronicle*, 4 June 1861.
24 'Faction Fight', *The Kerry Evening Post*, 1 June 1861.
25 'Faction Fighting in Kerry', *The Tralee Chronicle*, 4 June 1861.
26 'Killarney Petty Sessions – Wednesday', *Kerry Star*, 8 June 1861.
27 *Ibid.*
28 'Killarney Quarter Sessions', *Kerry Star*, 22 June 1861.
29 'Killarney Quarter Sessions. The Faction Fight at Molahiffe Fair', *The Kerry Evening Post*, 22 June 1861.
30 'Killarney Petty Sessions, Wednesday. Faction Fighting', *Kerry Star*, 1 June 1861.
31 'Killarney Petty Sessions – Wednesday', *Kerry Star*, 8 June 1861.
32 'Killarney Quarter Sessions. The Faction Fight at Molahiffe Fair', *The Kerry Evening Post*, 22 June 1861.

33 *Ibid.*
34 'Killarney Quarter Sessions', *The Cork Examiner*, 21 June 1861.
35 'Killarney Quarter Sessions. The Faction Fight at Molahiffe Fair', *The Kerry Evening Post*, 22 June 1861. 'Bad spleen': antipathy.
36 'Killarney Quarter Sessions', *The Cork Examiner*, 21 June 1861; *The Tralee Chronicle*, 28 June 1861.
37 'Killarney Quarter Sessions. The Faction Fight at Molahiffe Fair', *The Kerry Evening Post*, 22 June 1861.
38 'Molahiffe (Co. Kerry) Fair', *The Cork Examiner*, 29 May 1862.
39 'Faction Fighting in Kerry', *The Cork Examiner*, 29 May 1865.
40 'Molahiffe Fair', *The Kerry Evening Post*, 29 May 1872.
41 *The Tralee Chronicle*, 30 May 1876.
42 'Killarney Petty Sessions. Faction Fighting at Molahiffe Fair', *The Kerry Weekly Reporter and Commercial Advertiser*, 4 June 1887.
43 'Local Prejudice', NFCS 0432: 286.
44 'Local Prejudice of one district against another', NFCS 0232: 047.
45 'Local Prejudice', NFCS 0102: 245.
46 'Local Prejudice', NFCS 0432: 286.
47 *Chute's Western Herald*, 26 November 1812.
48 'Copies of Informations', SOC 1532/2.
49 'Soupers': during the Great Famine (1845–49) some hungry Catholics were fed in soup kitchens provided by Protestant missionaries who used the opportunity to pressure them to relinquish their faith and convert. Note: the folklore interviewee, speaking in the twentieth century, has retrospectively applied a judgement inspired by events of the 1840s onto people of 1812.
50 A wide variety of projectiles could be fired from the long-barrelled muzzle-loaded guns of the time.
51 Of Keel House. A son of Langford Rae, a prominent local landlord.
52 'A faction fight between Keel and Kiltallagh', NFCS 0432: 315a–17a.
53 *Chute's Western Herald*, 26 November 1812.
54 'A faction fight between Keel and Kiltallagh', NFCS 0432: 317a.
55 *Ibid.*
56 'A faction fight between Keel and Kiltallagh', NFCS 0432: 318a.
57 'Cnocán Na Marbh', NFCS 0432: 311–12.
58 Also Kieonaghs, Konoghs, Keonoughs.
59 'Faction Fighting', *The Kerry Evening Post*, 31 December 1845.
60 'Faction Fight', *The Kerry Evening Post*, 26 November 1845.
61 'Faction Fighting', *The Kerry Evening Post*, 31 December 1845.

62 'Faction Fight', *The Kerry Evening Post*, 26 November 1845; 'Killarney Sessions – Saturday. Faction Fights', *The Tralee Chronicle*, 10 January 1846.

63 'Faction Fight', *The Kerry Evening Post*, 26 November 1845. The village of Glenflesk was about twenty miles away, east of Killarney.

64 *Ibid.*

65 *Ibid.*; 'Killarney Sessions – Saturday. Faction Fights', *The Tralee Chronicle*, 10 January 1846.

66 'Faction Fighting', *The Kerry Evening Post*, 31 December 1845.

67 *Ibid.*

68 *The Kerry Evening Post*, 21 January 1846.

69 *The Cork Examiner*, 11 May 1846.

70 'Tralee Petty Sessions', *The Tralee Chronicle*, 29 August 1856.

71 *John Bull*, 17 June 1822.

72 'Faction Fight', *The Kerry Evening Post*, 26 November 1845; 'Killarney Sessions – Saturday. Faction Fights', *The Tralee Chronicle*, 10 January 1846.

73 'Faction Fighting', *The Kerry Evening Post*, 26 August 1846.

74 'Castlemain Fair', *The Kerry Evening Post*, 3 November 1849.

75 *The Tralee Chronicle*, 25 May 1858.

76 'Castlemain Fair', *The Kerry Evening Post*, 25 November 1857; 'Castlemain Fair', *The Tralee Chronicle*, 27 November 1857.

77 *The Kerry Evening Post*, 26 May 1858.

78 *The Tralee Chronicle*, 25 May 1858.

79 'Milltown Petty Sessions – Monday', *The Tralee Chronicle*, 11 June 1858.

80 *Ibid.*

81 'Milltown Petty Sessions', *The Kerry Evening Post*, 4 February 1863.

82 'Milltown Petty Sessions', *The Kerry Evening Post*, 12 September 1860: 'Several persons were bound to keep the peace, having shown a disposition at the late fair of Castlemaine to renew the often well-fought faction fight between the Flynns and Teahans.'

83 'Faction Fighting', *The Tralee Chronicle*, 30 April 1861.

84 *The Kerry Evening Post*, 24 November 1866.

85 *The Kerry Evening Post*, 19 May 1869.

86 'Milltown Petty Sessions', *The Kerry Evening Post*, 23 June 1869.

87 *Southern Reporter and Cork Commercial Courier*, 13 September 1825. Emphases in original.

88 'Fairs', *The Morning Register* (Dublin), 4 May 1829.

89 *Cork Constitution*, 28 June 1834.

90 *The Freeman's Journal*, 6 July 1836; 'Tralee Quarter Sessions', *The Kerry Evening Post*, 29 June 1836.

91 'Milltown Fair', *The Kerry Evening Post*, 26 August 1846.
92 'Faction Fighting', *The Kerry Evening Post*, 22 December 1847.
93 *The Kerry Evening Post*, 23 September 1863.
94 'Milltown Petty Sessions', *The Kerry Evening Post*, 31 July 1872.
95 'Feats of Strength', NFCS 0475: 109. (His surname may have been Sullivan – see 'Feats of Strength', NFCS 0475: 113–14.)
96 'Feats of Strength', NFCS 0475: 106–7.
97 'Feats of Strength', NFCS 0475: 109.
98 'Feats of Strength', NFCS 0475: 110.
99 *Ibid.*
100 'Feats of Strength', NFCS 0475: 110–11.
101 'Faction Fight', *The Kerry Evening Post*, 26 November 1845; 'Castlemain Fair', *The Kerry Evening Post*, 3 November 1849.
102 *Southern Reporter and Cork Commercial Courier*, 13 September 1825.
103 Hall and Hall (1841), p. 427. Emphasis in original.

10 'WHO'S AFRAID?'

1 Sayers, Peig, *An Old Woman's Reflections* (Oxford University Press, London, 1962), p. 21.
2 Mac Síthigh (1984), p. 106.
3 *Ibid.*, pp. 105–6.
4 'The Faction Fights at Ballinclare Fair', NFC 782: 276.
5 Mac Síthigh (1984), p. 110.
6 Ó Giolláin, Diarmuid, 'The Pattern', in Donnelly Jr., James S. (ed.), *Irish Popular Culture 1650–1850* (Irish Academic Press, Dublin, 1998), p. 202.
7 'A faction fight between Keel and Kiltallagh', NFCS 0432: 315a.
8 Mac Síthigh (1984), p. 107.
9 Roddy the Rover (Aodh de Blácam), 'Seen, heard and noted. May was gay so they say. The Man Who Taught the Cuts – Scéal ó Chiarraidhe', *Irish Press*, 5 May 1944. Story translated by de Blácam from information that came from Mac Síthigh. In that version the fight is dated to about the year 1824; in the version in Mac Síthigh's later book he states that it took place around the year 1817.
10 'The Faction Fights at Ballinclare Fair', NFC 782: 274.
11 'The Faction Fights at Ballinclare Fair', NFC 782: 275.
12 *The Kerry Evening Post*, 28 January 1829.
13 *The Kerry Evening Post*, 6 May 1835.
14 *The Kerry Evening Post*, 3 May 1837.
15 'Ballinclare Fair', *The Kerry Evening Post*, 5 October 1844.

16 'Aunascaul Petty Sessions – November 26', *The Kerry Evening Post*, 2 December 1863.
17 'Ballinclare Fair – October 4', *The Kerry Evening Post*, 6 October 1866; *The Kerry Evening Post*, 19 May 1866.
18 *The Kerry Evening Post*, 19 May 1866.
19 Bureau of Military History Witness Statement 1413, p. 3. Statement by Tadhg Kennedy.
20 *The Kerry Evening Post*, 20 April 1831.
21 'The Faction Fights at Ballinclare Fair', NFC 782: 276.
22 NFC 782: 277.
23 *Ibid.*
24 NFC 782: 275–6.
25 NFC 782: 278.
26 *Southern Reporter and Cork Commercial Courier*, 5 July 1825.
27 *The Kerry Evening Post*, 6 July 1833.
28 'The Faction Fights at Ballinclare Fair', NFC 782: 278.
29 'The Faction Fights at Ballinclare Fair', NFC 782: 279–81.
30 'The Faction Fights at Ballinclare Fair', NFC 782: 281.
31 'Ballinclare Fair – October 4', *The Kerry Evening Post*, 6 October 1866; *The Kerry Evening Post*, 19 May 1866.
32 'Milltown Petty Sessions – Monday', *The Kerry Evening Post*, 28 May 1870.
33 Mac Síthigh (1984), p. 108.
34 Ó Dubhda, Seán, *Duanaire Duibhneach: .i. bailiú d'amhránaibh agus de phíosaibh eile filidheachta a ceapadh le tuairim céad bliain i gCorca Dhuibhne, agus atá fós i gcuimhne agus i mbéaloideas na ndaoine ann* (Oifig Díolta Foillseacháin Rialtais, Baile Átha Cliath, 1976), p. 157. Originally published 1933.
35 'The Faction Fights at Ballinclare Fair', NFC 782: 281.
36 Foley, Patrick, *Irish Historical Allusions, Curious Customs and Superstitions, County of Kerry, Corkaguiny* (self-published, 1916), pp. 27–8. In 1907 Foley also self-published *History of the Natural, Civil, Military and Ecclesiastical State of the County of Kerry in Baronies … Corkaguiny.*
37 'Tralee Quarter Sessions', *The Kerry Evening Post*, 11 July 1840.
38 'The Faction Fights at Ballinclare Fair', NFC 782: 282. (For William Deane Freeman see *The Kerry Evening Post*, 31 December 1828 and 'Mr William Deane Freeman, and the County of Kerry', *The Kerry Evening Post*, 30 January 1836.)
39 'The Faction Fights at Ballinclare Fair', NFC 782: 281–2.

40 Foley (1916), p. 28. Gerald Fitzgerald, 15th Earl of Desmond, rebelled with his family and followers against Elizabethan control of his territory in North Kerry. Failing, he fled with a handful of followers to Glenagenty, where he was captured and decapitated on 11 November 1583 on the orders of a Moriarty of Castledrum, Castlemaine.
41 MacDonagh, Michael, *Irish Life and Character* (Hodder and Stoughton, London, 1898), pp. 56–7.
42 Ó Dubhda (1976), pp. 157–61. Note: what is presented are extracts from a longer work. The song went to the tune of 'The Rocky Road to Dublin'. The title signifies the 'hullaballoo', or commotions/ructions, of the Fitzgeralds. The Holy Stone was a large stone that lay on the side of a street in Dingle, and which was associated with the Catholic church in Chapel Lane. Translated by Unique Voice translation services, Tralee.
43 *Ibid.*, p. 157.
44 *The Kerry Evening Post*, 14 August 1833. A reference to Daniel O'Connell's praise of Irish countrymen as the finest peasantry on the face of the Earth. The phrase particularly irritated his opponents, who would repeat it sardonically on the occasion of any act of peasant violence or misbehaviour. Emphasis in original.
45 Mac Síthigh (1984), p. 108.
46 *Ibid.*, p. 109. ('Ach le géaga glasa na coille/Amach as neart a gcuisleann'.)
47 Sayers (1962), p. 21.
48 O'Crohan, Tomás, *The Islandman* (Oxford University Press, Oxford, 1977), p. 64.
49 Mac Neill (1962), p. 104.
50 Mac Síthigh (1984), p. 105.
51 Ó Dubhda (1976), p. 157.

AFTERWORD: FACTION AND FEUD ARE PASSING AWAY

1 'Dinner to Mr O'Connell, MP', *The Leinster Journal*, 23 August 1828. 'John Bull': a fictional figure who was intended to personify England, just as 'Uncle Sam' represented the United States. He was usually illustrated as a stout, well-off farmer. Emphases in original.
2 'Grand Provincial Dinner', *The Freeman's Journal*, 4 September 1827.
3 'Tranquillization of the Country', *The Weekly Waterford Chronicle*, 16 August 1828.
4 *The Morning Register* (Dublin), 19 July 1828.
5 von Pückler-Muskau (1832), pp. 295–6.
6 'Letter to the editor, by "Faucon"', *The Kerry Evening Post*, 17 December 1828.

7 *Chute's Western Herald*, 8 January 1829; *The Kerry Evening Post*, 18 July 1829.
8 Kerrigan, Colm, *Father Mathew and the Irish Temperance Movement: 1838–1849* (Cork University Press, Cork, 1992), p. 96.
9 'Pacification', *The Waterford Mail*, 30 July 1828. '*Spailpín*': an impoverished labourer who was forced to tramp far and wide in search of work. The word was often employed as a term of abuse.
10 'The Agitators', *Leinster Express*, 13 August 1836.
11 *Ibid.*
12 'General Association of Ireland', *The Freeman's Journal*, 23 August 1837.
13 *The Kerry Evening Post*, 27 May 1837.
14 'The Fine Pisantry', *The Kerry Evening Post*, 30 May 1838.
15 Logan (1986), p. 105.
16 Quoted in Broeker, Galen, *Rural Disorder and Police Reform in Ireland, 1812–36* (Routledge and Kegan Paul, London, 1970), p. 118.
17 Minutes of Evidence taken before the Select Committee of the House of Lords appointed to enquire into the State of Ireland since the year 1835 in respect of Crime and Outrage ... (House of Commons, 1839), p. 970.
18 *Ibid.*, p. 971.
19 *Ibid.*, p. 917.
20 *Ibid.*, p. 973.
21 'Roman Catholic Church. Lenten Pastoral of the Rt Rev Dr Moriarty', *The Tralee Chronicle*, 12 February 1858.
22 'Police Bill', (Belfast) *News Letter*, 24 March 1786. The speaker was Sir Edward Crofton, MP for County Roscommon.
23 Wells, S. R., *Father Mathew, the Temperance Apostle: His Character and Biography* (Fowler and Wells, New York, 1867), p. 10.
24 *The Kerry Evening Post*, 10 March 1841.
25 'Oh, How Bless'd They Lived', *The Kerry Examiner*, 30 March 1841.
26 'A Man Killed in a Faction Fight', *The Cork Examiner*, 3 January 1845.
27 *The Kerry Evening Post*, 22 January 1845.
28 'Temperance soiree in Killarney to John O'Connell, Esq., of Grena', *The Tralee Chronicle*, 24 January 1846.
29 Kerrigan (1992), p. 99.
30 'Killarney Sessions', *The Tralee Chronicle*, 10 January 1846.
31 *The Kerry Evening Post*, 10 January 1846.
32 'Faction Fighting', *The Kerry Evening Post*, 22 December 1847.
33 *The Kerry Evening Post*, 19 February 1848.
34 *The Kerry Evening Post*, 21 May 1853.

35 *Southern Reporter and Cork Commercial Chronicle*, 11 August 1862.
36 'A Change for the Better', *The Clare Journal and Ennis Advertiser*, 7 July 1864.
37 *The Freeman's Journal*, 18 February 1881. 'Faction and feud are passing away' was a reference to a popular song, 'Orange and Green Will Carry the Day', written by Thomas Davis in 1845.
38 NFCS 0358: 482.
39 'The Pattern Day', NFCS 0405: 301–2.
40 Club History, Ballinamere GAA Club, http://ballinamere.gaa.ie/pages/parishdistricthistory.aspx.
41 NFCS 0518: 173.
42 *The Kerry Evening Post*, 16 November 1887.
43 Rouse, Paul, *Sport and Ireland: A History* (Oxford University Press, Oxford, 2015), p. 181.
44 *The Kerry Evening Post*, 23 July 1890.
45 'The Language Cause. Great Revival Meeting in Castlegregory', *Kerry People*, 7 February 1914.
46 *Kerry Sentinel*, 9 October 1889.
47 Colum, Padraic, *A Treasury of Irish Folklore* (Crown Publishers, New York, 1954), p. 399.
48 'Brosna Petty Sessions', *The Kerry Weekly Reporter and Commercial Advertiser*, 8 September 1900; 'Serious Affray at Kilflynn. A Free Faction Fight', *The Kerry Evening Post*, 19 October 1901.
49 NFCS 0358: 483.
50 'East Kerry election. Exciting scenes. People batoned. Several injured', *Kerry People*, 22 January 1910.
51 *Kerry People*, July 1910: 'Throughout that entire district there was a survival of those faction fights, more remarkable in another part of Ireland.'
52 Murphy, Jeremiah, *When Youth Was Mine: A Memoir of Kerry 1902–1925* (Mentor Press, Dublin, 1998), pp. 51–2.
53 Jeremiah O'Keefe, 'A Shameful Day in History of Kerry', *The Liberator* (Tralee), 27 January 1917.
54 T. M. Donovan, 'Old Times in Oilean Ciarraighe. The Past Pastors of Castleisland', *The Kerryman*, 29 October 1927.
55 Birmingham, George, *The Lighter Side of Irish Life* (T. N. Fowlis, London and Edinburgh, 1914), p. 44. First published 1912.

BIBLIOGRAPHY

BOOKS AND ARTICLES

Anon., *Leaves from My Note-Book … by an Ex-Officer of the Royal Irish Constabulary* (Dean and Son, London, 1879)

Anon., 'Notes of a Journey in the Kingdom of Kerry', *Blackwood's Edinburgh Magazine*, January 1828

Anon., 'O'Donoghue of the Glenns', *Tait's Edinburgh Magazine*, No. VI (1832)

Anon., *Paddiana; or, Scraps and Sketches of Irish Life, Present and Past,* Vol. I (Richard Bentley, London, 1847)

Anon., *Songs of Ireland and Other Lands* (D. & J. Sadlier, New York, 1847)

Andrews, J. H., 'The French School of Dublin Land Surveyors', *Irish Geography*, Vol. 5, Issue 2 (1965)

Barlow, Stephen, *The History of Ireland, from the Earliest Period to the Present Time*, Vol. I (Sherwood, Neely and Jones, London, 1814)

Barrington, Sir Jonah, *Personal Sketches of His Own Times,* Vol. I (Henry Colburn and Richard Bentley, London, 1832)

Barrington, Sir Jonah, *Personal Sketches of His Own Times,* Vol. III (Henry Colburn and Richard Bentley, London, 1832)

Bary, Valerie, *Houses of Kerry* (Ballinakella Press, Whitegate, 1994)

Bigger, Francis Joseph, 'The Lake and Church of Kilmakillogue …', *Journal of the Royal Society of Antiquaries of Ireland*, Vol. VIII (1898)

Birmingham, George, *The Lighter Side of Irish Life* (T. N. Fowlis, London and Edinburgh, 1914)

Bossy, John, 'The Counter-Reformation and the People of Catholic Ireland, 1596–1641', in Williams, T. D. (ed.), *Historical Studies VIII: Papers Read Before the Irish Conference of Historians 27–30 May 1969* (Gill and Macmillan, Dublin, 1971)

Broeker, Galen, *Rural Disorder and Police Reform in Ireland, 1812–36* (Routledge and Kegan Paul, London, 1970)

Browne, Eamon, 'Faction Fighting in Kerry: Ballyeagh Strand, 1834', *The Kerry Magazine*, No. 9 (1998)

Burke, Eoin, 'The Irishman is no *lazzarone*', *History Ireland*, Vol. 5, No. 3 (1997)

Burke, Eoin (ed.) *'Poor Green Erin': German Travel Writers' Narratives on Ireland from Before the 1798 Rising to After the Great Famine* (Peter Lang,

Frankfurt am Main, 2011)

Carleton, William, 'The Battle of the Factions', in *Traits and Stories of the Irish Peasantry*, Vol. I (William Frederick Wakeman, Dublin, 1834)

Carleton, William, 'The Country Dancing-Master: An Irish Sketch', *Irish Penny Journal*, 29 August 1840

Carr, John, *The Stranger in Ireland: or, a Tour in the Southern and Western Parts of that Country in the Year 1805* (Samuel F. Bradford, Philadelphia, 1806)

Clark, Samuel, *Social Origins of the Irish Land War* (Princeton University Press, Princeton, 1979)

Colum, Padraic, *A Treasury of Irish Folklore* (Crown Publishers, New York, 1954)

Conley, Carolyn, 'The Agreeable Recreation of Fighting', *Journal of Social History*, Vol. 33, No. 1 (1999)

Conley, Carolyn, *Melancholy Accidents: The Meaning of Violence in Post-Famine Ireland* (Lexington Books, Maryland, 1999)

Corish, Patrick J., *The Catholic Community in the Seventeenth and Eighteenth Centuries* (Helicon, Dublin, 1981)

Croker, T. Crofton, *Legends of the Lakes*, Vol. II (John Ebers, London, 1829)

Cronin, Dan, 'An Ancient Characteristic of Ireland: Faction Fights', *Sliabh Luachra, Journal of Cumann Luachra*, Vol. 1, No. 14 (2010)

Cronin, Maura, 'Popular Politics, 1815–1845', in Kelly, James (ed.), *The Cambridge History of Ireland, 1730–1880*, Vol. III (Cambridge University Press, Cambridge, 2018)

Culhane, Thomas F., 'Traditions of Glin and its Neighbourhood', *Journal of the Kerry Historical and Archaeological Society*, Vol. 2 (1969)

Cullen, L. M., 'Economic Development', in Moody, T. W. and Vaughan, W. E. (eds), *A New History of Ireland, Vol. IV: Eighteenth-Century Ireland 1691–1800* (Clarendon Press, Oxford, 1986)

Curtin, Gerard, *West Limerick Crime, Popular Protest and Society 1820–1845* (Sliabh Luachra Books, Ballyhahill, Co. Limerick, 2008)

Dineen, Patrick S. (ed.) *Dánta Aodagáin Uí Rataille; the Poems of Egan O'Rahilly* (Irish Texts Society, London, 1911)

Dolan, Terence Patrick, *A Dictionary of Hiberno-English* (Gill and Macmillan, Dublin, 1999)

Donnelly, James S. Jr., 'Factions in Prefamine Ireland', in Eyler, Audrey S. and Garratt, Robert F. (eds), *The Uses of the Past: Essays on Irish Culture* (University of Delaware Press, Washington, 1988)

Edgeworth, Richard Lovell, and Edgeworth, Maria, *Essay on Irish Bulls* (J. Johnson, London, 1802)

Farrell, Stephen, 'Co. Kerry', in Fisher, D. R. (ed.), *The History of Parliament: The House of Commons 1820–1832* (Cambridge University Press, Cambridge, 2009)

Farrell, Stephen, 'Tralee', in Fisher, D. R. (ed.), *The History of Parliament: The House of Commons 1820–1832* (Cambridge University Press, Cambridge, 2009)

Fenton, Seamus, *It All Happened* (M. H. Gill, Dublin, 1949)

Ferris, Fr William, *Fr. Ferris's Parish Histories: BallymacElligott, Ballyseedy, O'Brennan and Nohoval* (Cló Staire Chiarraí, Tralee, 2018)

Foley, Kieran, *History of Killorglin* (Killorglin History and Folklore Society, Killorglin, 1988)

Froude, James Anthony, *The English in Ireland in the Eighteenth Century*, Vol. I (Longmans, Green and Co., London, 1872)

Garnham, Neal, 'Accounting for the Early Success of the Gaelic Athletic Association', *Irish Historical Studies*, Vol. 34, No. 133 (2004)

Garrow Green, G., *In the Royal Irish Constabulary* (James Blackwood, London, 1905)

Gaughan, J. Anthony, *Listowel and its Vicinity* (Mercier Press, Cork, 1973)

Hall, Rev. James, *Tour through Ireland; Particularly the Interior and Least Known Parts,* Vol. I (R. P. Moore, London, 1813)

Hall, Mr and Hall, Mrs S. C., *Ireland: its Scenery, Character*, Vol. I (How and Parsons, London, 1841)

Herbert, E., 'The Cooleens and the Lawlors – The Story of a Faction Feud', *The Irishman's Annual 1955* (Tralee, 1955)

Hurley, John W., *Shillelagh: The Irish Fighting Stick* (Caravat Press, Pipersville, 2007)

Hurley, John W., *Fighting Irish: The Art of Irish Stick-Fighting* (Caravat Press, Philadelphia, 2018)

Jupp, Peter and Magennis, Eoin, *Crowds in Ireland c. 1780–1920* (Macmillan Press, London, 2000)

Kelly, James, *The Liberty and Ormond Boys: Factional Riot in Eighteenth-Century Dublin* (Four Courts Press, Dublin, 2005)

Kerrigan, Colm, *Father Mathew and the Irish Temperance Movement: 1838–1849* (Cork University Press, Cork, 1992)

Kirby, Michael, *Skelligs Calling* (Lilliput Press, Dublin, 2003)

Larkin, Emmet (ed.), *Alexis de Tocqueville's Journey in Ireland: July–August, 1835* (Wolfhound Press, Dublin, 1990)

Le Fanu, W. R., *Seventy Years of Irish Life* (Edward Arnold, London, 1893)

Lewis, George Cornewall, *On Local Disturbances in Ireland* (B. Fellowes, London, 1836)

Logan, Patrick, *Fair Day: The Story of Irish Fairs and Markets* (Appletree Press, Belfast, 1986)

Lyne, Gerard J., 'Daniel O'Connell, Intimidation and the Kerry Elections of 1835', *Journal of the Kerry Historical and Archaeological Society*, Vol. 4 (1971)

Lyne, Gerard J., 'The Pattern of Kilmakilloge', *Journal of the Kerry Archaeological and Historical Society*, No. 22 (1989)

Mac an tSíthigh, Seán, 'St Michael's Well and Skellig Michael', in Crowley, John and Sheehan, John (eds), *The Iveragh Peninsula: A Cultural Atlas of the Ring of Kerry* (Cork University Press, Cork, 2009)

MacDonagh, Michael, *Irish Life and Character* (Hodder and Stoughton, London, 1898)

MacLysaght, Edward, *Irish Life in the Seventeenth Century* (Cork University Press, Cork, 1950)

Mac Neill, Máire, *The Festival of Lughnasa* (Oxford University Press, London, 1962)

Mac Síthigh, Tomás, *Paróiste an Fheirtéaraigh; Stairsheanchas an Cheantair i dtréimhse an Ghorta Mhóir* (Coiscéim, Baile Átha Cliath, 1984)

Mc Coluim, Fionán, 'An Old Man's Memories', *Béaloideas*, Iml. 4, Uimh 2 (1933)

McElroy, Martin, 'The Impact of the Parliamentary Elections (Ireland) Act (1829) on the Irish electorate *c.* 1829–1832', in Blackstock, Allan and Magennis, Eoin (eds), *Politics and Political Culture in Britain and Ireland 1750–1850* (Ulster Historical Foundation, Belfast, 2007)

McKay, Robert (ed.), *An Anthology of the Potato* (A. Figgis, Dublin, 1961)

McMahon, Richard, *Homicide in pre-Famine and Famine Ireland* (Liverpool University Press, Liverpool, 2013)

Matheson, Steve, *Maurice Walsh, Storyteller* (Brandon Books, Dingle, 1985)

Moraghan, Seán, *Puck Fair: A History* (History Press, Dublin, 2013)

Moraghan, Seán, 'The Fighting Irish: Faction Fighting in Cork', *The Archive; Journal of the Cork Folklore Project*, Issue 18 (2014)

Murphy, Jeremiah, *When Youth Was Mine: A Memoir of Kerry 1902–1925* (Mentor Press, Dublin, 1998)

Ní Chinnéide, Síle, 'A New View of Eighteenth-Century Life in Kerry', *Journal of the Kerry Archaeological and Historical Society*, Vol. 6 (1973)

Nicholson, Asenath, *Ireland's Welcome to the Stranger: or, Excursions through Ireland in 1844 & 1845* (Charles Gilpin, London, 1847)

Ó Cadhla, Stiofán, *The Holy Well Tradition: The Pattern of St Declan, Ardmore, County Waterford, 1800–2000* (Four Courts Press, Dublin, 2002)

O'Conner, Morgan, *Poems, Pastorals and Dialogues* (J. Thompson, Dublin, 1726)

O'Connell, Maurice R. (ed.), *The Correspondence of Daniel O'Connell 1792–1814*, Vol. 1 (Irish University Press, Shannon, 1972)

O'Crohan, Tomás, *The Islandman* (Oxford University Press, Oxford, 1977)

Ó Danachair, Caoimhín, 'Faction Fighting in County Limerick', *North Munster Antiquarian Journal*, Vol. 10 (1966)

O'Donnell, Patrick, *The Irish Faction Fighters of the 19th Century* (Anvil Books, Dublin, 1975)

Ó Dubhda, Seán, *Duanaire Duibhneach: .i. bailiú d'amhránaibh agus de phíosaibh eile filidheachta a ceapadh le tuairim céad bliain i gCorca Dhuibhne, agus atá fós i gcuimhne agus i mbéaloideas na ndaoine ann* (Oifig Díolta Foillseacháin Rialtais, Baile Átha Cliath, 1976)

Ó Duilearga, Séamus, 'Cnuasach Andeas: Scéalta agus Seanchas Sheáin Shé ó íbh Ráthach', *Béaloideas*, Iml. 29 (1961)

Ó Duilearga, Seamus (ed.), *Seán Ó Conaill's Book* (Comhairle Bhéaloideas Éireann, Dublin, 1981)

Ó Fiannachta, Donncha, 'Fraction [*sic*] Fight at Mastergeehy', *Barr na hAoine, Stories and Facts*, Vol. 1 (Dromid Heritage Group, Dromid, 2007)

Ó Giolláin, Diarmuid, 'The Pattern', in Donnelly Jr, James S. (ed.), *Irish Popular Culture 1650–1850* (Irish Academic Press, Dublin, 1998)

O'Neill Daunt, William J., *Personal Recollections of the Late Daniel O'Connell, MP,* Vol. I (Chapman and Hall, London, 1848)

O'Rourke, Kevan, 'The Fighting Irish: Faction Fighting as Leisure in the Writings of William Carleton', in Lane, Leeann and Murphy, William (eds), *Leisure and the Irish in the Nineteenth Century* (Liverpool University Press, Liverpool, 2016)

O'Sullivan, Niamh, *In the Lion's Den: Daniel MacDonald, Ireland and Empire* (Quinnipiac University Press, Hamden, Connecticut, 2016)

O'Toole, Terence, 'National Emblems', *Dublin Penny Journal,* 7 July 1832

Otway, Caesar, *Sketches in Ireland* (William Curry, Dublin, 1827)

Owens, Gary, 'A Moral Insurrection: Faction Fighters, Public Demonstrations and the O'Connellite Campaign, 1828', *Irish Historical Studies*, Vol. 30, No. 120 (1997)

Palmer, Stanley H., *Police and Protest in England and Ireland 1780–1850* (Cambridge University Press, Cambridge, 1988)

Reid, Thomas, *Travels in Ireland in the Year 1822* (Longman, Hurst, Rees, Orme and Brown, London, 1823)

Roberts, Paul E. W., 'Caravats and Shanavests: Whiteboyism and Faction Fighting in East Munster, 1802–1811', in Clark, Samuel and Donnelly

Jr, James S. (eds), *Irish Peasants: Violence and Political Unrest* (University of Wisconsin Press, Madison, Wisconsin, 1983)

Rouse, Paul, *Sport and Ireland: A History* (Oxford University Press, Oxford, 2015)

Sayers, Peig, *An Old Woman's Reflections* (Oxford University Press, London, 1962)

Share, Bernard, *Slanguage* (Gill and Macmillan, Dublin, 2003)

Smith, Babette, *The Luck of the Irish: How a Shipload of Convicts Survived the Wreck of the Hive to Make a New Life in Australia* (Allen & Unwin, Sydney, 2014)

Smith, Charles, *The Ancient and Present State of the County of Kerry: New Reader's Edition*, ed. Seán Moraghan (Bona Books, Killorglin, 2010)

Stewart, Alexander and Revington, George (eds), *Memoir of the Life and Labours of the Rev Adam Averell* (Methodist Book Room, Dublin, 1848)

Thackeray, William Makepeace, *The Irish Sketchbook, 1842* (Chapman and Hall, London, 1857)

Thuente, Mary Helen, 'Violence in Pre-Famine Ireland: the Testimony of Irish Folklore and Fiction', *Irish University Review*, Vol. 15, Nr 2 (1985)

Townsend, Horace, *Statistical Survey of the County of Cork* (Graisberry and Campbell, Dublin, 1810)

Trench, William Steuart, *Ierne: A Tale*, Vol. I (Longmans, Green and Co., London, 1871)

von Pückler-Muskau, Fürst Hermann, *Tour in England, Ireland, and France, in the Years 1828 & 1829*, Vol. I (Effingham Wilson, London, 1832)

Wagner, Paul and Rector, Mark (eds), *Highland Broadsword: Five Manuals of Scottish Regimental Swordsmanship* (Chivalry Bookshelf, Highland Village, Texas)

Wells, S. R., *Father Mathew, the Temperance Apostle: His Character and Biography* (Fowler and Wells, New York, 1867)

Williams, N. J. A., *Pairlement Chloinne Tomáis* (Dublin Institute for Advanced Studies, Dublin, 1981)

UNPUBLISHED/SELF-PUBLISHED

Foley, Patrick, *Irish Historical Allusions, Curious Customs and Superstitions, County of Kerry, Corkaguiny* (self-published, 1916)

O'Donovan, John, *Antiquities of the County of Kerry Collected During the Progress of the Ordnance Survey in 1841* (typescript of original manuscript, Killarney Library)

ARCHIVES

Bureau of Military History
Chief Secretary's Office Registered Papers, National Archives of Ireland
Fitzgerald Papers, Public Record Office of Northern Ireland
Local History and Archives Department, Kerry County Library
Killarney Library Archive
Main Manuscript Collection, National Folklore Collection
Schools' Collection, National Folklore Collection
State of the Country Papers, National Archives of Ireland

PARLIAMENTARY PAPERS

'County of Kerry. Number of Freeholders in the County of Kerry entitled to vote at the Election of Members of Parliament', in *Estimates, Accounts and Papers relating to Ireland, Session 3 February to 6 July 1825*, Vol XXII (House of Commons, 1825)

'Minutes of Evidence taken before the Select Committee of the House of Lords, appointed to examine into the Nature and Extent of the Disturbances which have prevailed in those Districts of Ireland which are now subject to … the Insurrection Act … 18 May–23 June, 1824', in *Selection of Reports and Papers of the House of Commons* (House of Commons, 1836)

'Minutes of Evidence taken before the Select Committee of the House of Lords, appointed to inquire into the State of Ireland … 24 March–22 June, 1825', in *Selection of Reports and Papers of the House of Commons* (House of Commons, 1836)

'Minutes of Evidence taken before the Select Committee of the House of Lords appointed to enquire into the State of Ireland since the year 1835 in respect of Crime and Outrage …' (House of Commons, 1839)

'Report from the Select Committee of the House of Lords, appointed to inquire into the State of Ireland in respect of crime … Part I', in *Reports from Committees State of Ireland: Crime*, Vol. XI (House of Commons, 1839)

NEWSPAPERS

(Belfast) News Letter
Bell's Life in London and Sporting Chronicle
Carlisle Journal
Chute's Western Herald
Cork Constitution
Finn's Leinster Journal
John Bull
Kerry Champion
Kerry News

Kerry People
Kerry Sentinel
Kerry Star
Leinster Express
Limerick Chronicle
Limerick Leader
Lincolnshire Echo
Mayo Constitution
Reading Mercury, Oxford Gazette and Berkshire County Paper
Saunders's News-Letter
The Atlas (London)
The Belfast Commercial Chronicle
The Clare Journal and Ennis Advertiser
The Cork Examiner
The Courier and Evening Gazette (London)
The Dublin Evening Post
The Dublin Weekly Register
The Freeman's Journal
The Globe (London)
The Kerry Evening Post
The Kerry Examiner
The Kerry Weekly Reporter and Commercial Advertiser
The Kerryman
The Leinster Journal
The Liberator (Tralee)
The Mail (Waterford)
The Monitor (Sydney)
The Morning Register (Dublin)
The Nation (Dublin)
The Northern Star and National Trades Journal (Leeds)
The Southern Reporter and Cork Commercial Courier
The Southern Star
The Spectator (London)
The Standard (London)
The Sydney Morning Herald
The Tablet
The Times
The Tipperary Vindicator
The Tralee Chronicle
The Waterford Mail
The Weekly Waterford Chronicle
The Wexford Conservative
The York Herald and General Advertiser
Tralee Mercury

WEBSITES

http://ballads.bodleian.ox.ac.uk
www.ballinamere.gaa.ie
www.bureauofmilitaryhistory.ie
www.doegen.ie
www.1641.tcd.ie

ACKNOWLEDGEMENTS

I wish to thank the staff of the National Folklore Collection, University College Dublin, particularly Director Críostóir Mac Cárthaigh for permission to quote from material in the National Folklore Collection (NFC) and the Schools' Manuscript Collection (NFCS), Dr Conchúr Mag Eacháin for advice on referencing, and Claire Ní Dhubhcháin for her always kind assistance.

I am grateful to the Deputy Keeper of the Records, the Public Record Office of Northern Ireland, for permission to quote from letters of Maurice Fitzgerald, Knight of Kerry (PRONI references MIC639/5, MIC639/8, MIC639/7/160).

I also thank the Director of the National Archives of Ireland for permission to quote from the State of the Country Papers.

I am indebted to the Local History section of Tralee Library, particularly Michael Lynch, and to Eamon Browne and the staff of Killarney Library, who helped to supply many rare books from the deep stacks of Ireland's library service.

Translations of Irish language material were provided by Thomas O'Sullivan and James O'Malley, as well as others, through Unique Voice translation services, Tralee.

The text benefited from observations by Tara Arpaia for which I am grateful. Helpful comments were also made by Nigel Baldock, Paddy O'Shea, Redmond Roche and Kieran McNulty.

INDEX